Dearborn™

Health Insurance

License Exam Manual

6th Edition

Dearborn
PASSTRAK™

This publication is designed to provide accurate and authoritative information in regard to the subject matter covered. It is sold with the understanding that the publisher is not engaged in rendering legal, accounting or other professional service. If legal advice or other expert assistance is required, the services of a competent professional person should be sought.

This text is updated periodically to reflect changes in laws and regulations. To verify that you have the most recent update, you may call Dearborn at 1-800-423-4723.

Published by Dearborn Financial Institute, Inc.®

Printed in the United States of America.

First printing, October 2004

Library of Congress Cataloging-in-Publication Data

PassTrak health insurance license exam manual.— 6th ed.
p. cm.
Includes bibliographical references and index.
ISBN 0-7931-9644-2 (pbk. : alk. paper)
1. Insurance, Health—United States—Examinations, questions, etc. 2. Insurance, Health—Law and legislation—United States—Examinations, questions, etc. I. Dearborn Financial Institute.
HG9396.P37 2004
368.38′2′0076—dc22 2004023901

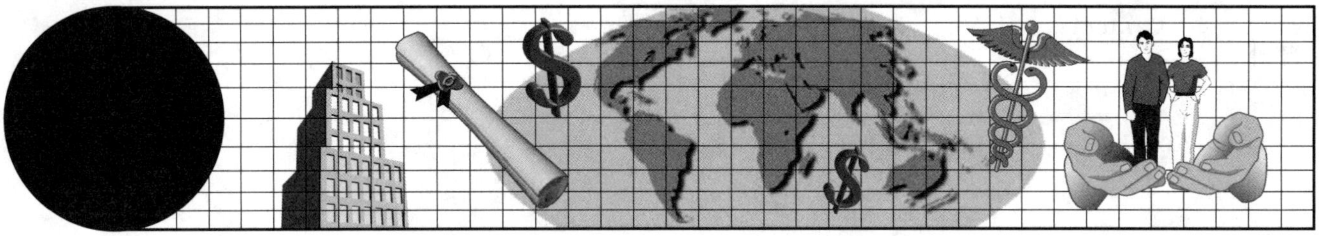

Contents

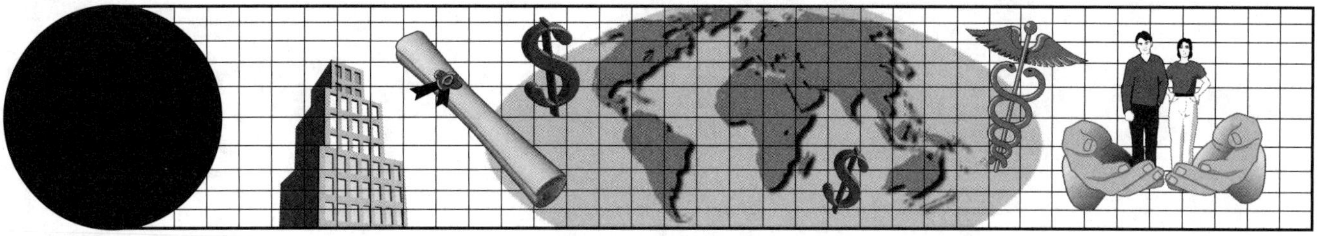

Acknowledgments

The publisher would like to acknowledge the following individuals for their contributions to the development of this text:

John Berti, Dearborn regional training manager (Northeast)
Barb Gavitt, Dearborn insurance instructor
Wes Schaller, Dearborn branch manager (Minnesota)
Anne Shropshire, CLU, Director of Insurance Products

Their efforts have resulted in a text that we believe will be an excellent source of knowledge and information about life, and accident and health insurance in these early years of the new millennium.

Arthur G. Carvajal, Esq.
Senior Legal Editor

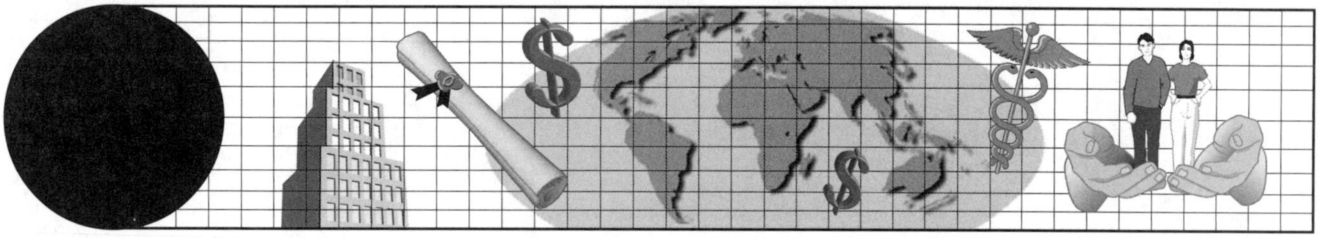

Introduction

Thank you for purchasing PASSTRAK® *Health Insurance License Exam Manual*. This brief introduction will help you get the most out of this book when preparing for your state licensing examination.

Most states require individuals to obtain some education in insurance before taking a state licensing exam. All states require individuals to take an exam to become licensed as an insurance agent or producer. There are some individuals who may be exempt from this licensing exam, usually on the basis of prior insurance education or experience. You can contact the department of insurance for your state to determine its precise licensing requirements.

This new edition includes information that we have added and expanded in the following topics: Medicare+Advantage programs, Medicare supplement policies, dental insurance, the Financial Services Modernization Act of 2000, the Economic Growth and Tax Relief Reconciliation Act of 2001, and the Medicare Prescription Drug and Modernization Act of 2003.

Examples and highlighted sections called Take Note and Test Topic Alert highlight key points in an easy-to-use format. Almost every unit contains at least one Quick Quiz that asks questions about the material covered in the previous section. Finally, review questions appear at the end of each unit, and the glossary has been updated. We hope that these changes will make this book easier to use and your study time more productive.

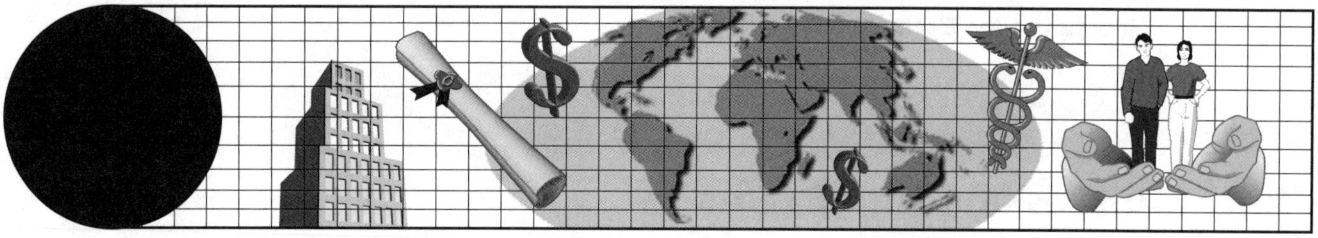

How to Use the License Exam Manual

PASSTRAK® *Health Insurance License Exam Manual* consists of units, unit exams, and practice final exams.

Here is an effective way to use this text for the greatest comprehension:

Throughout the text, you will see special notes to help your comprehension. These three types of notes have a specific purpose and are denoted with different text markers:

✓ ***Take Note:*** This note highlights an important point of fact, law, policy, or practice that you should know. By reading the Take Note sections by themselves after you have read the book, you can get a quick review of these important points just before you take the licensing exam.

Test Topic Alert

This note alerts you to important information that frequently appears in the licensing exam. This information comes directly from our classroom instructors, and highlights an important point that you should remember for the exam.

✓ ***For Example:*** This note illustrates the operation of important concepts and principles. It applies a principle or concept to a realistic situation.

Quick Quizzes and Unit Exams

1. Each unit contains periodic Quick Quizzes. Take these quizzes to ensure that you understand and retain the material covered in the preceding section.
2. At the end of each unit, you will find a Unit Exam. This review test covers all of the topics presented in the preceding unit. If you have mastered the Quick Quizzes, you should have no trouble successfully completing the Unit Exam.
3. Finally, when you have mastered the Quick Quizzes and Unit Exams, you are ready to take the Final Exam at the end of the book. Strive to get at least 80% of the questions correct after careful study of this book.

State insurance license exams are published by a private company or by the state. You can determine which test publisher—Promissor, Inc. or Experior, LLC—administers the exam in your state by visiting the publishers' web sites. For Promissor, go to **promissor.com**. For Experior, go to **experioronline.com**. You can also telephone Promissor at 1-888-204-6231 and Experior at 1-800-786-3926.

Access the content outlines and license candidate handbooks for your exam by visiting these sites. They will show which topics will be tested on your exam. In some cases, you will see that the exam content outline does not list a topic included in this book. If that is the case, the topic will not be tested on the exam. (It is included here because this book must cover topics that appear on either Promissor *or* Experior content outlines.)

If you do not see your state listed on the Promissor or Experior sites, your state does not retain either company and instead administers its own exams. Nevertheless, the topics on those exams are similar to those found in the Promissor and Experior content outlines, so you can use this book to prepare for those exams as well. Contact your state insurance department for more information about the exam.

The state insurance licensing exam is not easy. You must display considerable knowledge of the topics presented in this textbook and the law supplement, which covers state insurance laws and regulations. (If you do not have this law supplement for your state, contact Dearborn's customer service department at 1-800-423-4723.) If you thoroughly understand the information in this book and in the law supplement, you should be well-prepared to take the licensing exam.

Part One

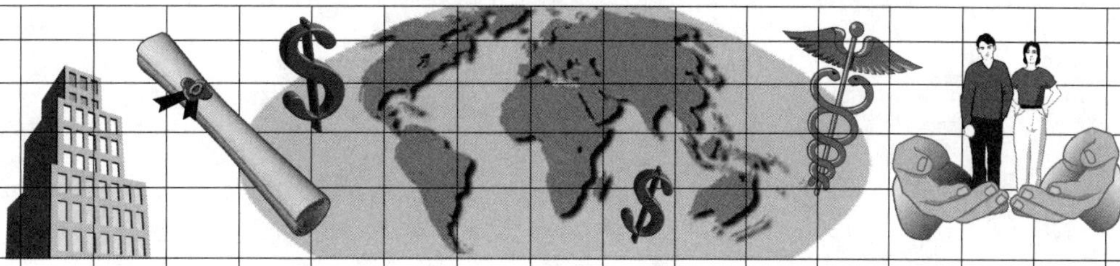

Principles of Insurance

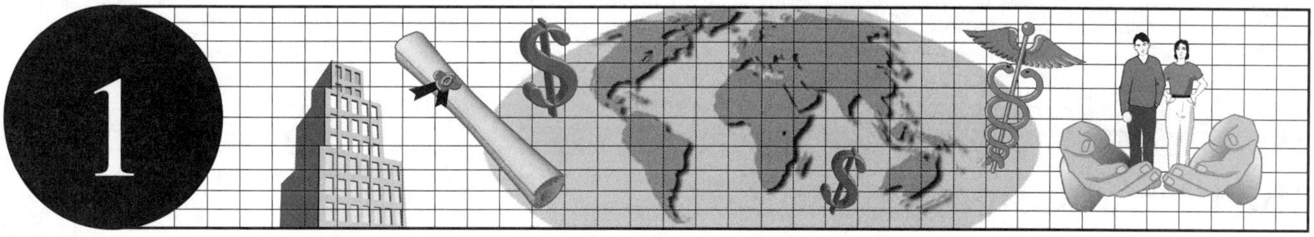

Purpose of Insurance

INTRODUCTION

Health insurance plays an important role in helping people attain financial and emotional security throughout life. For instance, health insurance protects individuals by assuming the risk that they will incur medical expenses. In this unit, we will examine the purpose of both types of insurance: providing economic protection against losses resulting from chance happenings like illness, accident, or death. We also will take a look at various types of risks and how insurance is designed specifically to replace the uncertainties of risk with guarantees.

UNIT OBJECTIVES

When you have completed this unit, you should be able to:

- explain why health insurance is important to people and to society as a whole;
- explain the concepts of risk pooling and the law of large numbers;
- define speculative risk, pure risk, peril, and hazard, and give an example of each;
- identify the four methods used to handle risk; and
- list and explain the elements of an insurable risk.

The Role of Insurance

We all have a compelling need for security, peace of mind, and freedom from worry. Unfortunately, achieving complete financial security historically has been elusive, in part because of universal problems such as death, sickness, accidents, and disability. These problems can strike at any time. The emotional stress they bring is increased by the financial hardships that almost certainly follow.

When death takes the life of a family provider prematurely, surviving family members suffer when they are left without adequate income or the means to provide basic necessities. On the other hand, some people face the unpleasant prospect of outliving their incomes—retirement may be forced on them before they have prepared adequately for a non-income-earning existence. Sickness and disability also can leave economic scars, often more expensive than death. An accident or illness can easily result in catastrophic medical bills or the inability to work for months or years.

Insurance evolved to provide a practical solution to the problem of such economic uncertainties and losses. **Health insurance** also evolved from scientific principles to provide funds for medical expenses due to sickness or injury and to cover loss of income during a period of disability. The true significance of insurance is its promise to substitute uncertainty with future economic certainty and to replace the unknown with a sense of security.

An Industry Overview

The insurance industry plays an important role in our nation's society. It is second only to the commercial banking industry as a source of investment funds because insurance companies invest the billions of premium dollars they receive annually in a wide range of investments.*

In 1999, 261.2 million Americans were covered under public and private health insurance, and 42.6 million were without health insurance. More than 194.6 million of the insured individuals were covered by private health insurers, including commercial insurance companies, Blue Cross and Blue Shield plans, self-funded employer plans, and prepayment plans such as health maintenance organizations (HMOs).

---

*One of the basic factors in health premiums is the interest earned by the insurance company on the premiums it receives and subsequently invests.

FIGURE 1.1 Life Insurance per Insured Household, 1970–1998

Year	*Life Insurance per Insured Household*	*Year*	*Life Insurance per Insured Household*
1970	$25,500	1985	$82,200
1971	$27,000	1986	$89,100
1972	$28,300	1987	$98,400
1973	$30,100	1988	$105,600
1974	$32,500	1989	$112,400
1975	$34,900	1990	$124,500
1976	$37,100	1991	$130,000
1977	$40,000	1992	$136,600
1978	$43,200	1993	$143,100
1979	$48,000	1994	$146,500
1980	$51,100	1995	$149,500
1981	$56,300	1996	$158,400
1982	$63,100	1997	$167,600
1983	$69,500	1998	$178,600
1984	$75,700	1999	$189,800

Source: *2000 Life Insurance Fact Book*

The rising cost of health care continues to be one of the most difficult problems facing our health care system. For example, according to the Health Insurance Association of America's *2002 Source Book of Health Insurance Data*, in 2000, Americans spent $1,299.5 billion for medical and health care services, research, and construction—$712 billion in private funds and $587.2 billion in public funds. In 2000, spending per person averaged $4,637, a 5.6% increase since 1999.

The Nature of Insurance

We are exposed to many perils. The purpose of any insurance is to provide economic protection against losses that may incur due to a chance happening or event, such as death, illness, or accident. This protection is provided through an insurance policy, which simply is a device for accumulating funds to meet these uncertain losses. The policy is a legally binding contract that sets forth the company's promise and obligations as follows:

> *Whereby, for a set amount of money (the premium), one party (the insurer) agrees to pay the other party (the insured or his or her beneficiary) a set sum (the benefit) upon the occurrence of some event.*

In the case of health or disability insurance, the benefit is paid if and when the insured incurs certain medical expenses or becomes disabled, as defined by the contract.

Basic Insurance Principles

Insurance is based on two fundamental principles: the spreading or pooling of risks (also known as **loss sharing**) and the law of large numbers. To understand these principles, consider the following examples.

Risk Pooling

✓ ***For Example:*** Assume that 1,000 individuals in the same social club agree that if any member of their group dies, all of the members will pitch in to provide the deceased's family with $10,000. This $10,000, it was determined, would provide the family with enough funds to cover the immediate costs associated with death and to provide a cushion for at least a few months. Because it is not known when any one individual within the group will die, the decision is made to pre-fund the benefit by assessing each member $10, thus creating the $10,000 fund. Without the agreement to help provide for each other's potential loss, each group member (and family) would have to face the economic cost of death alone. But by sharing the burden and spreading the risk of death over all 1,000 group members, the most any one member pays is $10.

This is, of course, a simplified example, but it explains the basic concept of loss sharing. By spreading a risk, or by sharing the possibility of a loss, a large group of people can substitute a small certain cost ($10 in our example) for a large unknown risk (the economic risk of dying). In other words, the risk is transferred from an individual to a group, each member of which shares the losses and has the promise of a future benefit. Insurance companies pool risks among thousands of insureds and apply mathematical principles to guarantee policyowners that the money will be there to pay a claim when it arises.

Law of Large Numbers

In addition to spreading risks, insurance relies on the principle that the larger the number of individual risks (or exposures) in a group, the more certain the amount of loss incurred in any given period. In other words, given a large enough pool of risks, an insurer can predict with reasonable accuracy the number of claims it will face during any given time, or the aggregate risk. No one can predict when any one person will die or if any one person will become disabled. However, it is possible to predict the approximate number of deaths or the likelihood of disability among a certain group during a certain period. This principle, known as the **law of large numbers**, is based on the science of probability and the experience of mortality (death) and morbidity (sickness) statistics. The larger and more homogeneous the group, the more certain the mortality or morbidity predictions.

✓ ***For Example:*** Statistics may show that among a group of 100,000 40-year-old males, 300 will die within one year. While it is not possible to predict who the 300 will be, the number will prove quite accurate. Conversely, with a small group, an accurate prediction is not possible. Among a group of 100 40-year-old males, it is not statistically feasible to predict if any in the group will die within one year. Because insurers cover thousands and thousands of lives, it is possible to predict when and to what extent deaths and disabilities will occur and, consequently, when claims will arise.

All forms of insurance—life, health, accident, property, and casualty—rely on risk pooling and the law of large numbers. These principles form the foundation on which insurance is based and allow for its successful operation.

The Concept of Risk

As we have learned so far, insurance replaces the uncertainty of risk with guarantees. But what exactly does the word *risk* mean? And how does insurance remove the uncertainty and minimize the adverse effects of risk?

Risk Defined

Risk is defined as the uncertainty regarding loss. Property loss, such as the destruction of a home due to fire, is an example of risk. Negligence or carelessness can give rise to a liability risk if there is potential injury to an individual or damage to property. The inability to work and earn a living due to a disability is another example of risk, as is loss of a family's income due to the death of the breadwinner. The loss inherent in all of these risks is characterized by a lessening (or disappearance) of value.

A class of risks is a homogenous group of loss exposures. Risks can be divided into two classes: speculative and pure.

- **Speculative risks** involve the chance of both loss and gain. Betting at the race track and investing in the stock market are examples of speculative risks.
- **Pure risks** involve only the chance of loss; there is never a possibility of gain or profit. The risk associated with the chance of injury from an accident is an example of pure risk. There is no opportunity for gain if the event does not occur—only the opportunity for loss if it does occur. Only pure risks are insurable.

✓ ***Take Note:*** The distinction between speculative and pure risks is important. Insurance does not protect individuals against losses arising out of speculative risks because these risks are undertaken voluntarily. However, not all pure risks are insurable.

With health insurance, the risk is not when, but if, illness or disability will strike. Losses associated with health risks include medical costs and loss of income.

Test Topic Alert! Insurance is designed to protect only against pure risk.

Perils and Hazards

Perils and hazards are factors that cause or give rise to risk.

A **peril** is the immediate specific event causing loss and giving rise to risk. It is the cause of a risk.

✓ ***For Example:*** When a building burns, fire is the peril. When a person dies, death is the peril. When an individual is injured in an accident, the accident is the peril. When a person becomes ill from a disease, the disease is the peril.

A **hazard** is any factor that gives rise to a peril. For purposes of life and health insurance, there are three basic types of hazards: physical, moral, and morale.

- **Physical hazards** are individual characteristics that increase the chance of peril. They may exist because of a person's physical condition, past medical history, or condition at birth. Blindness and deafness are physical hazards.
- **Moral hazards** are tendencies that increase risk and the chance of loss. Alcoholism and drug addiction are considered moral hazards.
- **Morale hazards** are also individual tendencies, but they arise from an attitude or state of mind that causes indifference to loss. For instance, driving recklessly without fear of death or injury is a morale hazard.

Treatment of Risk

How risks are treated varies greatly depending on the situation, the degree of potential loss, and the individual. Generally, there are four options: avoid, reduce, retain, or transfer the risk.

Risk Avoidance

One method of dealing with risk is **avoidance**—simply avoiding as many risks as possible. By choosing not to drive or own an automobile, one could avoid the risks associated with driving. By never flying, one could eliminate the risk of being in an airplane crash. By never investing in stocks, one could avoid the risk of a market crash.

✓ ***Take Note:*** Although risk avoidance may be an effective method of dealing with risk, it is not always practical. If risk avoidance were used extensively, society would ultimately suffer because some risk taking is necessary to achieve personal advancement and economic progress. For this reason, avoidance may be an unsatisfactory way of handling many risks.

Risk Reduction

Risk reduction is another means of dealing with risk. Because we cannot avoid risk entirely, we often attempt to lessen the possibility of loss by taking action to reduce the risk. Installing a smoke alarm in a home will not lessen the possibility of fire, but it may reduce the risk of loss from fire.

Risk Retention

Risk retention is another method of coping with risk. This means accepting the risk and confronting it if and when it occurs. One way to handle a retained risk is self-insurance, for instance, setting up a fund to offset the costs of a potential loss.

✓ ***Take Note:*** Risk retention may be voluntary or involuntary. For instance, a person who recognizes that a risk exists may agree voluntarily to assume the losses involved because the risk might lead to relatively small certain losses that can be borne easily. On the other hand, a person may not even recognize that a risk exists. In this case, the person involuntarily retains the possible financial loss without realizing it.

Risk Transference

The most effective way to handle risk is to transfer it so that the loss is borne by another party. Insurance is the most common method of transferring risk—from an individual or group to an insurance company. Though purchasing insurance will not eliminate the risk of death or illness, it relieves the insured individual or group of the losses these risks bring. Insurance satisfies both economic and emotional needs—it replaces the uncertainty surrounding risk with the assurance of guarantees, and it transfers the financial consequences of death, illness, or disability to the insurer.

Test Topic Alert!

A typical question on the license exam may ask you to identify the ways that individuals treat risk.

Quick Quiz 1.1

Match the following terms with the appropriate example below.

A. Speculative risk
B. Risk transference
C. Risk reduction
D. Risk avoidance

____ 1. Joan installs a sprinkler system in her new house.

____ 2. Because Mary is afraid of drowning and she never swims.

____ 3. Bob invests all of his investment money in technology stocks.

____ 4. Tom, a stuntman, purchases disability insurance.

Answers *1.* ***C*** *2.* ***D*** *3.* ***A*** *4.* ***B***

Elements of Insurable Risk

Though insurance may be one of the most effective ways to handle risk, not all risks are insurable. As noted earlier, insurers will insure only pure risks or those that involve only the chance of loss. However, not all pure risks are insurable. Certain characteristics or elements must be evident before a pure risk can be insured.

- **The loss must be due to chance.** To be insurable, a risk must involve a chance of loss that is fortuitous and outside the insured's control.
- **The loss must be definite and measurable.** An insurable risk must involve a loss that is definite as to cause, time, place, and amount. An insurer must be able to determine how much the benefit will be and when it will become payable.
- **The loss must be predictable.** An insurable risk must have occurrence that can be predicted statistically. This enables insurers to estimate the average frequency and severity of future losses and set appropriate premiums. Death, illness, and disability all are events whose rates of occurrence can be projected based on statistics.
- **The loss cannot be catastrophic.** Insurers typically will not insure risks that will expose them to catastrophic losses. There must be limits that insurers can be reasonably certain their losses will not exceed. For instance, an insurer would not issue a policy for $1 trillion on a single

life, because that one death would create a catastrophic loss to the company.

- **The loss exposures to be insured must be large.** An insurer must be able to predict losses based on the law of large numbers. Consequently, there must be a sufficiently large pool to be insured and those in the pool (the exposures) must be grouped into classes with similar risks. Individuals, for example, are grouped according to age, health, sex, occupation, and other classifications.
- **The loss exposures to be insured must be selected randomly.** Insurers must have a fair proportion of good risks and poor risks. A large proportion of poor risks would financially threaten the insurance company because there would be many claims without sufficient premiums to offset them. Keep in mind that there is a tendency, called **adverse selection**, for less favorable insurance risks (e.g., people in poor health) to seek or continue insurance to a greater extent than other risks.

Economic Basis of Health Insurance

To fully appreciate the purpose and function of insurance, it is important to understand that its roots lie in economics and the concept of human life value.

It has long been recognized that individuals have an economic value that can be measured in part by their future earning potential. This earning potential is the sum of one's net future earnings or, more precisely, the dollar value of an individual's future earning capability. The true significance of this earning potential extends beyond the individual to those who depend on the individual for their financial security. Thus, by definition, human life value is the value today of an individual's future earnings that are devoted to dependents.

In the abstract, human life value is the means by which homes are purchased, college educations are provided, monthly bills are paid—in short, it is the essence of an individual's or family's economic existence. Yet this value is subject to loss through death, retirement, disability, or poor health—any one of these perils affects earning capacity in some degree and, consequently, diminishes human life value. It is to conserve and protect human life value that life and health insurance exist.

Summary

Health insurance evolved to provide a practical solution to the economic losses associated with death, sickness, and accidents. It does so through an insurance policy, which is a device that accumulates funds to meet these losses. Insurance is based on risk pooling and the law of large numbers, principles that allow insurers to spread risks among thousands of individuals and to predict losses with reasonable accuracy.

Insurance transfers risk, which is one of the most effective ways to deal with risk and its losses. Not all risks are insurable, however. There are certain elements every risk must contain before it can be insured: it must be a pure risk; the loss it entails must be due to chance, definite, measurable, predictable, and noncatastrophic; and the loss exposure must be part of a large, randomly selected group.

The true worth of insurance lies in its ability to protect human life value—the value associated with an individual's earning potential—and to provide financial security.

Key Concepts

In preparing for their licensing examinations, students should be familiar with the following concepts:

- pure risk
- speculative risk
- law of large numbers
- elements of insurable risk
- hazard
- peril
- risk pooling
- methods of handling risk
- adverse selection

Unit Exam 1

1. Which of the following insurance concepts is founded on the ability to predict the approximate number of deaths or frequency of disabilities within a certain group during a specific time?
   A. Principle of large loss
   B. Quantum insurance principle
   C. Indemnity law
   D. Law of large numbers

2. The owner of a camera store is worried that new employees may help themselves to items from inventory without paying for them. What kind of hazard is this?
   A. Physical
   B. Ethical
   C. Morale
   D. Moral

3. All of the following actions are examples of risk avoidance EXCEPT
   A. refusing to fly
   B. refusing to invest in stocks
   C. paying an insurance premium
   D. refusing to drive

4. Which of the following statements is CORRECT?
   A. Only speculative risks are insurable.
   B. Only pure risks are insurable.
   C. Both pure risks and speculative risks are insurable.
   D. Neither pure risks nor speculative risks are insurable.

5. Which of the following statements does NOT describe an element of an insurable risk?
   A. The loss must not be due to chance.
   B. The loss must be definite and measurable.
   C. The loss cannot be catastrophic.
   D. The loss exposures to be insured must be large.

6. In the insurance business, risk can best be defined as
   A. sharing the possibility of a loss
   B. uncertainty regarding the future
   C. uncertainty regarding loss
   D. uncertainty regarding when death will occur

7. Buying insurance is one of the most effective ways of
   A. avoiding risk
   B. transferring risk
   C. reducing risk
   D. retaining risk

8. Which of the following best describes the function of insurance?
   A. It is a form of legalized gambling.
   B. It spreads financial risk over a large group to minimize the loss to any one individual.
   C. It protects against living too long.
   D. It creates and protects risks.

9. A tornado is an example of a
   A. physical hazard
   B. speculative risk
   C. peril
   D. moral hazard

10. An insured keeps a $50,000 diamond ring in a safe deposit box at a local bank. This is an example of
    A. avoidance
    B. reduction
    C. retention
    D. transference

Unit Exam 1 Answers & Rationale

1. **D.** The law of large numbers relies on the principle that, given a large enough pool of risks, an insurer can predict with reasonable accuracy the number of claims it will face during a specific time period. This principle is based on the science of probability and the experience of mortality (death) and morbidity (sickness) statistics.

2. **D.** The store owner is concerned about the tendency of her employees to be dishonest and steal inventory. The tendency to be dishonest is a moral hazard that increases risk and the chance of loss.

3. **C.** Risk avoidance occurs when a person simply avoids as many risks as possible. However, when Pat purchases insurance, he is not attempting to avoid risk; rather, he is transferring the loss from a potential risk to another party—the insurance company. Purchasing insurance, therefore, is considered risk transference, not risk avoidance.

4. **B.** Unlike speculative risk, pure risk involves only the chance of loss and never a possibility of gain or profit. Only this type of risk is insurable.

5. **A.** To be an insurable risk, the loss must be due to chance. A risk must involve the chance of loss that is fortuitous and outside the insured's control.

6. **C.** Risk is the uncertainty regarding loss.

7. **B.** Buying insurance enables a person to handle risk by transferring the risk of loss to another party—the insurance company. Although purchasing insurance does not eliminate the risk of death or illness, it relieves the insured of the losses that these risks bring by transferring them to a third party.

8. **B.** Insurance is based in part on risk pooling, which involves spreading risks among thousands of individuals to minimize the loss to any one individual.

9. **C.** A peril is the immediate specific event causing loss and giving rise to risk. In other words, a peril is the cause of a risk. Thus, when a town is destroyed by high winds, a tornado is the peril.

10. **B.** Placing a diamond ring in a safe deposit box is an example of risk reduction. Although the insured cannot avoid the risk of losing the ring altogether when not wearing it, the insured can reduce the risk of loss by putting it in a safe deposit box.

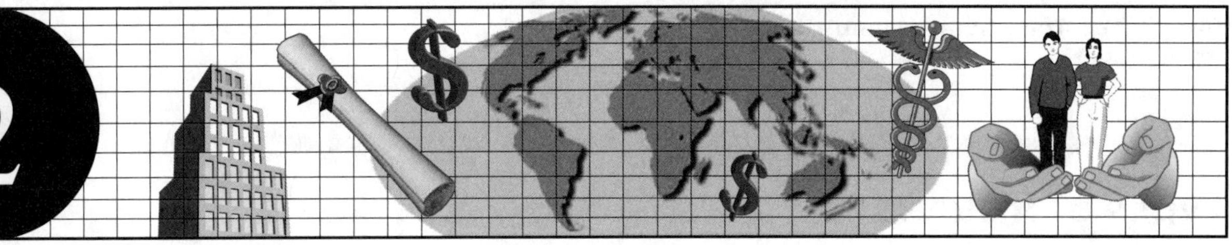

2 The Insurance Industry

INTRODUCTION

The insurance industry in the United States had more than 1,171 life insurance companies operating by the end of 2002. These firms employ over 2.3 million people and administer assets of more than $3.4 trillion. In this unit, we will examine the insurance industry in general and look at the different types of private insurers and government insurance programs. We also will examine how insurance is sold and the ways in which the industry is regulated at both the federal and state levels. Keep in mind, however, that each state has its own insurance laws and regulations that should be consulted.

UNIT OBJECTIVES

When you have completed this unit, you should be able to:

- list and describe the different types of private insurers and government insurance programs;
- describe the different types of systems through which insurance is sold, and the agent's role in these systems;
- describe the primary ways that insurance is regulated at the federal and state levels;
- define twisting, misrepresentation, misuse of premiums, replacement, and rebating, and give an example of each of these prohibited practices; and
- describe the roles of the National Association of Insurance Commissioners (NAIC), state guaranty associations, and the National Association of Health Underwriters (NAHU).

Types of Insurers

Although there are many ways to classify organizations that provide insurance, in the broadest of terms, there are two classifications: private and government. Within these two classes are many categories of insurance providers, as well as insurance plans and insurance producers.

Private Insurers

Private insurers offer many lines of insurance. Some sell primarily life insurance and annuities, some sell accident and health insurance, and some sell property and casualty insurance. Companies that write more than one line of insurance are known as **multiline insurers**.

Within this broad category of private insurers are specific types of insurance companies. A discussion of each type follows.

Stock Insurers

A **stock insurance company** is a publicly owned, private organization that is organized and incorporated under state laws for the purpose of making a profit for its stockholders. It is structured the same as any corporation. Stockholders may or may not be policyholders. When declared, stock dividends are paid to stockholders. In a stock company, the directors and officers are responsible to the stockholders.

Mutual Insurers

Mutual insurance companies also are organized and incorporated under state laws, but they have no stockholders. Instead, the owners are the policyholders. Anyone purchasing insurance from a mutual insurer is both a customer and an owner and has the right to vote for members of the board of directors. By issuing participating policies that pay policy dividends, mutual insurers allow their policyowners to share in any company earnings. Essentially, policy dividends represent a refund of the portion of premiums that remains after the company has set aside the necessary reserves and made deductions for claims and expenses. Policy dividends also can include a share in the company's investment, mortality, and operating profits.

Test Topic Alert!

Policy dividends are paid from participating policies usually sold by mutual insurers.

Occasionally, a stock company may be converted into a mutual company through a process called **mutualization**. Likewise, some mutual companies are **demutualizing** by converting to stock companies. Stock and mutual companies are often referred to as **commercial insurers**. They can both write life, health, and property and casualty insurance.

Assessment Mutual Insurers

Assessment mutual companies are typified by the way in which they charge premiums. A pure assessment mutual company operates on the basis of loss sharing by group members. No premium is payable in advance; instead, each member is assessed an individual portion of losses that actually occur. An advance premium assessment mutual company charges a premium in advance, at the beginning of the policy period. If the original premiums exceed the operating expenses and losses, the surplus is returned to the policyholders as dividends.

On the other hand, if total premiums are not enough to meet losses, additional assessments are levied against the members. Normally, the amount of assessment that may be levied is limited, either by state law or as a provision in the insurer's bylaws.

Reciprocal Insurers

Similar to mutual insurers, reciprocal insurers are organized on the basis of ownership by their policyholders. However, with reciprocal insurers it is the policyholders themselves who insure the risks of the other policyholders. Each policyholder assumes a share of the risk brought to the company by others. The insurer is a risk-sharing mechanism. Reciprocals are managed by an attorney-in-fact.

✓ ***Take Note:*** As a member of the group of reciprocal insurers, each policyowner is both an insured and an insurer. Each policyowner's premium is paid into a separate account and their share of any losses is paid from this account.

Lloyd's of London

Lloyd's of London is not an insurer, but rather an association of individuals and companies that individually underwrite insurance. Lloyd's can be compared to the New York Stock Exchange, which provides the arena and facilities for buying and selling public stock. The function of Lloyd's is to gather and disseminate underwriting information, help its associates settle claims and disputes, and through its member underwriters, provide coverages that might otherwise be unavailable in certain areas.

Reinsurers

Reinsurers make up a specialized branch of the insurance industry which insures insurers. Reinsurance is an arrangement by which an insurance company transfers a portion of a risk it has assumed to another insurer. Usually, reinsurance takes place to limit the loss any one insurer would face should a very large claim become payable. Another reason for reinsurance is to enable a company to meet certain objectives, such as favorable underwriting or mortality results. The company transferring the risk is called the **ceding** company; the company assuming the risk is the reinsurer.

Risk Retention Group

A **risk retention group (RRG)** is a mutual insurance company formed to insure people in the same business, occupation, or profession, such as pharmacists, dentists, or engineers.

Fraternal Benefit Societies

Insurance also is issued by fraternal benefit societies, which have existed in the United States for more than a century. Fraternal societies, noted primarily for their social, charitable, and benevolent activities, have memberships based on religious, national, or ethnic affiliations. Fraternals first began offering insurance to meet the needs of their poorer members, funding the benefits on a pure assessment basis. Today few fraternals rely on an assessment system, most having adopted the same advanced funding approach other insurers use.

To be characterized as a fraternal benefit society, the organization must be nonprofit, have a lodge system that includes ritualistic work, and maintain a representative form of government with elected officers. Fraternal society insurance may be sold only to members of the society. Most fraternals today issue insurance certificates and annuities with many of the same provisions found in policies issued by commercial insurers.

✓ ***Take Note:*** Fraternal societies primarily issue life insurance, although they sometimes sell sickness and accident insurance as well.

Service Insurers

Service insurers, or service providers, offer health insurance and health care services. One of the most well known service providers is Blue Cross and Blue Shield. These two organizations are nonprofit and differ from other insurers in that they sell medical and hospital care services, not insurance. These services are packaged into various plans, and those who purchase these plans are known as subscribers. Blue Cross offers prepayment plans to cover hospital expenses such as room and board and miscellaneous expenses. Blue Shield covers surgical expenses and other medical services performed by physicians.

Another type of service provider is the **health maintenance organization (HMO)**. HMOs offer a wide range of health care services to member subscribers. For a fixed periodic premium paid in advance of any treatment, these subscribers are entitled to the services of certain physicians and hospitals contracted to work with the HMO.

✓ ***Take Note:*** Unlike commercial insurers or Blue Cross and Blue Shield, HMOs provide financing for health care plus the health care itself. HMOs are known for stressing preventive health care and early treatment programs.

A third type of service provider is the **preferred provider organization (PPO)**. Under the usual PPO arrangement, a group desiring health care services—an employer or a union, for example—will obtain price discounts or special services from certain select health care providers in exchange for referring its employees or members to them. PPOs can be organized by employers or by the health care providers themselves. The contract between the employer and the health care professional, be it a physician or a hospital, spells out the kind of services to be provided. Insurance companies can also contract with PPOs to offer services to insureds. (Service providers will be discussed in detail in Unit 5.)

Home Service Insurers Insurance is also sold through a special branch of the industry known as home service (or debit) insurers. These companies specialize in a particular type of insurance called industrial insurance, which is characterized by relatively small face amounts (usually $1,000 to $2,000) with premiums paid weekly. (Industrial insurance will be discussed in Unit 4.)

Government as Insurer

As noted at the beginning of this unit, federal and state governments also are insurers, providing what are commonly called social insurance programs. Ranging from crop insurance to bank and savings and loan deposit insurance, these programs have far-reaching effects because they cover millions of people. The major difference between these government programs and private insurance programs is that the government programs are funded with taxes and serve national and state social purposes. Social insurance programs include:

- Old Age, Survivors, and Disability Insurance (OASDI), commonly known as Social Security;
- Social Security Hospital Insurance (HI) and Supplemental Medical Insurance (SMI), commonly known as Medicare;
- Medicaid; and
- workers' compensation.

The federal government has also established life insurance programs to benefit active members and veterans of the armed services. Three of the most notable programs are Servicemembers' Group Life, Veterans' Group Life, and National Service Life.

The government plays a vital role in providing social insurance programs. These programs pay billions of dollars in benefits every year and affect millions of people.

Self-Insurers

Though self-insurance is not a method of transferring risk, a discussion is appropriate here. Rather than transfer risk to an insurance company, a self-insurer establishes its own reserves to cover potential losses. Self-insurance is risk retention that is often used by large companies for funding workers' compensation and pension plans. Many times a self-insurer will look to an insurance company to provide insurance above a certain maximum level of loss, but will bear the amount of loss below that amount.

✓ ***Take Note:*** The use of self-insurance by businesses to deal with risks has grown significantly over the past 30 years. In some areas (such as employer-sponsored health plans), it has become a significant alternative to commercial insurance.

How Insurance Is Sold

Insurance is sold by a variety of companies through a variety of methods. Most consumers purchase insurance through licensed producers who present insurers' products and services to the public via active sales and marketing methods. Insurance producers may be either agents who represent a particular company, or brokers who are not tied to any particular company and can represent many companies' products.

✓ ***Take Note:*** In a sales transaction, agents represent the insurer and brokers represent the buyer. An agent has an agent's contract and a broker must have a broker's contract.

Agents also are classified as **captive** (or **career**) **agents** or **independent agents**. A captive agent works for one insurance company and sells only that company's insurance policies. An independent agent works for himself or for other agents and sells the insurance products of many companies.

There are also solicitors, consultants, and special agents. **Solicitors** act for agents by seeking prospects, receiving applications, or collecting premiums, but they usually do not have the authority to bind coverage. A **consultant** is an independent advisor specializing in the design, implementation, and administration of insurance sharing plans. Consultants are usually licensed agents. **Special agents**, who do not actually solicit insurance business, work as field representatives, helping a company's central office and the agency's force in their territory.

✓ ***Take Note:*** As the financial planning industry has grown rapidly in recent years, financial planners have also become an important source of information on personal risk management and insurance. Although these individuals do not actually sell insurance, their goal is to build their clients' wealth, minimize taxes, and protect their clients' estates, among other things.

The agent who solicits an insurance application represents the insurer and not the insured or beneficiary in any dispute between the insured or beneficiary and the insurer. In most states, however, the agent may represent as many insurers as will appoint her.

There are three systems that support the sale of insurance through agents and brokers. These are the **career agency system**, the **personal producing general agency system**, and the **independent agency system**.

Career Agency System

Career agencies are branches of major stock and mutual insurance companies that are contracted to represent the particular insurer in a specific area. In career agencies, insurance agents are recruited, trained, and supervised either by a manager-employee of the company or a **general agent (GA)** who has a vested right in any business written by agents. GAs may operate strictly as managers or they may devote a portion of their time to sales. The career agency system focuses on building sales staffs.

Personal Producing General Agency System

The **personal producing general agency (PPGA)** system is similar to the career agency system. However, PPGAs do not recruit, train, or supervise career agents. They primarily sell insurance, although they may build a small sales force to assist them. PPGAs are generally responsible for maintaining their own offices and administrative staff. Agents hired by a PPGA are considered employees of the PPGA, not the insurance company, and are supervised by regional directors.

Independent Agency System

The **independent agency system**, a creation of the property and casualty insurance industry, does not tie a sales staff or agency to any one particular insurance company; rather, independent brokers represent any number of insurance companies through contractual agreements. They are compensated on a commission or fee basis for the business they produce. This system also is known as the American agency system.

Other Methods of Selling Insurance

While most insurance is sold through agents or brokers under the systems described above, a large volume is also marketed through direct selling and mass marketing methods.

With the **direct selling** method, the insurer deals directly with consumers—no agent or broker is involved—selling its policies through vending machines, advertisements, or salaried sales representatives. Insurers that operate using this method are known as **direct writers** or **direct response insurers**.

A large volume of insurance is also sold through **mass marketing** techniques, such as direct mail or newspaper, magazine, radio, and television advertisements. Mass marketing methods provide exposure to large groups of consumers, often using direct selling methods with occasional follow-up by agents.

Quick Quiz 2.1

True or False?

_____ 1. Mutual insurance companies are owned by their policyowners.

_____ 2. A self-insurer transfers risk to an insurance company to cover all of its potential losses.

_____ 3. Career agencies are branches of major stock and mutual insurance companies that represent the insurer contractually in a particular area.

_____ 4. Blue Cross and Blue Shield are examples of home service insurers.

_____ 5. A fraternal benefit society sells insurance to individuals outside of the society as well as to society members.

_____ 6. Most insurance today is sold through direct selling and mass marketing.

_____ 7. With a reciprocal insurer, the policyholders insure the risks of the other policyholders.

Answers

1. ***True.***
2. ***False.*** *A self-insurer establishes its own reserves to cover potential losses, although it may use an insurance company to provide insurance above a certain maximum level of loss.*
3. ***True.***
4. ***False.*** *Blue Cross and Blue Shield are examples of service insurers. Service insurers offer health insurance and health care services, while home service insurers specialize in a particular type of insurance called industrial insurance.*
5. ***False.*** *Fraternal society insurance can be sold to members only.*
6. ***False.*** *Although a large amount of insurance is marketed through direct selling and mass marketing, most insurance today is sold through agents and brokers.*
7. ***True.***

Regulation of the Insurance Industry

The insurance industry is regulated by a number of authorities, including some inside the industry itself. The primary purpose of this regulation is to promote the public welfare by maintaining the solvency of insurance companies. Other purposes are to provide consumer protection and ensure fair trade practices, as well as fair contracts at fair prices.

History of Regulation

A brief overview of the history of insurance regulation will show a seesaw between the authority of the states and the federal government. Though a balance between these two bodies has been reached and maintained for many years, arguments favoring control by one governing authority over another are still being waged.

- *1868—Paul v. Virginia.* This case, which was decided by the US Supreme Court, involved one state's attempt to regulate an insurance company domiciled in another state. The Supreme Court sided against the insurance company, ruling that the sale and issuance of insurance is not interstate commerce, thus upholding the right of states to regulate insurance.
- *1905—The Armstrong Investigation.* Public outcry over abuses by insurers caused the New York state legislature to investigate life insurers in that state by creating the Armstrong Investigation. The result was the New York Insurance Code, which set a precedent and pattern for insurance regulation by other states throughout the country.
- *1944—United States v. Southeastern Underwriters Association (SEUA).* The decision of *Paul v. Virginia* held for 75 years before the US Supreme Court again addressed the issue of state versus federal regulation of the insurance industry. In the *SEUA* case, the Court ruled that the business of insurance is subject to a series of federal laws—many of which were in conflict with existing state laws—and that insurance is a form of interstate commerce to be regulated by the federal government. This decision did not affect the power of states to regulate insurance, but it did nullify state laws that were in conflict with federal legislation. The result of the *SEUA* case was to shift the balance of regulatory control to the federal government.
- *1945—The McCarran-Ferguson Act.* The turmoil created by the *SEUA* case prompted Congress to enact Public Law 15, the McCarran-Ferguson Act. This law made it clear that continued regulation of insurance by the states was in the public's best interest. However, it also made possible the application of federal anti-trust laws to the extent that the insurance business is not regulated by state law. This act led each state

to revise its insurance laws to conform to the federal law. Today, the insurance industry is state-regulated.

- *1958—Intervention by the Federal Trade Commission.* In the mid-1950s, the Federal Trade Commission (FTC) sought to control the advertising and sales literature used by the health insurance industry. In 1958, the US Supreme Court held that the McCarran-Ferguson Act disallowed such supervision by the FTC, a federal agency. The FTC has made additional attempts to force further federal control, but none have been successful.
- *1959—Intervention by the Securities and Exchange Commission.* In this instance, the question was whether variable annuities are insurance products to be regulated by the states, or securities to be regulated federally by the Securities and Exchange Commission (SEC). The US Supreme Court ruled that federal securities laws applied to insurers that issued variable annuities (and variable insurance contracts) and thus required these insurers to conform to both SEC and state insurance regulation. Producers who sell variable contracts must have a National Association of Securities Dealers (NASD) license as well as a life insurance license and must abide by NASD rules for sales and marketing practices.
- *1970—Fair Credit Reporting Act.* In an attempt to protect an individual's right to privacy, the federal government passed the Fair Credit Reporting Act, which requires fair and accurate reporting of information about consumers, including applications for insurance. Insurers must inform applicants about any investigations that are being made, and if any consumer report is used to deny coverage or charge higher rates, the insurer must furnish to the applicant the name of the reporting agency conducting the investigation. Any insurance company that fails to comply with this act is liable to the consumer for actual and punitive damages. (For specific provisions of this act, refer to the section entitled The Fair Credit Reporting Act of 1970 in Unit 8.)
- *1999—The Financial Services Modernization Act.* The Glass-Steagall Act of 1933, which barred common ownership of banks, insurance companies, and securities firms, and erected a wall of separation between banks and nonfinancial companies, came under repeated attack in the 1980s. In 1999, Congress enacted the Financial Services Modernization Act, which repealed the Glass-Steagall Act. Under the new legislation, commercial banks, investment banks, retail brokerages, and insurance companies may enter each other's lines of business.

The chronology of events cited above reflects the roles the courts and the federal government have played in regulating the insurance industry. What follows are some of the ways that individual states regulate this business and that the industry practices self-regulation.

State Regulation of the Insurance Industry

In addition to federal laws, the insurance industry is regulated at the state level by state insurance departments, divisions, or boards. These in turn are headed by a commissioner, director, or superintendent, depending on the state. Though specific duties vary from state to state, the head of a state insurance department generally is responsible for:

- issuing rules and regulations to enforce the state's insurance laws which are collectively referred to as the state's insurance code;
- licensing and supervising insurance companies formed within the state;
- licensing and supervising insurance agents and brokers;
- controlling the kinds of insurance contracts and policies that may be sold in the state;
- determining the amount of reserves an insurer must maintain;
- regulating the investment activity of insurers; and
- overseeing insurance companies' marketing practices and investigating consumer complaints.

Insurance Companies

All insurance companies doing business within a given state must be licensed or certified by that state. Thus, insurance companies are referred to as licensed or nonlicensed.

✓ ***Take Note:*** In some states, the terms used to designate whether or not a company is licensed are **authorized** and **nonauthorized**, or **admitted** and **nonadmitted**.

In addition, the following terms are frequently used to describe insurance companies and their site of incorporation:

- **Domestic insurers.** A company is a domestic insurer in the state in which it is incorporated.
- **Foreign insurers**. A foreign insurer is licensed to conduct business in states other than the one in which it is incorporated.
- **Alien insurers**. Alien insurers are companies incorporated in a country other than the United States, the District of Columbia, or any US territorial possession.

✓ ***Take Note:*** Whether companies are considered domestic, foreign, or alien, they must be licensed in each state where they conduct business. State laws restrict insurance companies that are not licensed, or authorized, from doing business within their borders.

Insurance Producers

Every state requires that people who sell insurance have a license from the state. However, before an insurance department will issue such a license—whether to a prospective agent or broker—the candidate must pass a producer licensing exam administered by the department. In some states, the agent's or broker's license is perpetual unless revoked; in other states, it must be renewed at stipulated intervals.

Individuals who sell variable contracts—variable annuities, variable life, and variable universal health—must also be licensed by the NASD. This requires passing the Series 6 (Investment Company/Variable Contracts Limited Representative) or the Series 7 (General Securities Representative) exam. Variable products are considered both securities and life insurance.

Agent Marketing and Sales Practices

Marketing and selling financial products such as life insurance and annuities require a high level of professionalism and ethics. Every state requires its licensed producers to adhere to certain standards designed to protect consumers and promote suitable sales and application of insurance products. Among these standards are the following.

- **Selling to needs.** The ethical agent determines what needs the client has and then determines the product best suited to address those needs. Two principles of needs-based selling are:
  - fact find (learn the client's situation and understand goals, needs, and concerns); and
  - educate (teach the client about insurance as a financial tool).
- **Suitability of recommended products.** The ethical agent assesses the correlation between a recommended product and the client's needs and capabilities by asking and answering the following questions:
  - What are the client's needs?
  - What product can help meet those needs?
  - Does the client understand the product and its provisions?
  - Does the client have the capability—financially and otherwise—to manage the product?
  - Is this product in the client's best interest?
- **Full and accurate disclosure.** The ethical agent makes it a practice to fully inform clients about all aspects of the recommended products including their limitations and their benefits. There should never be any attempt to hide or disguise the nature or purpose of the product, nor the company that is being represented. Insurance products are highly effective financial planning tools; they should be presented clearly, completely, and accurately.
- **Documentation.** The ethical agent documents each client meeting and transaction. He uses fact-finding forms and obtains the client's written

agreement as to the needs determined, the products recommended, and the decisions made. Some documentation is required by state law. Ethical agents know these laws and follow them precisely.

- **Client service.** The ethical agent knows that a sale does not mark the end of a relationship with a client, but the beginning. Routine follow-up calls are recommended to ensure that the client's needs always are covered and that the products in place still are suitable. When clients contact their agents for service or information, these requests are given top priority. Complaints are handled promptly and thoroughly.

Prohibited Practices

Just as there are standards governing appropriate and ethical sales and marketing practices, certain practices long have been viewed as inappropriate to the business of insurance and are prohibited in virtually all jurisdictions. Practically every state bans twisting, misrepresentation, misuse of premiums and rebating. These are known as prohibited practices.

- **Misrepresentation** is a false or misleading statement or representation made by a producer regarding his own policies or those of a competitor. Agents are not allowed to misrepresent a policy's terms, benefits, or the nature of the coverage it provides. If policy dividends are payable, they cannot be represented as guaranteed.
- **Twisting** is the act of persuading a policyowner to drop and replace an existing policy by misrepresenting the terms or conditions of another. Typically, the motivation for twisting is to induce the sale of a policy without any regard to the potential disadvantages to the policyowner. Not only is twisting illegal, it is highly unethical.
- **Misuse of premiums** includes diverting premium funds for personal use. Some states require that an agent establish a separate premium account if he or she holds the money for any time before turning it over to the insurer. Commingling premium funds with personal funds is prohibited.
- **Rebating** occurs if the buyer of an insurance policy receives any part of the agent's commission or if the agent gives the buyer anything of significant value in exchange for purchasing a policy. For instance, a $25 gift certificate given in exchange for the purchase of a policy would be rebating in some jurisdictions. Most states prohibit the practice of rebating, terming it an **illegal inducement**. Where rebating is allowed, strict guidelines have been imposed to control and monitor its practice.

Buyer's Guides and Policy Summaries

To help ensure that prospective insurance buyers select the most appropriate plan or plans for their needs and to improve their understanding of basic product features, most states require agents to deliver a buyer's guide to the consumer whenever they solicit insurance sales. These guides explain the various types of life insurance products in a way that the average consumer can understand. In addition, a policy summary containing information about the specific policy being recommended must be given to a potential buyer. Most states require this be done before the applicant's initial premium is accepted.

FIGURE 2.1 Insurance Company Rating Systems

A.M. Best Company

A++, A+	Superior; very strong ability to meet obligations
A, A–	Excellent; strong ability to meet obligations
B++, B+	Very good; strong ability to meet obligations
B, B–	Good; adequate ability to meet obligations
C++, C+	Fair; reasonable ability to meet obligations
C, C–	Marginal; currently has ability to meet obligations
D	Below minimum standards
E	Under state supervision
F	In liquidation
S	Suspended

S&P

AAA	Superior; highest safety
AA	Excellent financial security
A	Good financial security
BBB	Adequate financial security
BB	Adequate financial security; ability to meet obligations, may not be adequate for long-term policies
B	Currently able to meet obligations but highly vulnerable to adverse conditions
CCC	Questionable ability to meet obligations
CC, C	May not be meeting obligations; vulnerable to liquidation
R	Under a court order of liquidation; in receivership

Moody's

Aaa	Exceptional security
Aa	Excellent security
A	Good security
Baa	Adequate security
Ba	Questionable security; moderate ability to meet obligations
B	Poor security
Caa	Very poor security; elements of danger regarding payment of obligations
Ca	Extremely poor security; may be in default
C	Lowest security

Fitch

AAA	Highest claims-paying ability; negligible risk
AA+, AA, AA–	Very high claims-paying ability; moderate risk
A+, A, A–	High claims-paying ability; variable risk over time
BBB+, BBB, BBB–	Below average claims-paying ability; considerable variability in risk over time
BB+, BB, BB–	Uncertain claims-paying ability
CCC	Substantial claims-paying ability risk; likely to be placed under state supervision

The policy summary also contains cost indices that help the consumer evaluate the suitability of the recommended product. The **net payment cost comparison index** gives the buyer an idea of the cost of the policy at some future point, compared to the death benefit. The **surrender cost comparison index** compares the cost of surrendering the policy and withdrawing the cash values at some future time.

✓ ***Take Note:*** Because all states are interested in protecting the interests of the buying public, the actions of individuals soliciting insurance sales are strictly regulated. However, the laws regarding insurance marketing and trade practices vary from state to state. As a result, it is very important that you examine and understand your state's laws.

National Association of Insurance Commissioners

All state insurance commissioners or directors are members of the National Association of Insurance Commissioners (NAIC). This advisory organization has standing committees that work regularly to examine various aspects of the insurance industry and to recommend appropriate insurance laws and regulations.

The NAIC has four broad objectives:

- to encourage uniformity in state insurance laws and regulations;
- to assist in the administration of those laws and regulations by promoting efficiency;
- to protect the interests of policyowners and consumers; and
- to preserve state regulation of the insurance business.

The NAIC has been instrumental in developing guidelines and model legislation that help ensure that the insurance industry maintains a high level of public trust by conducting its business competently and fairly. This group also develops standards for policy provisions, helping ensure that policies are uniform across the country. Notable among the NAIC's accomplishments was the creation of the Advertising Code and the Unfair Trade Practices Act, which have been adopted by virtually every state.

Advertising Code

A principal problem of states in the past was regulating misleading insurance advertising and direct mail solicitations. Many states now subscribe to the Advertising Code developed by the NAIC. The code specifies certain words and phrases that are considered misleading and are not to be used in advertising of any kind and also requires full disclosure of policy renewal, cancellation, and termination provisions. Other rules pertain to the use of testimonials, statistics, special offers, and the like.

Unfair Trade Practices Act

Most jurisdictions also have adopted the NAIC's Unfair Trade Practices Act. This act, as amended in 1972, gives insurance commissioners the power to investigate insurance companies and producers, to issue cease and desist orders, and to impose penalties on violators. The act also gives commissioners the authority to seek a court injunction to restrain insurers from using any methods believed to be unfair or deceptive. Included as unfair trade practices are misrepresentation and false advertising, coercion and intimidation, unfair discrimination, and inequitable administration or claims settlements.

State Guaranty Associations

All states have established guaranty funds or guaranty associations to support insurers and to protect consumers if an insurer becomes insolvent. Should an insurer be financially unable to pay its claims, the state guaranty association will step in and cover the consumers' unpaid claims. These state associations are funded by insurance companies through assessments.

The NAHU

The **National Association of Health Underwriters (NAHU)** is an organization of health insurance agents that is dedicated to supporting the health insurance industry and advancing the quality of service provided by insurance professionals. The organization issues a code of ethics that stresses the high professional duty expected of underwriters toward their clients, as well as to their companies, and emphasizes that only by observing the highest ethical balance can conflict between these two obligations be avoided. (See the Appendix for the NAHU code of ethic.)

Rating Services

The financial strength and stability of an insurance company are vitally important to potential insurance buyers and to insurance companies themselves. Guides to insurance companies' financial integrity and claims-paying ability are published regularly by various **rating services**, such as A.M. Best, Inc., Standard & Poor's, and Moody's and Fitch. For example, in *Best's Insurance Reports,* companies are rated A++ to A+ (superior), A to A– (excellent), B++ to B+ (very good), B to B– (good), C++ to C+ (fair), C to C– (marginal), D (below minimum standards), E (under state supervision), and F (in liquidation). Experts generally recommend that insurance buyers purchase policies from companies that have a rating of A++ to A–, because these ratings indicate a strong ability to meet obligations to policyowners.

Summary

There are many types of insurance providers. State and local governments provide insurance, as do private insurers. Private insurers include stock companies, mutual companies, reciprocals, assessment mutuals, fraternal societies, home service insurers, and service providers. Special categories of insurers include reinsurers and Lloyd's of London.

Insurance is sold through a variety of methods, most commonly through licensed producers. The systems that support the sale of insurance through agents and brokers are the career agency system, the personal producing agency system, and the independent agency system.

To promote public welfare, the insurance industry is regulated by a number of authorities. These authorities include the:

- states and their departments of insurance;
- NAIC and its model legislation; and
- federal government through the application of antitrust laws and the Fair Credit Reporting Act.

All states have enacted laws and regulations that affect the business of insurance, always with consumer interest in mind. Insurance companies, as well as agents and brokers, are bound by these laws.

Key Concepts

In preparing for their licensing examination, students should be familiar with the following concepts:

- types of insurers
- NAIC
- NAHU
- McCarran-Ferguson Act
- Fair Credit Reporting Act
- federal regulation
- Financial Services Modernization Act
- state regulation
- prohibited practices
- insurance company rating systems
- organization and ownership of insurers
- types of marketing/distribution systems
- *United States v. Southeastern Underwriters Association*

Unit Exam 2

1. In some states, an insurance salesperson who offers a $100 gourmet dinner in exchange for the purchase of a life insurance policy would be considered to have committed which of the following prohibited sales practices?

   A. Twisting
   B. Replacement
   C. Rebating
   D. Churning

2. An insurance company organized and headquartered in Indiana can be described as what type of company when practicing in Indiana?

   A. Alien
   B. Home-based
   C. Foreign
   D. Domestic

3. Which of the following statements regarding types of insurers is NOT correct?

   A. Reinsurers work directly with individual policyowners.
   B. Stock insurance companies seek a profit for their shareholders.
   C. Mutual insurance companies are owned by their policyowners.
   D. Service providers generally specialize in health insurance and health care services.

4. Regarding landmark cases and laws involving the regulation of insurance, which of the following statements is NOT correct?

   A. Insurers are required to disclose when an applicant's consumer or credit history is being investigated.
   B. The Securities and Exchange Commission (SEC) may regulate insurers that sell variable annuities and variable life insurance.
   C. The Federal Trade Commission (FTC) directly supervises all insurance marketing activities.
   D. The New York Insurance Code has long been a model for state insurance regulation.

5. Which of the following statements regarding the National Association of Insurance Commissioners (NAIC) is NOT correct?

   A. It is empowered to prosecute and punish criminal violators in the insurance industry.
   B. It seeks to preserve state rather than federal regulation of the insurance industry.
   C. It promotes uniformity in state insurance laws and regulations.
   D. It seeks to promote efficient administration of insurance laws and regulations.

6. In an insurance transaction, licensed agents legally represent which of the following?

   A. The insurer
   B. The applicant and insured
   C. The state insurance department
   D. Themselves

7. In an insurance transaction, licensed brokers legally represent which of the following people?

   A. The insurer
   B. The applicant and insured
   C. The state insurance department
   D. Themselves

8. A life insurance company organized in Illinois, with its home office in Philadelphia, is licensed to conduct business in Wisconsin. In Wisconsin, this company would be considered which of the following types of insurers?

   A. Domestic
   B. Alien
   C. Foreign
   D. Regional

9. Which of the following is not a service insurer?

   A. HMO
   B. Blue Cross
   C. Lloyd's of London
   D. PPO

10. A reinsurer is a company that

    A. accepts all the risk from another insurer
    B. assumes a portion of the risk from another insurer
    C. cedes the risk from another insurer
    D. does not take any risk

11. The head of a state insurance department is responsible for all of the following EXCEPT

    A. licensing and supervising agents and brokers
    B. overseeing insurance companies' marketing practices
    C. issuing rules and regulations
    D. making insurance laws

12. In addition to the state, the organization that regulates variable life and variable annuities is the

    A. Federal Trade Commission (FTC)
    B. National Association of Insurance Commissioners (NAIC)
    C. Securities and Exchange (SEC)
    D. Federal Communications Commission (FCC)

13. Which of the following prohibited practices involves the diversion of insurance funds for personal use?

    A. Replacement
    B. Rebating
    C. Misrepresentation
    D. Misuse of premiums

14. What does the state guaranty association guarantee?

    A. That your policy will be issued
    B. That your claim will be paid if your insurer becomes insolvent
    C. That dividends will be paid
    D. Rates of return on your policy

Unit Exam 2 Answers & Rationale

1. **C.** Rebating occurs if an agent gives the buyer anything of significant value in exchange for purchasing a policy. A $100 gourmet dinner offered in exchange for purchasing an insurance policy, therefore, would be considered rebating.

2. **D.** An insurance company is considered a domestic insurer in the state in which it is incorporated. Thus, a company organized and headquartered in Indiana is considered a domestic company in Indiana.

3. **A.** Reinsurers insure other insurance companies. The purpose of reinsurance is to limit the loss an insurer would face if a very large claim became payable. Thus, reinsurers work directly with other insurance companies rather than with individual policyowners.

4. **C.** The FTC has attempted to control the advertising and sales literature used by the health insurance industry. However, in 1958 the Supreme Court held that the McCarran-Ferguson Act disallowed such supervision by the FTC.

5. **A.** Although the NAIC assists in administering state insurance laws and seeks to protect policyowners' interests, it does not have any legal authority to prosecute and punish criminal violators in the insurance industry.

6. **A.** A licensed insurance agent legally represents the insurer in a sales transaction and in any disputes between the insured or beneficiary and the insurer.

7. **B.** An insurance broker is not affiliated with any particular company and may represent different companies' products. In an insurance transaction, the broker represents the buyer and not the insurer.

8. **C.** To be considered a domestic company in Wisconsin, the insurance company must be incorporated there. However, because it was incorporated in Illinois and is merely authorized to transact business in Wisconsin, it is considered a foreign company in Wisconsin.

9. **C.** Service insurers such as Blue Cross, HMOs, and PPOs offer health insurance and health care services. Lloyd's of London, on the other hand, is not a service insurer but an association of individuals and companies that individually underwrite insurance.

10. **B.** A reinsurer assumes part, but not all, of the risk from another insurer to help limit the loss the insurer would face if a large claim became payable.

11. **D.** The head of a state insurance department is responsible for licensing and supervising agents and brokers, overseeing insurance companies' marketing practices, and issuing rules and regulations. However, the state legislature and not the head of the state insurance department is responsible for making insurance laws.

12. **C.** Because federal securities laws apply to insurers that issue variable annuities, they must conform to both SEC and state regulations. The SEC also regulates variable life insurance.

13. **D.** The prohibited practice of misusing premiums involves diverting premium funds for personal use.

14. **B.** If an insurer is insolvent or financially unable to pay its claims, the state guaranty association protects consumers by guaranteeing that its claims will be paid.

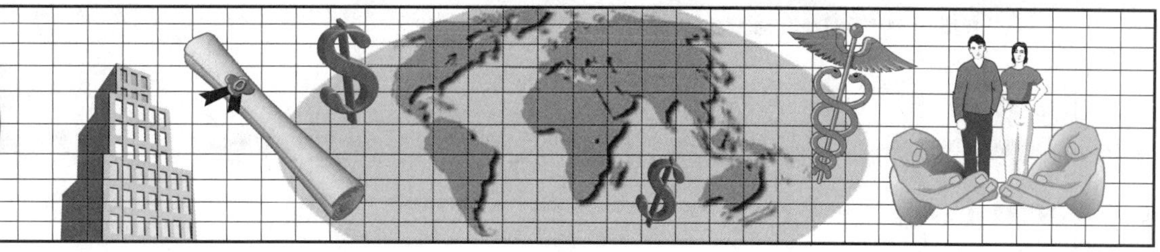

3

Law and the Insurance Contract

INTRODUCTION

Health insurance policies are legal contracts enforceable by law. As such, they are governed by many of the same legal principles that are applicable to the formation of any contract. However, in addition to these general principles, there are other characteristics that apply to insurance contracts specifically. We will begin this unit by reviewing the general requirements of an enforceable contract and then look at some of the other elements of an insurance contract in particular. We will also examine the agent's role in the creation of a contract and how the concepts of waiver, estoppel, and the parol evidence rule apply to the interpretation of contracts.

UNIT OBJECTIVES

When you have completed this unit, you should be able to:

- identify and describe the essential elements of a legally binding contract;
- list and describe the special features of insurance contracts;
- explain the general concepts of agency law, including the difference between express, implied, and apparent authority, and give an example of each; and
- explain how waiver, estoppel, and the parol evidence rule apply to insurance transactions.

General Law of Contracts

A **contract** is an agreement enforceable by law. It is the means by which one or more parties bind themselves to certain promises. With a life insurance contract, the insurer binds itself to pay a certain sum on the death of the insured. In exchange, the policyowner pays premiums.

For a contract to be legally valid and binding, it must contain certain elements: **an offer and acceptance, consideration, legal purpose,** and **competent parties**.

Offer and Acceptance

To be legally enforceable, a contract must be made with a definite, unqualified offer by one party and the acceptance of its exact terms by the other party. In many cases, the offer of an insurance contract is made by the applicant when he submits the application with the initial premium. The insurance company accepts the offer when it issues the policy as applied for. Sometimes the insurance company will not issue the policy as applied for but may counteroffer with the issuance of another policy at different premium rates or with different terms. The applicant has the right to accept or reject the counteroffer.

The applicant who does not submit an initial premium with the application is inviting the insurance company to make the contract offer. The insurer can respond by issuing a policy (the offer) that the applicant can accept by paying the premium when the policy is delivered.

Until an offer has been accepted, the person making the offer has the right to rescind it. Thus, if an applicant wishes to withdraw an application before the insurer accepts it, the offer is terminated, even if the initial premium has been submitted. The insurer must return the premium.

Consideration

For a contract to be enforceable, the promise or promises it contains must be supported by consideration. **Consideration** is something of value given in exchange for the promises sought. In an insurance contract, consideration is given by the applicant in exchange for the insurer's promise to pay benefits; this consideration consists of the application and the initial premium. This is why the offer and acceptance of an insurance contract are not completed until the insurer receives the application and the first premium.

Legal Purpose

To be legally enforceable, a contract must have a **legal purpose**. This means that the goal of the contract and the reason the parties enter into the agreement must be legal. A contract in which one party agrees to commit murder for money would be unenforceable in court because the goal or purpose of the contract is not legal.

✓ ***Take Note:*** In all jurisdictions, insurance is deemed to have a legal purpose.

Competent Parties

To be enforceable, a contract must be entered into by competent parties. With a contract of insurance, the parties to the contract are the applicant and the insurer. The insurer is considered competent if it has been licensed or authorized by the state (or states) in which it conducts business. The applicant, unless proven otherwise, is presumed to be competent, with the exception of:

- minors;
- the mentally infirm; and
- those under the influence of alcohol or narcotics.

Each state has its own laws governing minors and the mentally infirm entering into contracts of insurance. These laws are based on the principle that some parties are not capable of understanding the contract they agree to.

✓ ***Take Note:*** In many states, a minor is considered to be any person under age 21. However, in recent years, a majority of states have lowered this age to 18. With respect to insurance contracts, several states have enacted statutes that give minors of a certain age (varying from 14 to 18) the capacity to enter into valid and enforceable life insurance contracts. In the absence of such a statute, however, insurance contracts with minors are voidable at the minor's option.

It should be noted that beneficiaries and insureds (if different from the applicant) are not parties to an insurance contract. As such, they need not have contractual capability.

Other competent parties that may enter into contracts of insurance with an insurance company include business entities, trusts, and estates.

Test Topic Alert! Use this acronym to recall the four elements of a legal contract: **CLOC** (**C**ompetent parties, **L**egal purpose, **O**ffer and acceptance, and **C**onsideration).

Special Features of Insurance Contracts

The elements just discussed must be contained in every contract for it to be enforceable by law. In addition to these, insurance contracts have their own distinguishing characteristics that set them apart from other legally binding contracts.

Aleatory

An **aleatory contract** is conditioned on the occurrence of an uncertain event beyond the control of the parties involved. Insurance contracts are aleatory in that there is an element of chance for both of the contracting parties, and the dollar values exchanged need not be equal. Consequently, the benefits provided by an insurance policy may or may not exceed the premiums paid. For example, an individual who has a disability insurance policy will collect benefits if she becomes disabled; if no disability strikes, no benefits are paid.

✓ ***Take Note:*** The opposite of an aleatory contract is a commutative contract, in which there is no element of chance and the parties exchange goods of equal value. A real estate transaction is a commutative contract—the seller agrees to sell property for a certain sum and the buyer agrees to buy the property for the same sum.

Adhesion

Insurance contracts are contracts of **adhesion**. This means that the contract has been prepared by one party (the insurer), and the terms did not result from negotiation between the parties. In effect, the applicant adheres to the terms of the contract when he accepts it.

In contract law, and notably with respect to contracts of adhesion, the contract is to be viewed or interpreted most favorably for the party that did not draft it. The purpose is to overcome or balance any advantage on the part of the party that prepared the contract. Consequently, if there are any ambiguities in the contract, they will be interpreted in favor of the party that did not create the contract. For insurance contracts, any ambiguous provisions will be given the interpretation most favorable to the insured or beneficiary, not the insurer.

Unilateral

Insurance contracts are unilateral in that only one party—the insurer—makes any kind of enforceable promise. Insurers promise to pay benefits when or if a certain event, such as death or disability, should happen. The applicant makes no such promise—and does not even promise to pay premiums; likewise the insurer cannot require that they be paid. Of course, the insurer has the right to, and will, cancel the contract if premiums are not paid.

Test Topic Alert!

As a unilateral contract, an insurance policy is legally binding on the insurance company only. The terms may be enforced only against the insurance company, which is bound to perform its duties under the contract.

A **unilateral contract** can be contrasted to a bilateral contract, in which each contracting party makes enforceable promises.

Conditional

An insurance contract is conditional in that the insurer's promise to pay benefits is dependent on the occurrence of the risk insured against. If the risk does not materialize, no benefits are paid. Furthermore, the insurer's obligations under the contract are conditioned on the performance of certain acts by the insured or the beneficiary.

✓ ***For Example:*** The timely payment of premiums is a condition of the continuance of the contract. If premiums are not paid, the company is relieved of its obligation to pay a death benefit, though it is bound by other promises contained in the contract's surrender and reinstatement provisions. Providing proof of death (or proof of disability or medical expenses) is another condition. Until the insurer receives such proof, it is not liable for payment.

The significance of a condition is that, if the policyowner or beneficiary satisfies the condition, it legally binds the insurer to its obligations under the contract. If the condition is not met, the insurer is released from its obligations. However, conditions on a policyowner or beneficiary are not legally binding or enforceable. An insured who does not meet a contractual condition simply gives up the right to make a claim under the contract. If a policyowner stops paying premiums, for example, the insurance company cannot compel further payment. It can only cancel the policy. By contrast, an insurance company that does not meet its contractual obligations once the policyowner or beneficiary satisfies the conditions for making a claim may be liable to the insured for damages.

Valued or Indemnity

An insurance contract is either a valued contract or an indemnity contract. A valued contract pays a stated sum, regardless of the actual loss incurred, when the contingency insured against occurs. Life insurance contracts are valued contracts. If an individual acquires a life insurance policy insuring his life for $1 million, that is the amount payable at his death. There is no attempt to value actual financial loss.

An indemnity contract, on the other hand, pays an amount equal to the loss—it attempts to return the insured to his original financial position.

✓ ***For Example:*** Fire and health insurance policies are examples of indemnity contracts. An insured who owns a $100,000 fire insurance policy and suffers a $5,000 loss from fire will be able to collect up to $5,000, not $100,000.

The doctrine of **subrogation** is inherent to indemnity contracts. This means that in the event a claim is paid, the insurer acquires the insured's right to take legal action against any negligent third party that may have caused or contributed to the loss. The right of subrogation does not exist with life insurance contracts. An auto insurer has the right to take legal action against an individual who caused damage to one of the company's insured vehicles (up to the amount of the loss payment); a life insurer has no such recourse if the death of one of its insureds was caused by a negligent third party.

Utmost Good Faith

Insurance is a contract of utmost good faith. Both the policyowner and the insurer must know all material facts and relevant information. There can be no attempt by either party to conceal, disguise, or deceive. A consumer purchases a policy based largely on what the insurer and its agent claim are its features, benefits, and advantages; an insurer issues a policy based primarily on what the applicant reveals in the application.

The concepts of warranties, representations, and concealment are associated with this idea of utmost good faith. These represent grounds through which an insurer might seek to avoid payment under a contract.

Warranty

A **warranty** in insurance is a statement made by the applicant that is guaranteed to be true. It becomes part of the contract and, if found to be untrue, can be grounds for revoking the contract. Warranties are presumed to be material because they affect the insurer's decision to accept or reject an applicant.

Representation

A **representation** is a statement made by the applicant that they believe to be true. It is used by the insurer to evaluate whether or not to issue a policy. Unlike warranties, representations are not part of the contract and need be true only to the extent that they are material and related to the risk. Most states require that health insurance policies contain a provision that all statements made in the application be deemed representations, not warranties. If an insurance company rejects a claim on the basis of a representation, the company bears the burden of proving that the representation was material and related to risk.

Test Topic Alert!

Statements made by a person on an application for health insurance generally are representations, not warranties.

The practical distinction between a warranty and a representation is this: if a warranty is untrue, the insurer has the right to cancel the contract; if a representation is untrue, the insurer has the right to cancel the contract only if the representation was material to the creation of the contract.

✓ ***For Example:*** If an insured falsely stated in a health insurance application that her cancer was in remission when the insured was, in fact, terminally ill, this statement would be a misrepresentation. If the insurance company had known this information, it would either have rejected the application or issued the policy on substantially different terms. As a result, this misrepresentation may provide grounds for the insurer to cancel the contract. However, if an insured misstated the age at which a grandparent died, the insurer probably would not be able to rescind the contract because such misrepresentation would have had no influence on the terms of the contract.

Concealment

The issue of **concealment** is also important to insurance contracts. Concealment is defined as the applicant's failure to disclose a known material fact when applying for insurance. If the purpose for concealing information is to defraud the insurer (that is, to obtain a policy that might not be issued otherwise if the information were revealed), the insurer may have grounds for voiding the policy. Again, the insurer must prove concealment and materiality.

In most instances, health insurers have only a limited period of time to uncover false warranties, misrepresentations, or concealment. After that time period passes, the contract cannot be voided or revoked for these reasons.

✓ ***For Example:*** An applicant for homeowner's insurance does not disclose that he manufactures firecrackers in the basement as a hobby. Although the insurance company did not specifically ask about this hobby, the applicant has an obligation to disclose extraordinary facts such as these that are within his scope of knowledge. Not disclosing this fact would be considered concealment.

FIGURE 3.1 Elements of an Insurance Contract

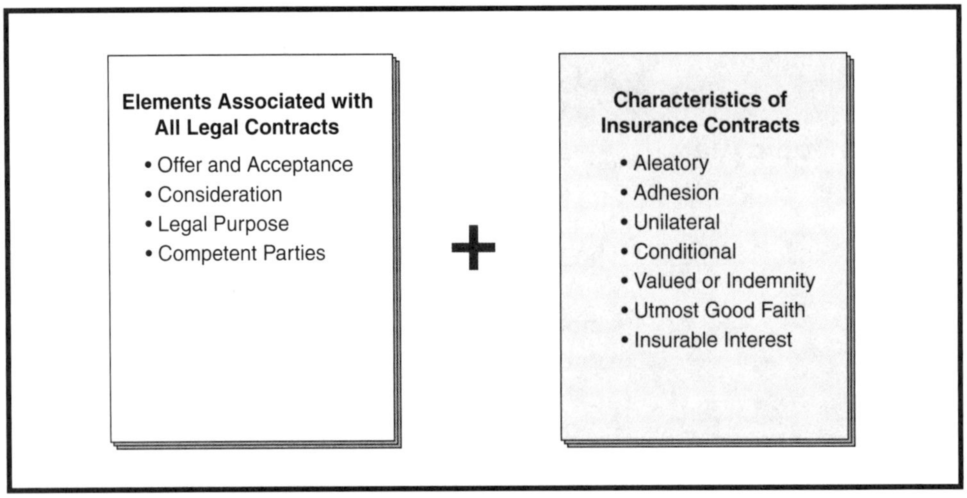

Insurable Interest

Another element of a valid insurance contract is insurable interest. This means that the person acquiring the contract (the applicant) must be subject to loss on the death, illness, or disability of the person being insured. A policy obtained by a person not having an insurable interest in the insured is not valid and cannot be enforced.

✓ ***Take Note:*** Many relationships provide the basis for an insurable interest. Husbands and wives have an insurable interest in each other as do partners in a partnership. Corporations have an insurable interest in their key executives as well.

When the applicant is the same as the person to be insured, there is no question that insurable interest exists—individuals are presumed to have insurable interest in themselves. Questions tend to arise when the applicant is not the person to be insured. As a general rule, the consent of the person to be insured is required before a policy is issued, even if the applicant has an insurable interest. Insurers have a legal responsibility to verify insurable interest and obtain the insured's consent.

Test Topic Alert! Insurable interest may have to exist between the policyowner, the insured, and the beneficiary for the insurance company to consider the risk a pure risk.

One important point about insurable interest with health contracts is that the interest must exist at the inception of the policy. It need not continue throughout the duration of the policy, nor must it exist at the time of the claim. This is in contrast to property and casualty insurance policies, for which insurable interest must exist at the time of claim.

Quick Quiz 3.1

1. To be legally binding, a contract must contain all of the following elements EXCEPT

   A. consideration
   B. offer and acceptance
   C. competent parties
   D. unilateral promises

2. An insured does not disclose a terminal illness when applying for life insurance. This is known as a

   A. guaranteed warranty
   B. concealment
   C. conditional disclosure
   D. revocation of warranty

3. A life insurance contract that pays a set $500,000 death benefit at the insured's death is what kind of contract?

   A. Indemnity
   B. Warranty
   C. Valued
   D. Personal

4. Which of the following parties makes an enforceable promise in an insurance contract?

   A. Insured
   B. Insurer
   C. Insured and the insurer
   D. Agent, the insured, and the insurer

5. If an insured makes a material warranty in an insurance application that is later found to be untrue, the insurance company can

   A. cancel the contract
   B. file a lawsuit
   C. increase premiums
   D. assign the contract

Answers

1. ***D.*** *To be legally binding, a contract must contain an offer and acceptance, consideration, a legal purpose, and competent parties. Some contracts, such as insurance contracts, are unilateral; that is, only one party makes any type of enforceable promise. However, this is not a required element for a contract to be legally binding.*

2. **B.** *Concealment occurs when an applicant fails to disclose a known material fact when applying for insurance.*
3. **C.** *A health insurance contract that pays a set benefit upon the insured's hospitalization is called a valued contract. A valued contract pays a stated sum, regardless of the actual loss incurred, when the contingency insured against occurs. In contrast, an indemnity contract pays an amount equal to the loss and attempts to return the insured to his original financial position.*
4. **B.** *In an insurance contract, only one party—the insurer—makes any kind of enforceable promise. The applicant makes no such promise and does not even promise to pay premiums.*
5. **A.** *Because the insured's warranties will affect the insurer's decision to accept or reject the application, the insurer can cancel the contract if it discovers an untrue warranty in the application.*

Agents and Brokers

Because insurance contracts are binding and enforceable, certain legal concepts extend to those who bring together the contract parties—the applicant and the insurer. In most cases, an agent or a broker brings the parties together. Unit 2 discussed some of the more important regulations that states impose on those who solicit and sell insurance; here we will focus on legal aspects of negotiating and placing insurance contracts.

The Concept of Agency

As noted earlier, an agent is an individual who has been authorized by an insurer to be its representative to the public and to offer its goods and services for sale. Specifically, this role entails:

- describing the company's insurance policies to prospective buyers and explaining the conditions under which the policies may be obtained;
- soliciting applications for insurance;
- in some cases, collecting premiums from policyowners; and
- rendering service to prospects and to those who have purchased policies from the company.

An agent's authority to undertake these functions is defined clearly in a **contract of agency** (or **agency agreement**) between the agent and the company. Within the authority granted, the agent is considered identical with the company. The relationship between an agent and the company he represents is governed by agency law.

Principles of Agency Law

By legal definition, an agent is a person who acts for another person or entity (known as the **principal**) with regard to contractual arrangements with third parties. The concept of power is implicit in this definition—an authorized agent has the power to bind the principal to contracts (and to the rights and responsibilities of those contracts). With this in mind, we can review the following main principles of agency law.

- The acts of the agent (within the scope of authority) are the acts of the principal.
- A contract completed by an agent on behalf of the principal is a contract of the principal.
- Payments made to an agent on behalf of the principal are payments made to the principal.
- The agent's knowledge regarding the principal's business is presumed to be the principal's knowledge.

Agent Authority

Note the above parenthetical explanation "within the scope of authority." Authority—that which an agent is authorized to do on behalf of his company—is another important concept in agency law. Technically, only those actions for which an agent is authorized can bind a principal. In reality, however, an agent's authority can be quite broad. There are three types of agent authority: express, implied, and apparent.

- **Express authority** is the authority a principal intends to—and does—give to its agent. Express authority is granted by means of the agent's contract, which is the principal's appointment of the agent to act on its behalf.

✓ ***For Example:*** The agency contract generally contains clauses dealing with the specific and general powers of the agent, the scale of commissions, and the ownership of contracts sold.

- **Implied authority** is authority that is not expressly granted but which the agent is assumed to have in order to transact the principal's business. Implied authority is incidental to express authority because not every detail of an agent's authority can be spelled out.

✓ ***For Example:*** An agent's contract may not specifically state that he can print business cards that contain the company's name, but the authority to do so is implied.

- **Apparent authority** is the appearance or assumption of authority based on the actions, words, or deeds of the principal, or because of circumstances the principal created.

✓ ***For Example:*** By providing an individual with a rate book, application forms, and sales literature, an insurance company creates the impression that an agency relationship exists between itself and the individual. The company will not be allowed later to deny that such a relationship existed.

✓ ***Take Note:*** Understand that apparent authority arises only when the buyer has no way of knowing that the agent has exceeded his authority. Also, even if the agent did not have the express or implied authority to take a particular action, his authority may be extended by ratification. **Ratification** occurs when the insurer accepts the agent's actions that were beyond the scope of his authority and acts as if the agent actually had authority to take such actions (e.g., it accepts the premium on coverage the agent wrote while exceeding express authority).

The significance of authority—whether express, implied, or apparent—is that it ties the company to the acts and deeds of its agent. The law will view the agent and the company as the same entity when the agent acts within the scope of her authority.

Agent as Fiduciary

Another legal concept that governs the activity of an agent is that of fiduciary. A **fiduciary** is a person who holds a position of special trust and confidence. Agents act in a fiduciary capacity when they accept premiums on behalf of the insurer or offer advice that affects people's financial security. Agents have fiduciary responsibilities to both their clients and the insurance companies they represent. Acting as a fiduciary requires that an agent:

- be fit and proper;
- be honest and trustworthy;
- have a good business reputation;
- be qualified to perform insurance functions;
- have knowledge of, and abide by, state laws and regulations; and
- act in good faith.

Brokers vs. Agents

As noted earlier, unlike agents, brokers legally represent the insureds and do not have the legal authority to bind the insurer. Brokers solicit and accept applications for insurance and then place the coverage with an insurer. The business is not in force and the insurance company is not bound until it accepts the application. Technically, brokers represent themselves in the solicitation of insurance policies; once prospects or clients request coverage, brokers represent their buyers.

In practice, the legal distinction between brokers and agents is insignificant. Both brokers and agents are licensed as insurance producers and both are subject to insurance laws and regulations. In fact, in some states any individual who solicits insurance and places a policy will be considered an agent of the insurer with regard to that policy.

Professional Liability

Just as doctors and lawyers should have malpractice insurance to protect against legal liability arising from their professional services, insurance agents need **errors and omissions (E&O)** professional liability insurance. Under this insurance, the insurer agrees to pay sums that the agent is legally obligated to pay for injuries resulting from professional services that she rendered or failed to render. Under E&O policies, the insurer will defend any suits covered by the policy, even if the suits are groundless, false, or fraudulent. Any claim arising from injuries, real or alleged, comes within the scope of this coverage.

Other Legal Concepts

In addition to the principles of contract and agency law, other legal concepts apply to insurance and the power of agents. These are waiver, estoppel, the parol evidence rule, void vs. voidable contracts, and fraud.

Waiver

Waiver is the voluntary giving up of a legal, given right. If an insurer voluntarily waives a legal right it has under a contract, it cannot later deny a claim based on a violation of that right.

✓ ***For Example:*** A health insurance contract specifies that premium payments are to be made by the policyowner directly to the company at the home office address. John, one of the company's insureds, has made his payments to his agent over the years and the company has accepted these payments. In so doing, the company has effectively waived the direct payment provision and cannot later deny payment of claim on John's policy on the grounds that premiums were not remitted directly to the company.

Estoppel

The concepts of waiver and estoppel are closely related. **Estoppel** prohibits one party from denying the consequences of its own actions or deeds if such actions or deeds result in another party acting in a specific manner or drawing certain conclusions. In other words, estoppel is the loss of defense.

✓ ***For Example:*** In the preceding example, if the insurer has waived its right to have premiums remitted to it directly, it will be estopped from denying John's claim because he gave his premium payments to his agent.

Another example of estoppel is if a company severs its agency relationship with an agent but later accepts an application from this individual, thereby reasserting the agency relationship. The company will be estopped from claiming an agency relationship did not exist at the time it entered into the contract with the insured.

Parol Evidence Rule

Parol evidence is oral or verbal evidence, or that which is given verbally in a court of law. The **parol evidence rule** states that when parties put their agreement in writing, all previous verbal statements come together in that writing, and a written contract cannot be changed or modified by parol (oral) evidence. This preserves the integrity of the written contract as the final embodiment of the parties' agreement.

✓ ***Take Note:*** There are a few exceptions to the parol evidence rule. Parol evidence may be admissible in court when the written contract terms are incomplete or ambiguous, or when there has been a mistake or fraud in preparing the written contract. Then parol evidence is used not to change the terms, but to explain or interpret them.

Void vs. Voidable Contracts

The terms *void* and *voidable* often are incorrectly used interchangeably. A **void** contract is simply an agreement without legal effect. In essence, it is not a contract at all, for it lacks one of the elements specified by law for a valid contract. A void contract cannot be enforced by either party.

A contract having an illegal object is void, and neither party to the contract can enforce it.

✓ ***For Example:*** Tom agrees to steal a car and sell it to Fred. The car is damaged during the theft; Fred refuses to pay the price they agreed upon. Tom cannot sue Fred to get the payment, and Fred cannot sue Tom to get another undamaged car.

In contrast, a **voidable contract** is an agreement which, for a reason satisfactory to the court, may be set aside by one of the parties to the contract. It is binding unless the party with the right to reject it wishes to do so. If a situation develops under which the insured has failed to comply with a condition of the contract (e.g., he ceased paying the premium), the contract is voidable, and the insurance company has the right to void the contract and revoke the coverage.

Fraud

In the event of fraud, insurance contracts run counter to a basic rule of contract law. Under most contracts, fraud is a reason to void a contract. With life insurance contracts, an insurer has a limited period of time (usually two years from date of issue) to challenge the validity of a contract. After that period, the insurer cannot contest the policy or deny benefits based on material misrepresentations, concealment, or fraud. (This is explained in more detail in *Time Limit on Certain Defenses*, Unit 11.)

Summary

An insurance policy is a legally binding contract between the applicant/owner and the insurance company. As such, it must contain an offer and acceptance, consideration, legal purpose, and competent parties—elements required of all enforceable contracts. In addition, insurance contracts are distinguished by other features unique to the purpose and scope of insurance. Among these special features is the element of insurable interest.

Agents and brokers—and the companies they conduct business with—operate under the concept of agency and the principles of agency law. One of the most important aspects of agency law is that it gives the agent the power to act on behalf of the principal (the insurer) and to bind it to contracts. Agents are empowered by three types of authority: express, implied, and apparent.

Finally, there are additional legal concepts that have direct application to insurance and insurance contracts. These include waiver, estoppel, the parol evidence rule, void versus voidable contracts, and fraud.

Key Concepts

In preparing for their licensing examination, students should be familiar with the following concepts:

- offer and acceptance
- legal purpose
- aleatory
- unilateral
- valued vs. reimbursement
- warranties
- concealment
- estoppel
- fraud
- express authority
- apparent authority
- consideration
- competent parties
- adhesion
- conditional
- insurable interest
- representations
- waiver
- parol evidence rule
- void vs. voidable contract
- implied authority

Unit Exam 3

1. Which of the following is the authority that an insurer gives to its agents by means of the agent's contract?

   A. Implied
   B. Express
   C. Fiduciary
   D. General

2. An insurance contract is prepared by one party, the insurer, rather than by negotiation between the contracting parties. This feature means that the insurance contract

   A. is an aleatory contract
   B. is a contract of acceptance
   C. is a contract of adhesion
   D. names only the insurer as the competent party

3. Which of the following statements regarding insurable interest is NOT correct?

   A. Insurable interest exists when the applicant is the insured.
   B. A policy obtained by a person without an insurable interest in the insured can be enforced.
   C. The applicant must be subject to loss on the death, illness, or disability of the insured.
   D. Generally, the person to be insured must give their consent before a policy is issued, even if the applicant has an insurable interest.

4. Which of the following statements is NOT correct?

   A. Express authority is granted by means of the agent's contract.
   B. Express authority is expressed orally.
   C. Implied authority is not overtly extended in the agent's contract, but does permit many of the agent's operations.
   D. Apparent authority is the appearance of authority based on the principal's actions, words, or deeds.

5. Which of the following statements regarding utmost good faith in insurance contracts is CORRECT?

   A. The concept of utmost good faith—that there is no attempt to conceal, disguise, or deceive—applies only to the insurer.
   B. Although a warranty is a statement, it is not technically part of the contract.
   C. A representation is a statement that the applicant guarantees to be true.
   D. Most state insurance laws consider statements made in an application for an insurance policy to be representations, not warranties.

6. Which of the following statements describes an insurable interest?

   A. The policyowner must expect to benefit from the insured's death.
   B. The policyowner must expect to suffer a loss when the insured dies or becomes disabled.
   C. The beneficiary, by definition, has an insurable interest in the insured.
   D. The insured must have a personal or business relationship with the beneficiary.

7. Which of the following statements describes the parol evidence rule?
   A. A written contract cannot be changed once it is signed.
   B. An oral contract cannot be modified by written evidence.
   C. A written contract cannot be changed by oral evidence.
   D. An oral contract takes preference over any earlier written contracts.

8. Which of the following is a special element of an insurance contract?
   A. Offer and acceptance
   B. Conditional
   C. Consideration
   D. Competent parties

9. An insurer is considered competent if it
   A. is registered with the NAIC
   B. is licensed or authorized by the state
   C. follows the state department of insurance's code of ethics
   D. is registered with the Securities and Exchange Commission

10. All of the following are considered to be competent parties who can enter into insurance contracts EXCEPT
    A. applicants
    B. trusts and estates
    C. business entities
    D. individuals under age 18

11. Which of the following is an example of consideration?
    A. Politeness
    B. Initial premium
    C. Legal purpose
    D. Offer and acceptance

12. With health contracts, when must an insurable interest exist?
    A. After the policy is issued
    B. Before the beneficiary is named
    C. While the policy is in force
    D. At the inception of the policy

13. An insurance company has how many years to challenge the validity of a health insurance contract?
    A. 1
    B. 2
    C. 3
    D. 4

14. Which of the following describes the voluntary giving up of known right?
    A. Estoppel
    B. Adhesion
    C. Waiver
    D. Unilateral

15. Bob and Tom enter into a contract in which Bob agrees to fraudulently induce sick people to sell their insurance contracts to Tom's company. Bob and Tom's contract can best be described as
    A. void
    B. competitive
    C. voidable
    D. conditional

Unit Exam 3 Answers & Rationale

1. **B.** Express authority is granted through the agent's contract in which the principal appoints the agent to act on its behalf.

2. **C.** Insurance contracts are contracts of adhesion. This means that the contract has been prepared by one party (the insurer) rather than as the result of negotiation between the parties.

3. **B.** If a person obtains a policy but does not have an insurable interest in the insured, the contract will not be valid and cannot be enforced.

4. **B.** Express authority is the authority the principal intends for and gives to its agent under a contract. It is not expressed orally.

5. **D.** According to most states, health insurance policies must contain a provision that all statements made in the application are deemed representations, not warranties. If a warranty or representation is untrue, the insurer may cancel the contract; however, the insurer may cancel the contract only if the representation was material to the creation of the contract.

6. **B.** In every insurance contract there must be an insurable interest. This means that the person acquiring the contract (the applicant) must be subject to loss on the death, illness, or disability of the person being insured.

7. **C.** According to the parol evidence rule, once an agreement is reduced to writing, it cannot later be modified by any parol (verbal) evidence.

8. **B.** An insurance contract is conditional in that the insurer's promise to pay benefits depends on the occurrence of the risk insured against. The insurer's obligations under the contract are also conditioned on whether the insured performs certain acts, such as paying premiums.

9. **B.** To have an enforceable contract, both the insurer and the applicant must be competent parties. The insurer will be considered competent if it has been licensed or authorized by the state (or states) in which it conducts business.

10. **D.** Applicants are presumed to be competent. However, there are three exceptions: minors, the mentally infirm, and those under the influence of alcohol or drugs.

11. **B.** To be enforceable, a contract's promises must be supported by consideration. Consideration means that value has been given in exchange for the promises sought. In the health insurance context, consideration is the initial premium that an applicant gives in exchange for the insurer's promise to pay benefits.

12. **D.** Although an insurable interest does not have to exist when a claim is made or throughout the duration of a policy, it must exist at the inception of the policy.

13. **B.** An insurer generally has two years from the date of issue to challenge the validity of a contract.

14. **C.** A person who voluntarily gives up a legal, given right is deemed to have waived that right.

15. **A.** Bob and Tom's contract would be considered a void contract because it lacks one of the elements specified by law for a valid contract. The contract has an illegal purpose (fraudulently inducing sick individuals to sell their insurance policies) and neither party to the contract can enforce it.

Part Two

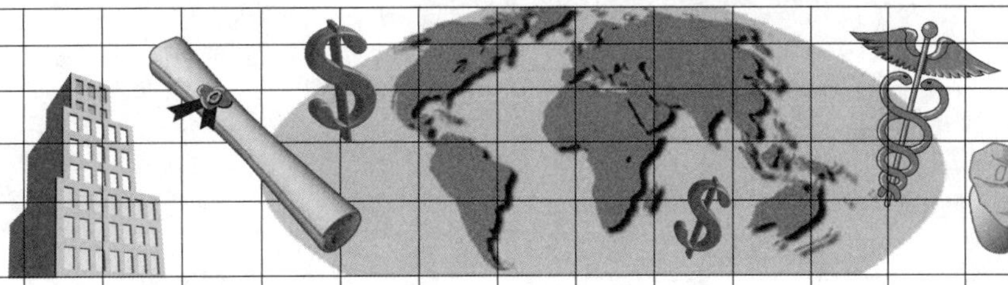

Principles of Health Insurance

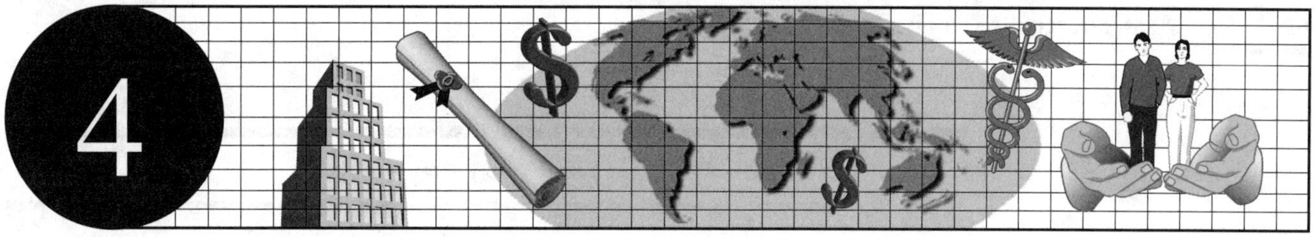

Introduction to Health Insurance

INTRODUCTION

The terms **health and accident insurance, accident and sickness insurance,** and **health insurance** are used interchangeably in the health insurance industry from state to state and company to company. But no matter how this type of insurance is referred to in the industry, it all means the same thing to consumers—a critically important type of insurance that provides financial protection from the high costs of illness and injury.

The remainder of this text is devoted to the principles of health insurance. We will take a look at the types of health insurance plans that exist (including plans for the elderly), the providers of health insurance coverages, policy provisions, underwriting standards, and more. This unit is designed to provide an overview of the broad field of health insurance, focusing on the basics.

UNIT OBJECTIVES

When you complete this unit you should be able to:

- explain the main features of medical expense insurance, disability income insurance, and accidental death and disability insurance;
- describe the typical ways in which individuals and families purchase health insurance; and
- explain the main ways in which health insurance differs from life insurance.

FIGURE 4.1 Health Coverages and What They Provide

Type of Coverage	*Provisions and Benefits*
Medical Expense Insurance	Provides benefits for the cost of medical care. Depending on the type of policy (and its specific provisions), coverage can range from limited (coverage for hospital costs only, for example) to very broad (coverage for all aspects of medical services and care).
Disability Income Insurance	Provides a specified periodic income to the insured—usually on a monthly basis—in the event he or she becomes disabled.
Accidental Death and Dismemberment Insurance	Provides a lump-sum payment in the event the insured dies due to an accident or suffers the loss of one or more body members due to an accident.

Basic Forms of Health Insurance Coverage

Health insurance (as it will be called in this text) refers to the broad field of insurance plans that provide protection against the financial consequences of illness, accidents, injury, and disability. Statistics reveal that approximately 261 million Americans were protected by one or more forms of health coverage at the end of 1999. Health insurance claims payments made to insureds amount to billions of dollars every year, and approximately half of these claims payments are made by commercial insurance companies.

Within the broad field of health insurance, three distinct categories of health coverage exist: **medical expense insurance, disability income insurance,** and **accidental death and dismemberment insurance**. Each of these coverages will be discussed in detail in subsequent units, but an introduction is appropriate here.

Medical Expense Insurance

Medical expense insurance provides financial protection against the cost of medical care by reimbursing the insured, fully or in part, for these costs. It includes many kinds of plans that cover hospital care, surgical expenses, physician expenses, medical treatment programs, outpatient care, and the like.

Medicare supplement insurance and long-term care insurance, two types of health insurance coverage designed for the elderly, are also examples of medical expense insurance plans and are discussed in detail in Unit 10.

Disability Income Insurance

Disability income insurance is designed to provide replacement income when wages are lost due to a disability. As such, it does not cover the medical expenses associated with a disability. Rather, it provides the disabled insured with a guaranteed flow of periodic income payments while she is disabled.

Accidental Death and Dismemberment (AD&D) Insurance

Accidental death and dismemberment insurance (AD&D) is the purest form of accident insurance, providing the insured with a lump-sum benefit amount in the event of accidental death or dismemberment under accidental circumstances.

✓ ***Take Note:*** AD&D coverage is typically part of a group insurance plan.

Within each of these three categories are many forms and variations of coverage that have evolved to meet unique insurance needs. Even the type of health insurance provider—of which there are many—can make a difference in the basic makeup of any of these kinds of coverages. Each of these basic coverages, as well as the many types of health insurance providers, will be discussed in later units. They are introduced here to help acquaint you with the health insurance field in general.

How Health Insurance Is Purchased

As is the case with life insurance, health insurance is available to individuals and families through individual plans and policies, or through group plans and policies including blanket policies and franchise policies.

Individual health insurance is issued by commercial insurers and service organizations as contracts between the insured and the company. Though all companies have standard policies for the coverages they offer, most allow an individual to select various options or benefit levels that will meet his needs most precisely. Individual health contracts require an application, and the proposed insured must usually provide evidence of insurability.

Group health insurance, also issued by commercial insurers and service organizations, provides coverage under a master contract to members of a specified group. Like group life plans, group health plans are available to employers, trade and professional associations, labor unions, credit unions, and other organizations. Insurance is extended to the individuals in the group through the master contract, usually without individual underwriting and usually without requiring group members to provide evidence of insurability. The employer or the association is the policyowner and is responsible for premium payments. The employer may pay the entire premium or may require some contribution from each member to cover the insurance cost.

✓ ***Take Note:*** In general, the provisions and coverages of group health insurance contracts are more liberal than individual health contracts.

Health insurance also is provided through state and federal government programs. At the state level, Medicaid is available to assist low-income individuals in meeting the costs of medical care. The federal government offers health insurance protection through Medicare and OASDI disability provisions, components of the Social Security system.

Characteristics of Health Insurance

Though closely related to life insurance in purpose, health insurance differs from it in several important ways. A review here of the distinguishing characteristics of health insurance will set the stage for more in-depth discussion to follow in later units.

Renewability Provisions

Life insurance (particularly whole life insurance) and annuities are characterized by their permanence. The policies cannot be cancelled by the insurer unless the policyowner fails to make a required premium payment. Even term life policies are guaranteed effective for the duration of the term, as long as premiums are paid. Health insurance is not as permanent in nature. Health insurance policies may contain any one of a wide range of renewability provisions which define the rights of the insurer to cancel the policy at different points during the life of the policy.

✓ ***Take Note:*** Five principal renewability classifications exist: cancellable, optionally renewable, conditionally renewable, guaranteed renewable, and noncancellable.

In general the more advantageous the renewability provisions are to the insured, the more expensive the coverage.

Premium Factors

Like life insurance, health insurance is funded by the regular payment of premiums. However, unlike life insurance relatively few payment options are available with a health policy. For instance, health policies do not offer any sort of limited payment option, as one would find with a 10-pay or paid-up-at-65 life policy. Health insurance policies are paid for on a year-by-year basis. Health premiums can be paid under one of several different payment modes, including annual, semiannual, quarterly, and monthly. Monthly premiums often are paid through some form of preauthorized check method, by which the insurer automatically obtains the premium directly from the policyholder's checking account.

✓ ***Take Note:*** Except for the noncancellable type of policy cited previously, health insurance premium rates are subject to periodic increases.

Various factors enter into premium calculations for health insurance. These include interest, expense, types of benefits, and morbidity. Morbidity is the expected incidence of sickness or disability within a given age group during a given period of time; it is to health insurance what mortality is to life insurance. Other health insurance premium factors are claims experience and the age, sex, and occupation of the insured. All of these factors are discussed in detail in Unit 12.

Participating vs. Nonparticipating Policies

Health insurance policies may be written on either a participating or nonparticipating basis. Most individual health insurance is issued on a nonparticipating basis. On the other hand, group health insurance generally is participating and provides for dividends or experience rating.

Group health plans issued by mutual companies usually provide for dividends, while stock companies frequently issue experience-rated plans. A group policy that is experience-rated may make premium reductions retroactive for 12 months. Premium increases for such policies are not retroactive. Experience-rated refunds may be contingent upon renewal of the master policy, but the payment of dividends usually is not contingent upon renewal.

Cost-accounting formulas are complex and vary from insurer to insurer. However, the two major factors that influence whether or not dividends or experience-rated refunds are payable are expenses and claims costs of the insurer. If these cost items are less than anticipated, the group policyowner benefits by receiving a dividend or refund credit. If expenses and claims costs are higher than expected, the group policyowner may not qualify for a dividend or refund credit.

Reserves

Reserves are set aside by an insurance company and designated for the payment of future claims. Part of each premium is designated for the reserves.

Two types of health insurance reserves are **premium reserves** and **loss** (or **claims**) **reserves**. Premium reserves reflect the liability of the insurer for losses that have not occurred, but for which premiums have been paid. Reserves earmarked as loss (or claims) reserves represent the insurer's liability for losses that have occurred, but for which settlement is not yet complete. The details of how reserves are handled and recorded by the company are very technical. State laws dictate the minimum requirements for reserves for both life and health insurance. The annual statements required by state insurance departments break down a company's reserves in considerable detail.

Claims

The role of the health insurance claims examiner differs somewhat from that of the life insurance claims examiner. In the case of life insurance, most claims are fairly well defined: the amount of insurance coverage is readily determined by the policy and benefits are payable if the insured has died. With health insurance, though, the claims process is not as clearly defined. Medical expense insurance, for example, is typically based on a **reimbursement contract,** meaning that the benefit an insured receives is not fixed but instead is dependent on the amount of the loss. Its purpose is to reimburse the insured for the amount of loss sustained (within limits). This is in contrast to life insurance, AD&D, and disability income insurance, which all are **valued contracts** which pay the amount stated in the contract if a defined event occurs, such as death or disability.

The health claims examiner also must decide if, in fact, a loss actually has occurred. This is especially challenging in disability income cases, where a subjective assessment of disability can create misunderstandings.

Summary

This unit introduced the important field of health insurance. Many hybrid plans offer health protection in three different forms: medical expense, disability income, and accidental death and dismemberment. Health insurance is available to individuals and families on an individual basis, through a group plan or through the federal government. It is distinguished by many factors, including its provisions for renewability, premium factors, whether or not the contract is participating, reserves, and its claims procedures. In the following units, we will review the different types of health insurance and health insurance providers in greater detail.

Key Concepts

In preparing for their licensing examination, students should be familiar with the following concepts:

- medical expense insurance
- reserves
- morbidity
- accidental death and dismemberment insurance
- disability income insurance
- valued vs. reimbursement contracts
- renewability provisions
- participating vs. nonparticipating policies

Unit Exam 4

1. Which of the following statements pertaining to health insurance policy premium factors is CORRECT?

   A. A *policy fee* is another term for policy premium.
   B. A policyowner has an individual health plan, therefore the policy most likely is a participating policy.
   C. Age and sex of the individual insureds would have the most influence on a group health insurance policy's experience rating refund credit.
   D. Pearl files a claim against her major medical policy for a $9,800 hospital bill. The claim likely will be paid out of the insurer's reserves.

2. All of the following are basic forms of health insurance coverage EXCEPT

   A. medical expense
   B. limited pay health
   C. disability income
   D. accidental death and dismemberment

3. Which of the following premium factors is distinctive to health insurance (as opposed to life insurance)?

   A. Age
   B. Sex
   C. Morbidity
   D. Interest

4. Which of the following statements regarding health insurance is CORRECT?

   A. Once issued, health insurance policies cannot be cancelled by the insurer.
   B. Numerous premium payment options are available with health insurance policies.
   C. Most medical expense policies are contracts of reimbursement.
   D. Disability income policies are designed to pay the medical expenses associated with a disability.

5. Assume a health insurance contract states that it will pay $350 a month to the insured should she become totally disabled. Which term most aptly defines this kind of contract?

   A. Participating
   B. Valued
   C. Inclusive
   D. Reimbursement

Unit Exam 4 Answers & Rationale

1. **D**. Each health insurance company must set aside reserves that are designated for paying future claims. If Pearl files a claim for a $9,800 hospital bill, the claim likely will be paid out her insurance company's reserves.

2. **B**. Three distinct categories of basic health insurance coverage exist: medical expense, disability income, and accidental death and dismemberment.

3. **C**. One factor that enters into premium calculations for health insurance but not life insurance is morbidity. Morbidity is the expected incidence of sickness or disability within a given age group during a given period of time.

4. **C**. Most medical expense insurance pays for medical care by reimbursing the insured, either fully or in part, for his costs.

5. **B**. A valued contract pays an amount stated in the contract if a defined event, such as death or disability, occurs. Therefore, a contract that pays $350 a month to the insured upon her total disability would be considered a valued contract.

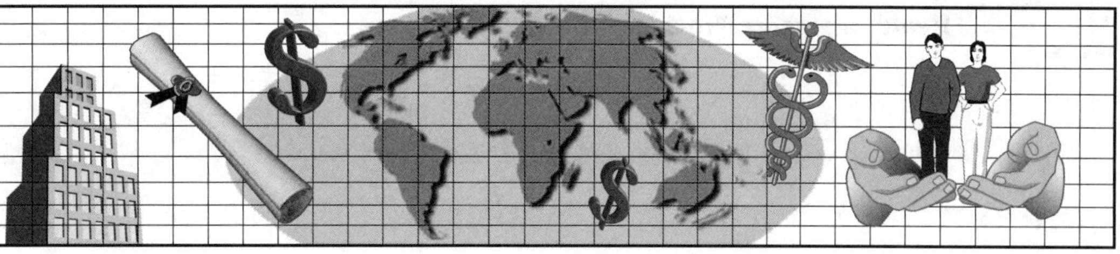

5 Health Insurance Providers

INTRODUCTION

Most Americans regard medical insurance as the most important form of insurance protection to own, and with good reason. As the cost of medical care increases, an uninsured illness or injury could result in financial disaster for many families.

A number of sources are available for individuals seeking health insurance protection. In general, health insurance providers can be divided into three main categories: commercial insurers, service providers, and state and federal governments. In all cases the objective is the same: to provide protection against the financial costs associated with illness, injury, or disability. In this unit we will look at some of the specific types of providers in each of these groups. We will also introduce Medicare and Medicaid, which play an important role in providing health insurance for a large segment of our population.

UNIT OBJECTIVES

When you have completed this unit, you should be able to:

- explain the main characteristics of Blue Cross and Blue Shield, HMOs, and PPOs, and describe how they differ from each other;
- identify the purpose of Medicare, Social Security Disability Income, Medicaid, and state workers' compensation programs, and explain how each program works; and
- describe how self-insured plans, multiple employer trusts, and MEWAs are used to provide health insurance.

Commercial Insurance Providers

Health insurance may be written by a number of commercial insurers, including life insurance companies, casualty insurance companies, or monoline companies that specialize in one or more types of medical expense and disability income insurance. This includes both individual and group insurance policies. Among life insurance companies, health insurance is offered by ordinary companies as well as debit (or home service) companies. (Recall that debit companies sell what are known as industrial policies.)

Commercial insurance companies function on the reimbursement approach. That is, policyowners obtain medical treatment from whatever source they feel is most appropriate and, per the terms of their policy, submit their charges to their insurer for reimbursement. The right-of-assignment built into most commercial health policies lets policyowners assign benefit payments from the insurer directly to the health care provider, thus relieving the policyowner of first having to pay the medical care provider. However, the right to assign a policy's benefits does not change the fact that the policy is reimbursing the insured for covered medical expenses.

Service Providers

Service providers are not insurers per se. Rather, they operate on the principle that their subscribers (the term used in place of policyholders) receive medical care services as a result of their payment of premiums. Subscribers typically are not billed for services rendered by a medical care provider. Instead, the care provider, who has entered into an agreement with the service organization to provide medical care, is paid by the service organization directly.

✓ ***Take Note:*** As you can see, this is the opposite of the cash reimbursement approach taken by commercial insurers. Under the service approach, the subscriber receives benefits in the form of medical services for which payment already has been made via the premium.

This service approach is used primarily by three types of organizations: **Blue Cross** and **Blue Shield organizations, health maintenance organizations (HMOs)**, and **preferred provider organizations (PPOs)**.

Blue Cross and Blue Shield

Blue Cross and Blue Shield are voluntary not-for-profit health care service organizations. Blue Cross offers prepayment plans designed to cover hospital services. Blue Shield covers surgical expenses and other medical services performed by physicians.

Generally, Blue Cross and Blue Shield plans work in close cooperation with each other, within a given state or region within a state. In fact, in the past few years most Blue Cross and Blue Shield plans merged into single plans. Unlike commercial insurance companies, Blue Cross and Blue Shield organizations have contractual arrangements with hospitals and physicians. These contracts provide for payments for services rendered to subscribers with agreed-upon rates or fee schedules.

Consequently, to obtain full value from their service plans, subscribers usually are required to utilize the contracted hospitals and physicians for medical care. Payments for services are made by Blue Cross or Blue Shield directly to the hospitals and physicians; subscribers are responsible only for services not covered by their particular plans. (Blue Cross and Blue Shield plans offer a broad and comprehensive range of services from which the subscriber can choose.)

✓ ***Take Note:*** Blue Cross and Blue Shield plans are available on an individual, family, or group basis.

Health Maintenance Organization (HMO)

A health maintenance organization (HMO), is another type of organization offering comprehensive prepaid health care services to its subscribing members. HMO participants can be members under a group insurance plan, an individual, or family members.

HMOs are distinguished by the fact that they not only finance health care services for their subscribers on a prepayment basis, but also organize and deliver the health services. Subscribers pay a fixed periodic fee to the HMO (as opposed to paying for services only when needed) and are provided with a broad range of health services, from routine doctor visits to emergency and hospital care. This care is rendered by physicians and hospitals that participate in the HMO.

Test Topic Alert! HMOs are known for stressing preventative care, with the objective of reducing the number of unnecessary hospital admissions and duplication of services.

Unlike commercial insurers and Blue Cross and Blue Shield organizations, HMOs rarely assess deductibles. When they do, the charges are nominal, such as $2 for prescription drugs or $5 for an office visit.

Two basic types of HMOs exist:

- **Open-panel HMO.** An open-panel HMO is characterized by a network of physicians who work out of their own private offices and participate in the HMO on a part-time basis.
- **Closed-panel HMO.** A closed-panel HMO is represented by a group of physicians who are salaried employees of the HMO and work out of its facilities.

Health maintenance organizations may be self-contained and self-funded based on dues or fees from their subscribers, or they may contract for excess insurance or administrative services provided by insurance companies. In fact, some HMOs are sponsored by insurance companies.

The Health Maintenance Act of 1973, which provided some federal funding for these organizations, spurred the HMO movement forward. One of its provisions requires employers with 25 or more employees to offer enrollment in an HMO if they provide health care benefits for their workers.

Preferred Provider Organization (PPO)

Another relatively new type of health insurance provider is the preferred provider organization (PPO). A preferred provider organization is a collection of health care providers such as physicians, hospitals, and clinics, who offer their services to certain groups at prearranged prices. In exchange, the group refers its members to the preferred providers for health care services.

Unlike HMOs, preferred provider organizations usually operate on a fee-for-service-rendered basis, not on a prepaid basis. Members of the PPO select from among the preferred providers for needed services. Also in contrast to HMOs, PPO health care providers are normally in private practice. They have agreed to offer their services to the group and its members at fees that are typically less than what they normally charge. In exchange, the providers broaden their patient and service base because the group refers its members to the PPO.

Test Topic Alert!

One feature that attracts groups to PPOs is the discounted fees that are negotiated in advance. Although an insured can receive treatment from any doctor of her choice, the benefit will be reduced if the doctor is not in the PPO.

Groups that contract with PPOs often are employers, insurance companies, or other health insurance benefits providers. While these groups do not mandate that individual members must use the PPO, a reduced benefit is typical if they do not. For instance, individuals may pay a $100 deductible if they use PPO services and a $500 deductible if they go outside the PPO for health care services.

Government Insurance Programs

For many people, health care cost protection is made available through a state or federal government program. At the federal level, Medicare is the primary source of health insurance. It is a part of the Social Security program that also provides disability income to qualified workers under OASDI. At the state level, Medicaid offers protection to financially needy individuals, and state workers' compensation programs provide benefits for workers who suffer from occupational injuries or illnesses. (Because of their significance to the health care needs of seniors, a detailed discussion of Medicare and Medicaid is included in Unit 9.)

Medicare

The federally administered Medicare program took effect in 1966. Its purpose is to provide hospital and medical expense insurance protection to those aged 65 and older, to those of any age who suffer from chronic kidney disease, or to those who are receiving Social Security disability benefits.

Social Security Disability Income

In addition to Medicare, the federal government also provides disability-related benefits through the Social Security OASDI program. Although this subject was covered in Unit 11, let's review some of the important points here.

Disability income benefits are available to covered workers who qualify under Social Security requirements. One of the requirements is that the individual must be so mentally or physically disabled that she cannot perform any substantial, gainful work. In addition, the impairment must be expected to last at least 12 months or result in an earlier death. The determination of disability for Social Security purposes is usually made by a government agency. In addition to meeting the definition of disabled, the individual must have earned a certain minimum number of quarters of coverage under Social Security. A five-month waiting period is required before an individual will qualify for benefits, during which time she must remain disabled.

✓ ***For Example:*** Jerry became disabled in January. He must wait five full months—February through June—before he will qualify for disability benefits. His first benefit payment would be for July, and it would be paid in August. No second five-month waiting period is required if the disabled worker recovers and then is disabled again within five years.

Medicaid

Medicaid is Title XIX of the Social Security Act, added to the Social Security program in 1965. Its purpose is to provide matching federal funds to states for their medical public assistance plans to help needy persons regardless of age. If family income is below a specified level, Medicaid benefits are generally available. Although each state has some leeway in establishing eligibility requirements, Medicaid benefits are generally payable to low-income individuals who are blind, disabled, or under age 21. The benefits may be applied to Medicare deductibles and copayment requirements.

State Workers' Compensation Programs

All states have workers' compensation laws, which were enacted to provide mandatory benefits to employees for work-related injuries, illnesses, or death. Employers are responsible for providing workers' compensation benefits to their employees and do so by purchasing coverage through state programs, private insurers, or by self-insuring.

Although each state's laws differ with regard to procedures, requirements, and minimum benefits, there is uniformity with respect to the following.

- If a worker is killed in an industrial accident, the law provides for payment of burial expenses (subject to a maximum amount) and compensation for the surviving spouse or other dependents of the worker at the time of death.
- Regardless of any negligence by the employer, he is liable for work-related disabilities that employees suffer.
- Under the law, a disabled employee is entitled to benefits as a matter of right, without having to sue the employer for benefits. However, in return for the benefits provided under the law, the employee gives up the right to sue the employer.
- Under most laws, a disabled employee is paid benefits on a weekly or monthly basis, rather than in a lump sum.
- The employer must provide the required benefits; the employee does not contribute to the plan.

The law provides for a schedule of benefits, the size of which is based on such factors as the severity of the disability and the employee's wages.

Quick Quiz 5.1

True or False?

_____ 1. Tina, age 30, is unemployed and has been blind since birth. She would probably would qualify for workers' compensation benefits.

_____ 2. If Mary obtains her health insurance through a commercial insurer, she must submit her medical charges to the insurer for reimbursement.

_____ 3. Blue Cross and Blue Shield plans are available to individuals, families, and groups.

_____ 4. With a PPO, a reduced benefit will be paid if a member uses a doctor who is not part of the network.

_____ 5. In January, Tom becomes disabled while working and begins receiving Social Security disability income benefits five months later. He recovers and returns to work that fall. If Tom re-injures himself a year later, he can receive Social Security benefits only after another five-month waiting period passes.

Answers

1. ***False***. *Workers' compensation benefits are available to employees who suffer work-related injuries, illness, or death. Although Tina would not be eligible for these benefits because she is unemployed, she might be eligible for Medicare or Medicaid.*
2. ***True***.
3. ***True***.
4. ***True***.
5. ***False***. *If a disabled worker recovers but then becomes disabled again within five years, a second five-month waiting period is not required. As a result, Tom could immediately begin receiving Social Security benefits the second time he becomes disabled.*

Alternative Methods of Providing Health Insurance

As the cost of health insurance has increased, businesses and individuals have turned to nontraditional methods of providing health insurance including self-insured plans, Multiple Employer Trusts (METs) and Multiple Employer Welfare Arrangements (MEWAs).

Self-Insurance

For businesses and individuals, an alternative to a commercial or service health insurance plan is self-insurance. Large corporations especially will self-insure their sick-leave plans for their employees. Labor unions, fraternal associations, and other groups often self-insure their medical expense plans through dues or contributions from members. Others may self-insure part of a plan and use insurance to protect against large, unpredictable losses.

Many of these self-insured plans are administered by insurance companies or other organizations that are paid a fee for handling the paperwork and processing the claims. When an outside organization provides these functions, it is called an **administrative services only (ASO)** or **third-party administrator (TPA)** plan.

To bolster a self-insured plan, some groups adopt a **minimum premium plan (MPP)**. These plans are designed to insure against a certain level of large, unpredictable losses, above and beyond the self-insured level. As the name implies, MPPs are available for a fraction of the insurer's normal premium.

Multiple Employer Trust (MET)

As mentioned in Unit 9, a method of marketing group benefits to employers who have a small number of employees is the MET. METs can provide a single type of insurance (such as health insurance), or a wide range of coverages (for example, life, medical expense and disability income insurance). In some cases, alternative forms of the same coverage are available (such as comprehensive health insurance or basic health insurance).

An employer who wants to get coverage for employees from a MET first must become a member of the trust by subscribing to it. The employer is issued a joinder agreement, which spells out the relationship between the trust and the employer and specifies the coverages to which the employer has subscribed. An employer need not subscribe to all the coverages offered by a MET.

A MET may either provide benefits on a self-funded basis or fund benefits with a contract purchased from an insurance company. In the latter case, the trust rather than the subscribing employers is the master insurance contractholder. In either case, the employees of subscribing employers are provided with benefit descriptions (certificates of insurance) in a manner similar to the usual group insurance agreement.

In addition to alternative methods of funding benefits, METs can be categorized according to how they are administered, whether by an insurance company or a third-party administrator.

Multiple Employer Welfare Arrangements

A MEWA is a type of MET for union employees. MEWAs are self-funded and tax exempt. Employees covered under a MEWA are required by law to have an employment-related common bond.

Test Topic Alert!

METs are often fully funded and claims are guaranteed. In contrast, MEWAs often are self-funded and claims are not guaranteed.

The Employee Retirement Income Security Act (ERISA) and Group Health Insurance

Health insurance presents a ripe area for fraud by unauthorized insurance companies. This abuse tends to increase when the economy is in difficult times. Perpetrators have become more sophisticated as well, creating more complex schemes that are difficult to discern.

Unauthorized health-insuring entities began to proliferate around 1974 with the enactment of the Employee Retirement Income Security Act, otherwise known as ERISA (29 USCA 1001, *et seq*). The United States Department of Labor enforces the Act.

Application of ERISA

ERISA deals with employee health and welfare benefit plans. It addresses matters concerning employer-sponsored health-insurance-type plans and retirement plans. The cause for concern lies in the health insurance aspect of the Act.

A goal of ERISA was to encourage individual employers to establish employee health plans. It did this by allowing employers to self-insure the plans. An employer could establish a health plan for its employees and dependents.

In a self-insured plan, the employer uses its own money to cover the health claims of its employees. By self-insuring, the employer can make the benefits more affordable because the employer does not need to absorb the operating costs of an insurance company, which are otherwise included in the premium.

Alternatively, the employer can establish a health plan in which an insurance company will pay covered claims.

Insurance regulators monitor insurers' activities out of a concern for:

- patterns of fraud;
- potential for criminal activity within the insurance business;

- adverse economic impact upon authorized insurers and other insurance licensees;
- potential for large quantity of unpaid claims due to dishonesty and actuarial unsoundness of unauthorized insurers;
- a lack of state or federal guaranty funds to pay unpaid claims;
- adverse impact on future insurability of participants under statutes mandating guaranteed-issue health coverage (i.e., creditable coverage);
- adverse economic impact upon health-care providers resulting from unpaid claims;
- a lack of comprehensive federal oversight, including licensure and regulation similar to that of state insurance codes; and
- public perception that state insurance regulators are supposed to protect them from improper insurance schemes, ensure that benefits are paid when due, and ensure the availability and affordability of legitimate insurance.

ERISA Pre-Emption and State Regulation

The primary issue involved in the unauthorized health insurance problem is the claim that a health plan and the entity sponsoring it are not subject to state insurance regulation. This concept is referred to as **pre-emption.**

✓ ***Take Note:*** The concept of pre-emption refers to language within ERISA that states ERISA "supersede[s] any and all state laws insofar as they...relate to any employee benefit plan...." Sec. 514(a).

The scope of pre-emption is much narrower than unauthorized health insurers represent. ERISA makes clear that it does not pre-empt any state law that regulates insurance.

In fact, ERISA clarifies the scope of its application by providing that no employee benefit plan or trust "...shall be deemed to be an insurance company or other insurer ...or to be engaged in the business of insurance."

In other words, the fact that ERISA maintains state regulatory authority over insurance does not mean that a legitimate ERISA plan providing health benefits can be deemed to be insurance. Despite the similarity of benefits afforded by the plan and by a health insurer, a genuine single-employer ERISA plan is not subject to direct state insurance regulation.

The net effect of the statutory provisions is that while ERISA governs an employee benefit plan, its jurisdiction is not exclusive. For example, state insurance regulation still applies to the insurer that is financially responsible for the payment of claims in an insured ERISA plan, and to the forms utilized by that insurer to provide the insurance.

ERISA and MEWAs

MEWAs are regulated by state insurance departments and must possess a certificate of authority.

✓ ***Take Note:*** By definition, a MEWA is a type of MET, or multiple-employer trust. As such, a MEWA cannot be a single-employer plan so as to exempt it from state insurance regulation.

In general, ERISA applies to certain types of MEWAs. [29 USCA 1002(40)(A)]. Therefore, MEWAs are regulated by both the states and the federal government. Clearly, MEWAs are not exempt from state insurance regulation.

MEWAs as Employee Benefit Plans

MEWAs that fall within the ERISA definition and are employee welfare benefit plans are subject to certain rules of pre-emption.

- A fully-insured MEWA is subject to state insurance laws that require the MEWA to maintain specific levels of reserves and contributions in order to ensure the MEWA's ability to pay benefits when due.
- A partially-insured MEWA is subject to state insurance laws that are consistent with ERISA, unless exempted from them under other regulations of the Department of Labor. If the MEWA is exempted from ERISA regulation, it is subject to state insurance regulation in the same manner as a fully-insured MEWA.

✓ ***Take Note:*** If the MEWA is not an employee benefit plan, there is no pre-emption at all. It is subject to full state insurance regulation.

Unique Situations

Union plans can fall outside the definition of a MEWA and therefore lie beyond concurrent state and federal regulation. However, this exception may only apply if the Department of Labor expressly finds that the collective bargaining agreements between that union and the employers are genuine and in good faith. Without such a determination, a union plan is still subject to state regulation as a MEWA.

Association Plans are not exempt from state insurance regulation because:

- there is no employer-employee relationship; and

- they must be fully insured (which means that at least the insurer is subject to regulation).

Professional Employer Organization (PEO) is the term used for what is also known as an Employee Leasing Company. This type of organization has been the target of unauthorized insurers. Despite the appearance of a "co-employer" relationship between the employer and the PEO, the PEO handles administrative functions while the original employer continues to exercise the usual practices of employment, such as:

- hiring and firing employees;
- evaluating employee performance;
- disciplining employees;
- determining compensation; and
- determining the hours, location, nature, and method of the work.

A PEO-sponsored health plan is not exempt from state insurance regulation under ERISA for two reasons.

- There is no employer and employee relationship between the employee and the PEO, as noted above.
- Some states prohibit PEOs from sponsoring self-insured health plans. Because only those plans that are fully self-insured may be potentially exempt from the state's insurance code, the exemption cannot exist with respect to a PEO-sponsored plan.

Determining Whether a Plan is Subject to Regulation

If a plan engages in some risk-bearing activity, including financial responsibility for the payment of claims of the employees or their dependents of at least two unrelated employers, the plan is a MEWA or an insurer. It must be licensed by the state and is subject to state regulation. In other words, the entity that is responsible for payment of claims filed by employees or their dependents must be licensed by the state's insurance department.

If the funds of several unrelated employers are commingled at any level (primary insurance, re-insurance, or stop-loss insurance), the plan is subject to state insurance regulation.

Penalties

Those who assist or act as an unauthorized insurer may be subject to conviction on a felony charge, liability for all unpaid claims, and suspension or revocation of all insurance licenses.

Summary

People seeking health insurance protection have a number of resources. Commercial insurance companies, which include life insurance companies as well as monoline and casualty insurance companies, are one source. Service providers, including the Blue Cross and Blue Shield organizations and the more recently introduced health maintenance organizations, are others. Preferred provider organizations provide an additional option by contracting their services with employer groups or insurers.

For many people, health insurance protection is obtained through a government-sponsored program. At the federal level, the Social Security program (OASDI) provides both disability income benefits and medical expense protection, the latter through the Medicare program.

At the state level, medical expense insurance is provided through the Medicaid program to financially needy citizens who are blind, disabled, or under age 21. Because Medicaid is state-administered (and only partially federally supported), each state has some leeway in setting the qualification standards for its program. All states also have enacted workers' compensation programs, which provide benefits to workers for occupational illnesses and disabilities.

Some large employers prefer to retain the risk of covering at least part of their employees' medical care expenses, and thus self-insure their plan.

Key Concepts

In preparing for their licensing examination, students should be familiar with the following concepts:

- commercial health insurers
- health maintenance organizations (HMOs)
- third-party administrator (TPA) plans
- self-insured plans
- Social Security disability income
- workers' compensation
- service providers
- preferred provider organizations (PPOs)
- administrative services only (ASO) plans
- Medicare
- Medicaid
- multiple employer trusts (METs)
- multiple employer welfare arrangements (MEWAs)

Unit Exam 5

1. HMOs are known for stressing

   A. preventative medicine and early treatment
   B. state-sponsored health care plans
   C. in-hospital care and services
   D. health care services for government employees

2. Which of the following statements regarding Blue Cross and Blue Shield organizations is CORRECT?

   A. Blue Cross provides surgical expense prepayment plans.
   B. Blue Shield provides hospital expense prepayment plans.
   C. Both Blue Cross and Blue Shield plans are available on a group basis.
   D. Reimbursement for hospital and medical expenses is made by Blue Cross and Blue Shield directly to the subscriber.

3. Which of the following organizations would make reimbursement payments directly to the insured individual for covered medical expenditures?

   A. Blue Cross/Blue Shield
   B. Commercial insurer
   C. Preferred provider organization
   D. Health maintenance organization

4. Marty just received his first Social Security disability payment. From this, we can assume

   A. he had applied for Medicaid previously
   B. he is at least age 65
   C. his disability is expected to last at least 12 months
   D. his disability commenced 3 months ago

5. Which of the following statements about health maintenance organizations is CORRECT?

   A. An insurance company that also markets group health insurance is known as an HMO.
   B. If a person joins an HMO and undergoes a physical examination, he will be billed for the exam and each subsequent medical service as it is performed.
   C. An insurance company may sponsor an HMO or assist an HMO by providing contractual services.
   D. Like commercial insurers, HMOs generally assess deductibles.

6. The waiting period before qualifying for Social Security disability benefits is how many months?

   A. 3
   B. 5
   C. 6
   D. 12

7. Which of the following statements regarding workers' compensation plans is CORRECT?

   A. Benefit amounts are mandated by the federal government.
   B. A worker will qualify for benefits only if her disability or illness was a result of employer negligence.
   C. Benefits may be financed by private insurers, state funds, or self-insurance.
   D. If a worker is killed in an industrial accident, her family is entitled only to a specified benefit amount to pay for burial expenses.

8. Which of the following statements about Medicaid is NOT correct?
   - A. It provides federal matching funds to states for medical public assistance plans.
   - B. Its purpose is to help eligible needy persons with medical assistance.
   - C. Medicaid benefits may be used to pay the deductible and coinsurance amounts of Medicare.
   - D. It limits financial assistance to persons age 65 or older who are in need of medical services they cannot afford.

9. Jerry is injured while working for his employer. Under state workers' compensation laws, we can assume that
   - A. his employer will not be liable for Jerry's work-related disabilities if the employer's negligence did not contribute to the injuries
   - B. Jerry will probably receive workers' compensation benefits on a monthly or weekly basis
   - C. Jerry must sue his employer to receive workers' compensation benefits
   - D. both Jerry and his employer are required to contribute to the cost of workers' compensation coverage

Unit Exam 5 Answers & Rationale

1. **A.** HMOs are known for stressing preventative care, the objective being to reduce the number of unnecessary hospital admissions and duplication of services.

2. **C.** Blue Cross and Blue Shield plans are available on a group basis as well as to individuals. While Blue Cross offers prepayment plans to cover hospital services, Blue Shield covers surgical expenses and other medical services performed by physicians. Payments for services are made directly to the hospitals and physicians.

3. **B.** Commercial insurance companies use the reimbursement approach. Policyowners obtain medical treatment from whatever source they want and, per the terms of their policy, submit their charges to their insurer for reimbursement.

4. **C.** To receive Social Security disability payments, Marty's disability must be expected to last at least 12 months.

5. **C.** HMOs may contract for excess insurance or administrative services provided by insurance companies. Some HMOs are also sponsored by insurance companies.

6. **B.** There is a 5-month waiting period before an individual will qualify for benefits. During this time, the individual must remain disabled.

7. **C.** Employers are responsible for providing workers' compensation benefits to their employees and do so by purchasing coverage through state programs, private insurers, or by self-insuring.

8. **D.** Medicaid benefits generally are payable to low-income individuals who are blind, disabled, or under age 21. Medicaid does not only benefit persons age 65 or older.

9. **B.** If Jerry is injured while working for his employer, he will probably receive workers' compensation benefits on a weekly or monthly basis rather than in a lump sum. Jerry need not sue his employer to receive benefits, nor is he required to contribute to the cost of such program. Finally, Jerry's employer will be liable for his work-related disabilities, regardless of whether he was negligent.

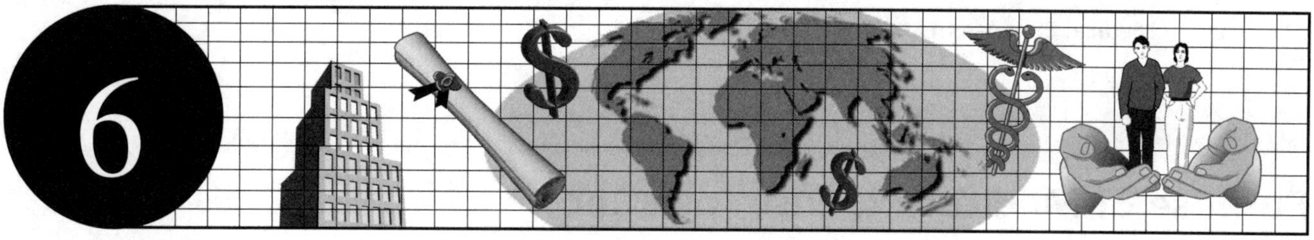

Medical Expense Insurance

INTRODUCTION

When people speak of their health insurance, they are usually referring to insurance that protects against the costs of medical care. Medical expense insurance, which is available in several different forms, reimburses policyowners for part or all of the costs of obtaining medical care. It is a vital form of insurance considered by many to be the one type of insurance they cannot do without.

UNIT OBJECTIVES

When you complete this unit you should be able to:

- describe the different types of coverage available under basic medical expense plans;
- explain the difference between supplementary major medical and comprehensive major medical plans;
- list and describe the three types of major medical deductibles;
- explain the concepts of coinsurance, stop-loss features, and pre-existing conditions; and
- describe the main features of hospital indemnity policies and limited risk policies.

Purpose of Medical Expense Insurance

Medical expense insurance provides financial protection against the cost of medical care for accidents and sickness. In this broad context, medical care includes hospital care, physician services, surgical expenses, drugs, nursing and convalescent care, diagnostic treatment, laboratory services, rehabilitative services, dental care, and physical therapy—in short, all medical treatment and services. The extent to which a given medical expense policy covers medical care—the specific types of services and treatments covered and the benefits provided—depends on the policy. In general, medical expense insurance is available through one of two different policy plans: **basic medical insurance** or **major medical insurance**. Basic medical insurance limits coverage to select types of medical care. Major medical insurance, which can work either as a supplement to a basic plan or as a comprehensive stand-alone plan, provides broader, more complete coverage.

Reimbursement vs. Indemnity Approach

Medical expense plans typically pay benefits as a reimbursement of actual expenses, although some benefits are paid as fixed indemnities, regardless of the actual loss.

✓ ***For Example:*** Karl owns a reimbursement-type medical expense policy that pays a maximum benefit of $200,000. He is hospitalized for 10 days and incurs covered medical expenses totaling $10,000. The policy would provide benefits of $10,000 (the expenses incurred).

✓ ***For Example:*** Doris owns an indemnity-type medical expense policy that provides a $100-per-day benefit for each day of hospitalization. She is hospitalized for ten days, incurring medical expenses of $10,000. Her policy will indemnify her by providing benefits of $1,000: ten days at $100 per day. Indemnity medical expense policies do not pay expenses or bills; they merely provide the insured with a stated benefit amount for each day she is confined to a hospital as an inpatient. The money may be used by the insured for any purpose.

With this foundation, we are ready to take a look at the two kinds of medical expense insurance policies: **basic** and **major medical**. Many types of plans fall within these two categories.

Basic Medical Expense Plans

Basic medical expense insurance sometimes is called first dollar insurance because, unlike major medical expense insurance, it provides benefits up front without requiring the insured to satisfy a deductible first. For many years it was the leading type of medical expense insurance sold, but today it is overshadowed by major medical insurance. This is due largely to the fact that basic medical expense policies limit the type and duration of services covered and dollar amounts that will be paid (or reimbursed) to the insured. Major medical plans are not as limiting.

Test Topic Alert! Basic medical expense insurance often is referred to as first dollar insurance.

Basic medical expense policies classify their coverages according to general categories of medical care: hospital expense, surgical expense, and physicians' (nonsurgical) expense. Additional plans cover nursing expenses and convalescent care. While it is common to find all categories contained under the umbrella of one policy, they can be written as separate coverages.

Basic Hospital Expense

Basic hospital expense insurance reimburses policyowners for the cost of hospital confinement. (Many policies today also provide coverage for outpatient care if it is provided in lieu of hospitalized care.) Basic hospital policies cover costs associated with daily room and board and other miscellaneous expenses.

Daily Room and Board Basic hospital expense policies cover the daily cost of room and board. These policies follow no set standards. They vary by daily amount payable and by the length of time the benefits are payable.

✓ ***For Example:*** Some policies will pay an in-hospital benefit for as long as 365 days, while others pay benefits for 90 days or 30 days only. Some policies reimburse the insured for the daily room and board charge up to a specified dollar amount. Others provide a service type of benefit, paying an amount equal to the hospital's daily charge for a semiprivate room.

Miscellaneous Expenses In addition to room and board, basic hospital expense policies cover hospital extras, or miscellaneous charges, up to a specified limit. Covered miscellaneous expenses include drugs, x-rays, anesthesia, lab fees, dressings, use of the operating room, and supplies.

In general, the maximum miscellaneous expense benefit is expressed as a multiple of the daily room and board benefit (e.g., 10 × room and board or

20 x room and board) or it may be a stated dollar amount. Some policies may even specify individual maximums for certain expenses within the maximum miscellaneous benefit.

✓ ***For Example:*** The overall maximum for the miscellaneous expense benefit may be $1,000, with maximums of $150 for use of the operating room, $125 for anesthesia, $75 for drugs and so on, but the total miscellaneous benefit would be limited to $1,000.

It is important to note that physicians' services are not covered under a basic hospital expense policy, even in the case of surgery. The cost for a physician is covered under a basic surgical expense or basic physicians' (nonsurgical) expense policy.

Basic Surgical Expense

Basic surgical expense policies provide coverage for the cost of a surgeon's services, whether the surgery is performed in the hospital or out. The surgeon's fees, anesthesiologist's fees, and any postoperative care generally are included in the coverage.

Three different approaches are used by insurers in providing this type of coverage and determining the benefits payable. These are the **surgical schedule** approach, the **reasonable and customary** approach, and the **relative value scale** approach.

Test Topic Alert! The approach used by an insurer in providing basic surgical expense coverage and determining the benefits payable is described in the back of the policy.

Surgical Schedule

Under the surgical schedule method, every surgical procedure is assigned a dollar amount by the insurer. Although the policy itself will contain only a representative sampling of common surgical procedures and their prices, a complete listing of all established surgical procedures is maintained in the insurer's claims department for use by its claims examiners. When a claim is submitted to the insurer, the claims examiner reviews the policy to determine the amount payable. If the surgeon's bill is more than the allowed charge set by the insurer, it is up to the insured to pay the surgeon the difference. If the surgeon's bill is less than the allowed charge, the insurer will pay only the full amount billed; the claim payment never will exceed the amount charged.

Reasonable and Customary Approach

Whereas the surgical schedule method pays up to a stated dollar amount regardless of the actual charge, the reasonable and customary approach is more open in its determination of benefits payable. Under this approach, the surgical expense is compared to what is deemed reasonable and customary for the geographical part of the country where the surgery was performed. If the charge is within the reasonable and customary parameters, the expense is usually paid in full.

Take Note: If the charge for a procedure is more than what is reasonable and customary, the patient must absorb the difference.

Relative Value Scale The relative value scale is similar to the surgical schedule method, except that instead of a flat dollar amount being assigned to every surgical procedure, a set of points is assigned.

The number of points assigned to any one procedure is relative to the number of points assigned to a maximum procedure.

For Example: An operation like a triple heart bypass typically would be considered a maximum procedure and assigned a high number of points (usually 500 or 1,000). Every other procedure is assigned a set of points relative to that. An appendectomy, which is a major procedure but not as serious as a triple bypass, might be assigned 200 points. Setting a broken finger might rate five points.

How are benefit amounts determined? The policy will carry a stated dollar-per-point amount, known as the **conversion factor**, to determine the benefit. For example, a plan with a $5-per-point conversion factor would pay $1,000 for a 200-point procedure. Generally, the larger the conversion factor, the larger the policy's premium.

Basic Physicians' (Nonsurgical) Expense

Basic physicians' expense insurance provides benefits for nonsurgical physicians' services. Examples of services covered include office visits and the care by a physician while the insured is hospitalized for a nonsurgical reason. Benefits are usually based on the indemnity approach.

✓ ***For Example:*** A plan might pay a flat fee of $50 per visit (not to exceed the actual charge, if less).

These policies typically carry a number of exclusions, such as x-rays, drugs, and dental treatment.

Other Basic Plans

Two other basic medical expense plans are worth noting: **nurses' expense benefits** and **convalescent care facility benefits**.

Nurses' expense benefits coverage is generally limited to private duty nursing care arranged in accordance with a doctor's order while the insured is a hospital patient. It may cover both registered professional and licensed practical nurses.

FIGURE 6.1 Basic Medical Expense Coverages

Medical Expense Category	*What Is Covered*
Hospital expense	• Daily room and board • Miscellaneous expenses
Surgical expense	• Cost of surgeon's services • Anesthesiologist
Physicians' expense	• Office visits • Nonsurgical care by a physician while hospitalized
Nurses' expense	• Private duty nursing care
Convalescent care expense	• Skilled nursing facility expenses

Basic medical expense policies provide coverage according to general categories of medical care. Policies covering all categories are available, as are policies that cover only select categories.

Convalescent care facility benefit coverage provides a maximum daily benefit for confinement in a skilled nursing facility for a specified recovery period following discharge from a hospital. Rest cures and normal custodial care are not covered.

Major Medical Expense Plans

Major medical expense insurance, often simply called major medical, has made it possible for many people to achieve substantial protection against the high cost of medical care. It offers broad coverage under one policy, typically paying benefits for hospital room and board, hospital extras, nursing services in-hospital or at home, blood, oxygen, prosthetic devices, surgery, physicians' fees, ambulance services, and more. In addition, it provides for high benefit limits. It generally is available on both an individual basis and a group basis.

The services and supplies covered under a major medical policy must be performed or prescribed by a licensed physician and necessary for the treatment of an insured's illness or injury. The benefit period may be defined on a calendar-year basis or may be specified as a two- to five-year period. In contrast to basic medical expense insurance, major medical policies provide total maximum lifetime benefits to individual insureds from $250,000 to $1 million or more.

Major medical expense insurance usually picks up where basic medical expense insurance leaves off in one of two ways: as a supplement to a basic plan or as a comprehensive stand-alone plan.

Supplementary Major Medical

A supplementary major medical plan covers expenses not included under a basic plan. It also provides coverage for expenses that exceed the dollar maximums specified in the basic policy, as well as those expenses no longer covered by the basic plan because the benefits have been exhausted.

With a supplemental plan, major medical coverage is coordinated with various basic medical expense coverages picking up where the basic plan leaves off.

✓ ***For Example:*** A basic plan may provide for hospital room and board benefits for a maximum of 45 days. If that basic plan were supplemented with a major medical plan, the supplementary major medical plan would cover hospital room and board expenses beginning on the 46th day. Or, if a basic plan provides a maximum benefit of $1,500 for a specific surgical procedure and the actual cost of the procedure was $2,000, a major medical supplement would cover the additional $500.

In addition, because of the broad coverage associated with most major medical supplements, a supplement will likely cover expenses that are either beyond the scope of the basic plan or excluded from its coverage.

Comprehensive Major Medical

The second type of major medical plan is the comprehensive major medical plan. Comprehensive plans are distinguished by the fact that they cover virtually all medical expenses—hospital expenses, physician and surgeon expenses, nursing care, drugs, physical therapy, diagnostic x-rays and laboratory services, medical supplies and equipment, transfusions, and more, all under a single policy.

Major medical plans, whether supplementary or comprehensive, typically include two important features: deductibles and coinsurance. Both of these features require the insured to absorb some of the cost of his medical expenses, thus allowing the insurer to avoid small claims and keep the cost of premiums down.

✓ ***Take Note:*** A basic medical plan usually does not include either a deductible or coinsurance. Instead it imposes limitations in the form of maximum benefit amounts that will be paid.

Deductibles

A deductible is a stated initial dollar amount that the individual insured is required to pay before insurance benefits are paid.

✓ ***For Example:*** If a plan has a flat $250 annual deductible, the insured is responsible for the first $250 of medical expenses every year. Covered expenses exceeding $250 then are paid by the major plan (subject to any coinsurance).

Depending on the type of major medical policy, the deductible may be one of three kinds: **flat, corridor,** or **integrated.**

Flat Deductible

A flat deductible is a stated amount that the insured must pay before policy benefits become payable.

✓ ***For Example:*** If an insured has a policy with a $500 deductible and incurs $2,000 of covered medical expenses, she must pay $500 toward the total. The insurer will then base its payments on the remaining $1,500.

Quite often, policies will include a family deductible, usually equal to three times the individual deductible amount. For example, in a family of four if three members each satisfied the individual deductible in one year, no deductible would be applied to medical expenses incurred by the fourth member.

Corridor Deductible

A corridor deductible is typical for a supplementary major medical policy that works in conjunction with a basic medical expense policy. The first covered medical expenses the insured incurs are paid by the basic policy. After the basic policy benefits are exhausted, the insured pays the full deductible, and then the major medical benefits are payable.

✓ ***For Example:*** Linda has a supplementary major medical policy that provides for a corridor deductible of $500. The deductible applies after full payment of up to $2,000 by the basic medical expense policy and before additional expenses are shared on a coinsurance basis by the insurer and Linda (see *Coinsurance* in this unit). Linda incurs a medical bill of $8,500. Responsibility for payment is as follows.

Total expenses:	$8,500
Basic medical expense pays:	–2,000
	$6,500
Corridor deductible paid by Linda:	– 500
Basis for major medical expense payment and coinsurance:	$6,000

As you can see, the basic medical expense policy paid for the first $2,000 of Linda's medical bills. The corridor deductible, which the insured is responsible for, is applied next. To the extent that additional medical expenses

FIGURE 6.2 Types of Major Medical Deductibles

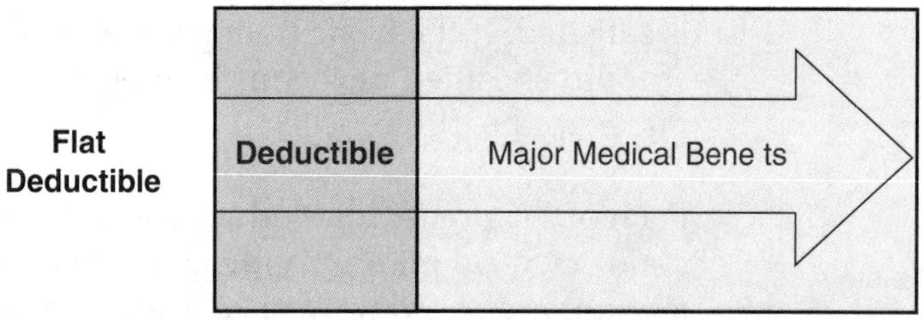

Typically used with comprehensive policies, a at deductible is a stated amount that the insured must pay before any policy bene ts are paid.

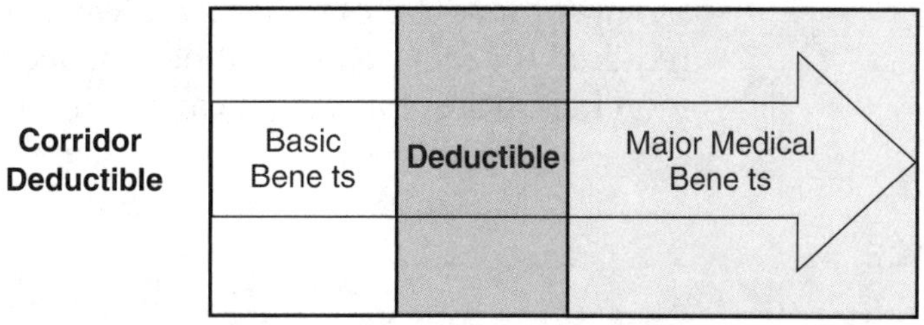

Typically used with supplemental plans, a corridor deductible is the deductible imposed after all basic bene ts have been paid but before any major medical bene ts will be paid.

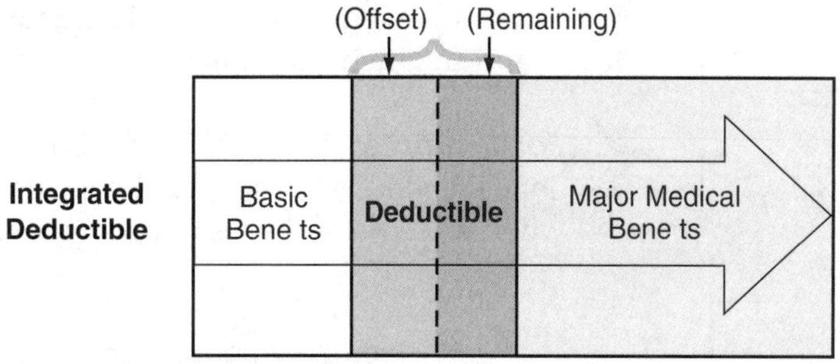

Occasionally used with supplemental plans, this deductible is the amount that must be satis ed before major medical bene ts are paid, but it is "offset" dollar-for-dollar by any bene ts paid under the basic plan.

remain—in this case, $6,000—they become the basis for the major medical payment. This usually is accomplished on a coinsurance or copayment basis, whereby the insured shares some percentage of the cost. This process is explained on the following page.

Test Topic Alert!

It is important to know when a deductible applies to the basic benefits policy and when a deductible applies after that policy's benefits are exhausted and before the supplementary major medical policy pays benefits.

Integrated Deductible

An integrated deductible is also used with a supplementary major medical plan, but it is integrated into the amounts covered by the basic plan. For example, if a supplementary plan carries a $500 deductible and the insured incurs $500 or more of covered expenses under the basic plan, the deductible is satisfied. If the basic policy benefits do not cover the entire deductible amount specified in the major medical policy, the insured is compelled to make up the difference.

Each of the preceding deductibles may be figured on one of two bases. If a major medical plan provides for a calendar year deductible, the deductible amount is applied only once during each calendar year. Once the deductible has been met in a calendar year, all claims submitted will be treated for the balance of the year without regard to any deductibles.

If a major medical plan has a per cause deductible, separate deductibles are required for each separate illness or accident. Per cause deductibles are common in policies that define causes of loss as each sickness or each injury.

Coinsurance

Coinsurance, or percentage participation, is another characteristic of major medical policies. It is simply a sharing of expenses by the insured and the insurer. After the insured satisfies the deductible, the insurance company pays a high percentage of the additional (covered) expenses—usually 75 or 80%—and the insured pays the remainder.

✓ ***For Example:*** Joe has an 80%/20% major medical policy, with a $200 flat annual deductible. This year, he incurs $1,200 in medical expenses, all of which are covered by his policy. The responsibility for payment would be as follows:

Total expenses:	$1,200
Deductible Joe pays:	– 200
Basis for insurer's payment:	$1,000
	× .80
Amount insurer pays:	$ 800
Coinsurance amount Joe pays:	$ 200

Thus, the insurer will pay 80% of the charges after the deductible has been satisfied, or $800. Joe must pay the $200 deductible and 20% of the remaining expenses, for a total cost share of $400.

Now let's assume that Joe experiences two separate medical problems this year. The first, which required hospitalization and surgery, totaled $7,500. Under his major medical policy, Joe submitted his claim and paid his $200 deductible. The policy would pay 80% of the charges above the deductible, or $5,840; Joe is responsible for the remaining $1,460. Three months later, Joe incurs another round of medical expenses amounting to $900. Because his policy stipulates a flat annual deductible which Joe has paid already, the policy will base its 80% payment on the full $900; Joe must pay the remaining 20%, or $180.

Coinsurance provisions are effective throughout the duration of a policy.

Stop-Loss Feature

To provide a safeguard for insureds, most major medical policies contain a stop-loss feature that limits the insured's out-of-pocket expenses. Once the insured has paid a specified amount toward her covered expenses—usually $1,000 to $2,000—the company pays 100% of covered expenses.

How a stop-loss cap is defined depends on the policy. For instance, one policy may stipulate that the contract will cover 100% of eligible expenses after the insured incurs $1,000 in out-of-pocket costs. Another policy may specify that the coinsurance provision applies only to the next $5,000 of covered expenses after the deductible is paid, with full coverage for any remaining expenses.

✓ ***For Example:*** Bill has a major medical policy with a stop-loss feature. It calls for a $500 deductible, followed by an 80%/20% coinsurance on the next $5,000 in covered expenses. Amounts more than that are fully absorbed by the policy. If Bill were to incur hospital and surgical bills of $20,000 this year, this is how payment would be assigned.

Total expenses:	$20,000
Deductible Bill pays:	– 500
	$19,500
Coinsurance Bill pays (20% of the next $5,000 in expenses):	– 1,000
Amount insurer pays:	$18,500

Thus, with a $500 deductible and $1,000 in coinsurance for the next $5,000, Bill's plan provides for a maximum out-of-pocket expenditure by the insured of $1,500.

Pre-existing Conditions

Another feature of most major medical policies is the exclusion for pre-existing conditions. For individual plans, a pre-existing condition is an illness or physical condition that existed before the policy's effective date and one that the applicant did not disclose on the application. (A condition that is noted on the application may be excluded by rider or waiver.) Consequently, medical costs incurred due to a pre-existing condition are excluded from coverage under plans that contain this exclusion. However, the exclusion applies for only a limited time. After that time limit passes, any existing conditions no longer are considered pre-existing and will be covered in full, subject to any other policy limitations. (See also *Time Limit on Certain Defenses,* Unit 11.)

✓ ***Take Note:*** The rules regarding pre-existing conditions are different for group health insurance plans. On July 1, 1997, the Health Insurance Portability and Accountability Act limited the ability of employer-sponsored groups and insurers to exclude individuals from health insurance coverage due to pre-existing medical conditions. These rules will be discussed in more detail in Unit 13.

Test Topic Alert!

The exclusion for pre-existing conditions is designed to protect insurers against adverse selection by those who know they have a medical ailment and are facing certain medical costs.

Quick Quiz 6.1

True or False?

_____ 1. If Susan has surgery, the cost of services provided by her doctor will not be covered under a basic hospital policy.

_____ 2. Tom has an appendectomy that costs $5,000. Under his insurance policy, $4,000 to $4,500 is considered a reasonable and customary charge for this procedure. Because the cost of Tom's surgery falls outside this parameter, his insurance will not pay for his operation.

_____ 3. If Mark has surgery, the costs of surgical care provided by his doctor will be covered under a physicians' expense policy.

_____ 4. Jane is hospitalized. Her nurses' expense benefits plan will cover the cost of the private duty nursing care she receives.

_____ 5. Bill is in the hospital for 10 days. His daily room and board expenses will be covered by his basic hospital expense insurance.

Answers

1. ***True***.
2. ***False***. *Even though Tom's surgery costs more than what is considered reasonable and customary, his insurance still will pay for part of the cost of operation. However, Tom must pay for the amount that is not covered by insurance.*

3. ***False***. *If Mark has surgery, the cost of his surgeon's services will not be covered by physicians' expense insurance. Instead, a surgical expense policy will cover the cost of his surgeon's services.*
4. ***True***.
5. ***True***.

Other Types of Medical Expense Coverage

As we've discussed, basic medical expense plans and major medical expense plans are the two primary kinds of health policies that provide coverage for accidents and illness. However, a discussion of medical expense plans would not be complete without mentioning a couple of other plans, most notably **hospital indemnity policies** and **limited risk** (or **dread disease**) **policies**.

Hospital Indemnity Policy

A hospital indemnity policy simply provides a daily, weekly, or monthly indemnity of a specified amount based on the number of days the insured is hospitalized.

✓ ***Take Note:*** A hospital indemnity plan may provide the insured $100 a day for every day she is confined in a hospital irrespective of the actual expenses incurred. The insured can apply the benefits to any purpose.

This insurance has been available for many years but has been promoted more heavily in recent years largely due to rapidly increasing health care costs. Many companies can offer high benefit indemnity plans at reasonable premiums because underwriting and administration are greatly simplified, and claim costs are not affected by increases in medical costs.

Benefits may run as high as $4,500 per month, based on a daily hospital confinement benefit of $150, and some are even higher. Maximum benefit periods range from about six months to several years or for a lifetime. Benefits are payable directly to the insureds and may be used for any purpose. Hospital indemnity policies also are usually exempt from most state laws that apply to specific kinds of insurance contracts.

Limited Risk Policy

Policies that provide medical expense coverage for specific kinds of illnesses are known as limited risk or dread disease policies. They are available primarily due to the high costs associated with certain illnesses, such as cancer or heart disease. However, some states prohibit the sale of these policies because they invite questionable sales and marketing practices that take advantage of people's fear of these diseases.

Limited risk policies that cover specified accidents also are available and are discussed in Unit 8.

Managed Care

Managed care plans, such as health maintenance organizations (HMOs), preferred provider organizations (PPOs), and point-of-service (POS) plans offer comprehensive medical services to their members. Managed care plans also apply financial incentives that encourage providers to keep both the quantity and cost of services in check and motivate members to select cost-effective providers.

Managed care has been able to halt the growth of health insurance premiums by means of a series of strategies that:

- encourage the use of cost-effective health care providers by employees;
- reward cost-effective health care delivery by providers;
- foster efficiency in health care delivery by ensuring services are appropriate but not excessive;
- promote wellness by emphasizing primary and preventative care; and
- assure high-quality care by evaluating the outcomes of care and monitoring the ways in which services are provided.

Selecting and Using Cost-Effective Providers

Some HMOs hire health care providers to serve their members. However, most managed care plans contract with individual or groups of health care providers, including primary care as well as specialty physicians, hospitals, home care agencies, hospices, nursing homes, and ancillary health personnel. The use of salaried providers by HMOs lowers costs because the providers have no financial incentive to prescribe additional and possibly unnecessary treatment. Managed care plans that contract with providers save money by purchasing health services for their enrolled populations at a discount. In the contracting process, managed care plans negotiate payments that are below the providers' usual and customary fees.

✓ ***Take Note:*** Part of the attractiveness of managed care for providers is the assurance that they will have a specific volume of patients to care for. When hospitals, physicians, and ancillary services agree to become preferred or participating panel or network providers for a managed care organization, they gain direct access to the employees who have enrolled in managed care.

Managed care plans actively encourage their enrollees to obtain managed care from panel providers in several ways. A particularly effective way is by using financial incentives, such as deductibles, copayments, and coinsurance.

Deductibles

Deductibles are familiar aspects of traditional indemnity health insurance. They require the employee to absorb some of the cost of his own medical expenses so the insurer can avoid small claims and keep the cost of premiums down. A deductible is a stated dollar amount that the insured is required to pay before the insurer begins paying for designated benefits. Some employers try to entice employees to use managed care panel providers, such as PPOs or POSs, by reducing the amount of their deductible.

Coinsurance

Coinsurance, or percentage participation, is another characteristic of major medical policies. It is a sharing of expenses by the employee and her health insurer. After the employee satisfies the deductible, the insurance company pays a higher percentage of any additional covered expenses—usually 75% or 80%—and the employee pays the remainder.

Copayment

Copayments are commonly used in managed care, particularly by HMOs when employees seek treatment from a health care provider on their own. Copayments are set amounts of money that must be paid at the time an employee sees a provider. Copayment levels vary with the type of service that is provided. The same amount in copayment is required each time an employee receives a particular service.

✓ ***Take Note:*** Copayment amounts are restricted by law for federally qualified HMOs. Total annual copayments for basic benefits, such as physician services, outpatient treatment, hospital care, and the like in a federally qualified HMO cannot exceed 200% of the total annual premiums charged by a comparable benefit plan that did not include copayments.

Medical Cost Management

Medical cost management is an effective means of controlling claims experience. It is the process of controlling how policyholders utilize their policies. Insurers use several approaches to manage costs.

Mandatory Second Opinion

In an effort to reduce unnecessary surgical operations, many health policies contain a provision requiring the insured to obtain a second opinion before receiving non-life-threatening surgery. Benefits are often reduced if a second opinion is not obtained.

Precertification Review

To control hospital claims, many policies require policyholders to obtain approval from the insurer before entering a hospital on a non-emergency basis. Even if the admission is for an emergency, most policies with this type of provision require the insured to notify the insurer within a short time (usually 24 hours) after admission. The insurer will then determine how much of the hospital stay it will cover, depending on the reason for the admission. If the insured wants to stay longer, the additional expense is his responsibility, not the insurer's.

Ambulatory Surgery

Advances in medicine now permit many surgical procedures to be performed on an outpatient basis rather than in a hospital. To encourage employees to utilize less expensive outpatient care, many policies offer some sort of inducement.

✓ ***For Example:*** For example, a policy may waive the deductible or coinsurance if the employee elects to have surgery on an outpatient basis.

Case Management

Case management involves a specialist within the insurance company, such as a registered nurse, who reviews a potentially large claim as it develops and discusses treatment alternatives with the employee along the way. The case manager reviews the patient's progress with each of his providers on a regular basis to obtain an understanding of the patient's condition, coordinate services so health care delivery is smooth and seamless, and identify changes in the patient's status that require prompt attention.

The purpose of case management is to involve the employee in the management of what could become a very expensive claim. Additional benefits from case management include an integrated plan for restoring an individual to the functional status she enjoyed before the illness, detect complications or setbacks that need quick medical response, and facilitate communication among all health care providers.

Utilization Management

Utilization management differs in the several types of managed care organizations. PPOs generally have less comprehensive utilization management programs than HMOs, and some HMO models are more utilization management-conscious than others. Some utilization management programs are characteristic of managed care, however, such as the use of primary care physician gatekeepers, clinical practice guidelines or protocols, prescription drug formularies, alternative health care settings, and utilization review.

Primary Care Gatekeepers

Employees who decide to join a managed care organization that is not a point-of-service plan are expected to see their primary care physician before they receive any medical care. The primary care physician then either provides the care an employee needs directly or refers the employee to a medical specialist, a hospital, or an ancillary health professional. In so doing, the primary care physician acts as a guide, or a **gatekeeper**, for patients through the health care system.

Physician gatekeeper programs control the utilization of health services by preventing employees from going to costly specialists or hospital emergency rooms when they can receive the treatment they need at less cost elsewhere. It helps to assure that employees do not receive inappropriate or unnecessary services. It also keeps down the cost of health care delivery by steering employees to specialist physicians and other health care providers who have demonstrated their cost effectiveness.

Members of HMOs and gatekeeper PPOs must usually have the approval of their primary care physician gatekeepers before they obtain any type of treatment. However, members of less tightly controlled PPOs may have to obtain approval only for elective procedures from an administrator at the PPO.

Characteristics of HMOs

HMOs differ from insurance companies and Blue Cross and Blue Shield plans in the comprehensiveness of the care they offer, as well as their delivery of health services and cost control mechanisms.

Comprehensiveness of Care

HMOs offer their subscribers a comprehensive package of health care services, generally including benefits for outpatient care as well as for hospitalization. Subscribers usually get these services at no cost except the periodically required premium (referred to as a capitation payment because it is a set flat rate that is "capitated" for each member). The capitated amount of money that is received or paid out is based on the number of members in the HMO. Therefore it is expressed as the amount per member per month, or PMPM. However, in some cases a modest copayment, such as $5 per physician visit or $3 per drug prescription, may be imposed.

Delivery of Medical Services

HMOs provide for the delivery of medical services, which in many cases is performed by salaried physicians and other personnel employed by the HMO. This approach is in contrast with the usual fee-for-service delivery of health care. However, many HMOs contract with providers on a fee-for-service basis.

✓ ***Take Note:*** Subscribers are required to obtain their care from providers of medical services who are affiliated with the HMO. Because HMOs may operate in a geographic region no larger than a single metropolitan area, this requirement may result in limited coverage for subscribers if treatment is received elsewhere. Most HMOs have out-of-area coverage, but only in the case of medical emergencies, with the exception of point-of-service plans.

Types of HMOs

The earliest HMOs can best be described as closed-panel plans under which subscribers must use physicians who are employed by the plan or by an organization with which the plan contracts. With most closed-panel plans having several general practitioners, subscribers usually can select their physician from among those who accept new patients and make medical appointments just as if the physician was in private practice. However, there is frequently little choice among specialists because a plan may have a contract with only one physician or a limited number of physicians in a given specialty.

The number of closed-panel plans is relatively small, accounting for about 30% of all HMO subscribers. The three different types of closed-panel plans—staff model HMOs, group-model HMOs, and network-model HMOs—are discussed below in more detail.

Many newer HMOs have been formed as **individual practice associations**, which can be considered an open-panel type of plan. Open panel plans have more flexibility with respect to subscribers' choice of physicians and physicians' participation in the plan. Most of the remaining subscribers to HMOs receive their coverage in a variety of way under mixed-model plans.

Staff-Model HMOs

Under a **staff-model** plan, the HMO hires its own physicians. The HMO may own hospitals, laboratories, or pharmacies, or it may contract for these services. The HMO also may have contracts with specialists to treat subscribers if it is not large enough to justify hiring specialists in a given medical field.

Providers who are employed by the staff-model HMO receive a salary and possibly incentive bonuses for controlling expenditures. A staff-model HMO offers a great degree of control over costs because it controls the salaries of its physicians, who may lose their jobs with the HMO if the organization is unprofitable or if they do not provide care within the cost and utilization parameters of the HMO.

Group-Model HMOs

The most common type of closed-panel plan is the **group-model** HMO. Under this arrangement, physicians (and other medical personnel) are employed by another legal entity that has a contractual relationship with the HMO to provide medical services for its subscribers. In most cases this relationship is exclusive, so the physicians in the group treat only HMO subscribers. The physicians also typically operate out of one or more common health care facilities.

Under a group-model plan, the HMO may contract with a single provider of medical services or with different providers for different types of services. The HMO usually pays for services on a capitation basis, which means the provider gets a predetermined fee per year for each subscriber and must provide any and all covered services for this capitation fee. The fee is independent of the way in which the provider compensates its own employees. Under a capitation arrangement, providers share financial risk with the HMO because they stand to lose money if utilization is higher than expected but to make money is lower than anticipated. Therefore, the provider has a strong incentive to control costs.

Network-Model HMO

A **network-model** HMO differs from a group-model HMO in that it contracts with two or more independent groups of physicians to provide medial services to its subscribers. Physician groups that enter into this type of arrangement often treat non-HMO patients on a fee-for-service basis.

Individual Practice Associations

In **individual practice associations (IPAs)**, participating physicians practice individually or in small groups at their own offices. In most cases the physicians accept non-HMO patients on a traditional fee-for-service basis, and HMO subscribers. IPAs are often referred to as open-panel plans because subscribers choose from a list of participating physicians.

Several methods may be used to compensate physicians who participate in an IPA. The most common is through a fee schedule that is based on the services provided to subscribers. To encourage physicians to be cost effective, plans commonly reduce payments to physicians when their experience is worse than expected. On the other hand, the physicians may receive a bonus if the experience of the plan is better than expected.

IPAs do not usually own their own hospitals. Rather, they enter into contracts with local hospitals to provide hospital care for their subscribers.

Mixed-Model HMOs

Increasing numbers of HMOs are operating as **mixed-model** plans, which means that the organization of the plan is a combination of two or more of the approaches described above. Such a combination generally occurs as a plan continues to grow. Some mixed models also have resulted from the merger of two plans that each used a different organizational form.

Point-of-Service Plans

A hybrid of HMOs and PPOs, **point-of-service** (POS) plans provide more freedom to subscribers in their choice of health care providers than HMOs do. However, POS plans also exert more control over costs than PPOs.

✓ ***Take Note:*** A POS plan is a hybrid arrangement that combines aspects of a traditional medical expense plan with an HMO or a PPO. Unlike a multiple plan option that ties an employee into a benefits plan for a year, participants in a POS plan decide whether they want to receive treatment from an HMO or PPO network physician at the time they seek care.

There are two basic types of POS plans: the open-access and the network plan. An open-access POS can take the basic form of any type of HMO. However, it allows a subscriber to go outside the HMO network of medical care providers at any time. A network POS plan requires the PPO participant to choose a primary care physician the same way an HMO does. This physician acts as a gatekeeper to control utilization and refer members to specialists within the PPO network.

Summary

The need for medical expense insurance—commonly referred to as health care insurance—is greater today than at any time in the past because of the high cost of medical care. Basic medical expense insurance, once the predominant form of health insurance, is now overshadowed by major medical insurance in terms of premium dollars and total coverage. Offered as individual and group policies, medical expense insurance is an indispensable part of a total insurance portfolio.

Key Concepts

In preparing for their licensing examination, students should be familiar with the following concepts:

- deductibles
- pre-existing condition
- basic medical expense policies
- basic surgical expense
- basic physicians' (nonsurgical) expense
- basic hospital expense
- stop-loss feature
- hospital indemnity policy
- limited risk policy
- coinsurance
- supplementary and comprehensive major medical expense policies

Unit Exam 6

1. The miscellaneous expense benefit in a basic hospital expense policy normally will cover
   A. physicians' bedside visits
   B. private duty nursing care
   C. drugs and medicine administered in the hospital
   D. hospital room and board

2. Clarence is to enter the hospital for a thyroidectomy. His basic medical expense policy includes a relative value schedule for surgical expense. The schedule lists 55 units for a thyroidectomy and a conversion factor of $8. How much will the policy pay?
   A. $400
   B. $440
   C. $540
   D. $550

3. Which of the following statements about deductible provisions in medical insurance policies is NOT correct?
   A. They help to eliminate small claims.
   B. They provide that initial expenses up to a specified amount are to be paid by the insured.
   C. They are most common in basic medical expense policies.
   D. They help to hold down premium rates.

4. An insured has a basic hospital/surgical expense policy, which provides benefits of $50 per day for up to 30 days of hospitalization and $750 for miscellaneous charges. It bases its surgical benefits on a schedule approach. The insured is hospitalized for a severely broken leg that requires surgery. The surgical procedure has been assigned $500 by the policy, although the customary charge in the area is $600. The insured incurs the following covered expenses:

   $80 per day for 7 days hospital charge
   $675 for the surgical procedure
   $800 for miscellaneous expenses

   The insured's policy will pay
   A. $1,600
   B. $1,700
   C. $1,810
   D. $2,035

5. When a medical expense policy pays benefits on an indemnity basis, it pays
   A. a certain percentage of whatever the hospital room charges are
   B. for total hospital expenses, less a deductible
   C. a flat amount per day for hospital room and board
   D. only for surgery and miscellaneous hospital expenses

6. Wilbur's basic medical expense policy limits the miscellaneous expense benefit to 20 times the $90 daily room and board benefit. During his recent hospital stay, Wilbur's miscellaneous expenses totaled $2,100. How much, if any, of this amount will Wilbur have to pay?
   A. $0
   B. $210
   C. $300
   D. $2,100

7. Which of the following examples about major medical policy deductibles is CORRECT?

   A. Eric's major medical policy has a $500 flat deductible provision. He incurs covered expenses totaling $350. He will pay nothing and his major medical policy will pay $350.
   B. Sarah has a major medical policy with a $500 flat deductible and an 80/20 coinsurance provision. Her covered expenses total $1,800. Of that amount, she will pay $500 and her insurance will pay $1,300.
   C. Valerie incurs a hospital bill of $8,300. Her basic medical expense insurance pays $2,400. Valerie pays a $200 deductible and her major medical plan takes care of the balance of covered expenses. Her deductible would be classified as a corridor deductible.
   D. An integrated deductible amount is $2,000. With this deductible, after the basic policy benefits are exhausted, the insured pays the full $2,000 deductible and then the major medical benefits are payable.

8. Arthur incurs total hospital expenses of $9,500, all of which are covered by his major medical policy. The policy includes a $500 deductible and a 75/25 coinsurance feature. Of the total expense, how much will Arthur have to pay?

   A. $2,375
   B. $2,750
   C. $2,875
   D. $6,675

9. All of the following are types of deductible provisions associated with major medical policies EXCEPT

   A. corridor
   B. integrated
   C. flat
   D. stop-loss

10. If the coinsurance feature in a major medical insurance policy is 75/25 with a $100 deductible, how much of a $2,100 bill would the insured pay?

    A. $100
    B. $500
    C. $600
    D. $1,500

Unit Exam 6 Answers & Rationale

1. **C.** In addition to room and board, hospital expense policies cover miscellaneous charges such as drugs, x-rays, anesthesia, lab fees, and supplies.

2. **B.** To determine the amount that Clarence's policy will pay for his operation, he would take the number of points assigned to the procedure (55) and multiply it by the conversion factor ($8). Using this calculation, the policy will pay $440.

3. **C.** Basic medical expense plans do not require the insured to satisfy a deductible first. Instead, they impose limitations in the form of maximum benefit amounts that will be paid.

4. **A.** Under a basic hospital/surgical expense policy, limits are imposed on the maximum amount of benefits that will be paid. Any expenses incurred above these dollar amounts must be paid by the insured. In this case, the insured's policy will pay $1,600, broken down as follows: $50/day for 7 days = $350; $500 for the surgical procedure; and $750 for miscellaneous expenses.

5. **C.** Under a medical expense policy, when benefits are paid on an indemnity basis the policy will pay a flat amount per day for hospital room and board.

6. **C.** If Wilbur's basic medical expense policy limits the miscellaneous expense benefit to 20 times the $90 daily room and board benefit, it will pay $1,800 (20 × $90) for such expenses. Wilbur must pay any amount above this limit. In this case, he will have to pay $300 ($2,100 – $1,800).

7. **C.** Valerie's deductible would be considered a corridor deductible. With this type of deductible, the first covered medical expenses ($2,400) that Valerie incurs are paid by her basic medical expense policy. After that, she pays her full deductible ($200) and then her major medical plan takes care of the remaining covered expenses.

8. **B.** Arthur will have to pay $2,750. After he pays his $500 deductible, his insurance company would pay 75% of the remaining $9,000 in expenses while Arthur would pay 25% of this amount, or $6,750 and $2,250, respectively.

9. **D.** Major medical policies may use one of three types of deductible: flat, corridor, or integrated. A stop-loss deductible does not exist.

10. **C.** In an insurance policy with a 75/25 coinsurance feature and a $100 deductible, the insured would pay $600 of a $2,100 bill. This would be calculated as follows: $100 deductible plus $500 (25% of $2,000, the remaining amount of the bill).

7

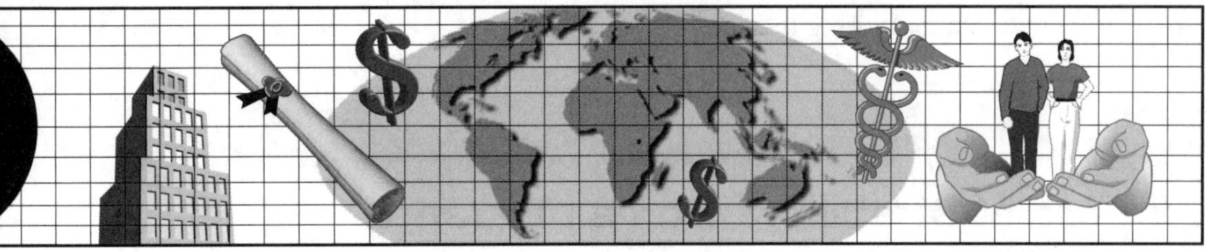

Disability Income Insurance

INTRODUCTION

All too often, what is thought to be a well-planned insurance program—a program consisting of life insurance, annuities, and medical expense coverage—is proven completely inadequate when disability, the one risk not covered, materializes. The risk associated with disability is not merely the loss of income; there also is the additional cost of caring for a disabled breadwinner who no longer can earn an income. Because a disability can be permanent, the financial consequences rank in severity with the death of the wage earner. The sudden loss of income resulting from a disabling accident or illness would, in most cases, lead to serious financial consequences. Fortunately, protection is available. The purpose of this unit is to describe the important role disability income insurance serves and to explain the different features found in these types of policies.

UNIT OBJECTIVES

When you complete this unit you should be able to:

- explain how the percent-of-earnings and flat amount methods are used to determine the amount of disability income benefits;
- compare and contrast the *any occupation* and *own occupation* definitions of total disability;
- describe how partial disability benefits are determined;
- list and describe the standard provisions typically found in a disability income policy; and
- list and describe the different types of riders that may be purchased with disability income policies.

Purpose of Disability Income Insurance

Disability income insurance is designed to provide an individual with a stated amount of periodic income in the event he cannot work due to a disabling illness or accident. Statistics prove that the probability of disability greatly exceeds the probability of death during an individual's working years. The need for protection against the economic consequences of a wage earners death cannot be overemphasized, and it is this need that disability income insurance fills.

Disability income policies provide coverage for disabilities resulting either from accidents alone or from accidents and sickness. Because sickness-related disabilities represent only a small fraction of all disabilities, it is not economically feasible to issue sickness-only disability policies. To obtain sickness income protection, one normally has to purchase accident income coverage as well.

Disability income policies are available as individual plans and group plans. They also serve a very important function for businesses and business owners. In this unit, we will focus on the basics of individual disability policies. Group disability will be discussed in Unit 13 and business uses of disability income insurance will be discussed in Unit 14.

Disability Income Benefits

The benefits paid under a disability income policy are in the form of monthly income payments. Unlike life insurance, which insurers will issue for almost any amount the applicant applies and qualifies for, disability income insurance is characterized by benefit limits. Insurers typically place a ceiling on the amount of disability income protection they will issue on any one applicant, defined in terms of the insured's earnings. And with few exceptions, this benefit ceiling is less than the insured's regular income.

✓ ***Take Note:*** Without a benefit ceiling, a disabled insured could conceivably receive as much income as she did while working, with little incentive to return to work and much incentive to prolong the disability.

Test Topic Alert! Disability income benefits are based on the insured's earnings and are designed to replace lost income.

Insurers use two methods to determine the amount of benefits payable under their disability income policies. The first method determines the benefit using a percentage of the insured's predisability earnings, and takes into account other sources of disability income.

✓ ***For Example:*** An individual earning $2,000 a month may be limited by Company A to a monthly benefit of 60% of income, or $1,200. If that individual already has an existing disability income policy from Company X that provides for $400 in monthly income, the amount payable by Company A would be limited to $800 each month.

Some policies that use the percent-of-earnings formula provide a benefit that varies with the length of the disability. For instance, the benefit amount may equal 100% of the insured's predisability earnings for the first month and then reduce the benefit amount to 70% thereafter.

The second method used to establish disability benefits is the flat amount method. Under this approach, the policy specifies a flat income benefit amount that will be paid if the insured becomes totally disabled. Normally, this amount is payable regardless of any other income benefits the insured may receive.

✓ ***Take Note:*** The percent-of-earnings approach typically is used in group disability income plans. The flat amount method is more common in individual plans.

Disability Defined

With one exception (partial disability), an insured must be totally disabled before benefits under a disability income policy are payable. What constitutes total disability varies from policy to policy. The insured must meet the definition set forth in his policy. Basically, there are two definitions: **any occupation** or **own occupation**.

Any Occupation

The any occupation definition of total disability requires the insured to be unable to perform any occupation for which she is reasonably suited by reason of education, training, or experience to qualify for disability income benefits.

Own Occupation

The own occupation definition of total disability requires that the insured be unable to work at his own occupation as a result of an accident or sickness.

✓ ***Take Note:*** Obviously from a policyowner's point of view, an own occupation disability income policy is more advantageous. It also is more expensive and difficult to qualify for.

Disability income policies often qualify total disability in two stages, using both the own occupation and any occupation definitions. These policies will provide initial benefits based on the own occupation definition for a

FIGURE 7.1 Distribution of Disability Claims by Impairment

Disability Claims, 1996

Impairment	Claims	Percent of total
Back	13,243	18.2
Emotional/psychiatric	9,216	12.7
Neurological	8,201	11.3
Extremities	6,582	9.0
Heart	3,003	4.1
Diabetes	2,605	3.6
Substance Abuse	2,437	3.3
Hearing	2,094	2.9
Vision	1,911	2.6
Blood disorders (including HIV)	1,883	2.6
Cancer	1,706	2.3
Asthma	1,266	1.7
Other	18,560	25.7
Total	72,687	100.0

Source: Equal Employment Opportunity Commission, HIAA *Sourcebook of Health Insurance Data 1999-2000*

specified period of time (for example, during the first two years of the disability), then change the qualifying basis to the any occupation definition.

Test Topic Alert!

From the insured's viewpoint, the any occupation definition is more restrictive than the own occupation definition. The insurer is less likely to pay a benefit if the insured's disability must prevent him from engaging in *any* reasonably suitable occupation.

Presumptive Disability

Most policies today contain a presumption of disability provision. Basically, this provision specifies certain conditions that automatically qualify the insured for the full benefit, because the severity of the conditions presumes the insured is totally disabled even if he is able to work. Presumptive disabilities include blindness, deafness, loss of speech, and loss of two or more limbs.

✓ ***For Example:*** If Janet has a stroke and loses her ability to speak, she has suffered a presumptive disability and would be entitled to total disability benefits for the rest of her policy's benefit period.

Partial Disability

The exception to the total disability requirement is a policy that also pays benefits in the event of a partial disability. It is not uncommon for disability income policies to make provision for partial disability, either as part of the basic coverage or as an optional rider for an additional premium. By most definitions, partial disability is the inability of the insured to perform one or more important duties of her job or the inability to work at that job on a full-time basis, either of which results in a diminished income.

✓ ***Take Note:*** Normally, partial disability benefits are payable only if the policyowner first has been totally disabled. This benefit is intended to encourage disabled insureds to get back to work, even on a part-time basis, without fear that they will lose all their disability income benefits.

The amount of benefit payable when a policy covers partial disabilities depends on whether the policy stipulates a **flat amount** or a **residual amount**.

Flat Amount Benefit

A flat amount benefit is a set amount stated in the policy. Usually this amount is 50% of the full disability benefit.

✓ ***For Example:*** Helen, who has a disability income policy with an own occupation definition, is severely injured after falling down a flight of stairs. She is unable to work for four months, during which time her disability income policy pays a full benefit. After four months she is able to return to work, but only on a part-time basis, earning substantially less than she did before her injury. If her policy did not contain a partial disability provision, her benefits would cease entirely because she no longer meets the definition of totally disabled. However, if her policy provides for partial disability benefits to be paid as a flat amount, she will be able to work on a part-time basis and continue to receive half of her disability benefits.

Residual Amount Benefit

A residual amount benefit is based on the proportion of income actually lost due to the partial disability, taking into account the fact that the insured is able to work and earn some income. The benefit usually is determined by multiplying the percentage of lost income by the stated monthly benefit for total disability.

✓ ***For Example:*** If the insured suffered a 40% loss of income because of the partial disability, the residual benefit payable would be 40% of the benefit that the policy would provide for total disability. This percentage is subject to change as the disabled insured's income varies.

Generally, residual benefits are provided through a rider to the policy, which specifies that no residual benefits are paid if the loss of income is less than 20 or 25%. Usually, residual benefits are payable even if the insured was not first totally disabled.

✓ ***For Example:*** Larry, a printer, suffered a severe back injury following a car accident. Though he was able to continue working, it was on a limited part-time basis, at only 60% of his predisability salary. If Larry's disability income policy provided for residual disability benefits, he would receive monthly payments from the insurer equal to 40% of the total disability benefit.

Insurers require proof of an insured's total or partial disability before they will pay benefits. To be eligible for benefits, the disabled insured must be under the care of a physician.

Cause of Disability

Another important aspect of disability income policies is the way in which they define the cause of disability. As noted above, disability income insurance policies cover accidents only, or accidents and sickness. Thus, how a disability occurs is an important consideration for disability income policies, as well as any other kind of policy covering injury due to accident.

Generally, disability income policies state that benefits are payable when injuries are either caused by external, violent, and accidental means, or result in accidental bodily injury.

Policies that use the **accidental means provision** require that the cause of the injury must have been unexpected and accidental. Policies that use the accidental bodily injury provision require that the injury itself must be unexpected and accidental. This also is known as the **results provision**.

✓ ***For Example:*** Jim, the insured, took an intentional dive off a high, rocky ledge into a lake. He struck his head on some rocks and was partially paralyzed. If his policy had an accidental means provision, the benefits probably would not be payable because the cause of his injury, the dive, was intentional. However, if his policy had an accidental bodily injury (or results) provision, benefits would be payable because the result of the accident, his injury, was unintentional and accidental.

Today, most disability income policies (and other policies providing accident protection) use the accidental bodily injury or results provision, which is far less restrictive than the accidental means provision. In fact, many states now require all accident-based insurance benefits to be based on the accidental bodily injury provision.

Disability Income Policy Provisions

In addition to specifying the amount of benefit payable and the circumstances under which a benefit is payable (plus complying with required provisions standards), disability income policies contain a number of other important provisions. The most notable of these are as follows.

Probationary Period

The probationary period specified in a disability insurance policy is the period of time that must elapse following the effective date of the policy before benefits are payable. It is a one-time-only period that begins on the policy's effective date and ends 15 or 30 days after the policy has been in force. The purpose of the probationary period is to exclude pre-existing sicknesses from coverage and provide a guidepost in borderline cases when there is a question as to whether an insured became ill before or after the effective date of the policy. Just as important, it helps protect the insurer against adverse selection, because those who know they are ill are more likely to try to obtain insurance coverage.

✓ ***Take Note:*** A disability income probationary period applies to sickness only; it does not apply to accidents. Whereas a person may be able to anticipate a sickness-related disability (e.g., after a visit to the doctor), it is not possible to anticipate an accident.

Elimination Period

Similar in concept to a deductible, the elimination period is the time immediately following the start of a disability when benefits are not payable. Elimination periods eliminate claims for short-term disabilities for which the insured usually can manage without financial hardship and save the insurance company from the expense of processing and settling small claims. This helps keep premiums down. The longer the elimination period, the lower the premium for comparable disability benefits. An elimination period can be compared to a deductible because both are cost-sharing devices that can have a direct bearing on the amount of premium required of the policyowner.

Depending on the policy, elimination periods may apply only to disabilities caused by sickness and not to disabilities caused by accident. In either event, elimination periods usually range from one week to one year or longer, but most are at least 30 days.

Test Topic Alert! An elimination period begins after a disability occurs and is not retroactive. Like a deductible, it is a cost-sharing device that can affect the amount of the premium.

Benefit Period

The benefit period is the maximum length of time that disability income benefits will be paid to the disabled insured. The longer the benefit period, the higher the cost of the policy. For individual policies, there are basically two types of benefit periods and accordingly they serve to classify a disability income policy as either short term or long term. Individual short-term policies provide benefits for six months to two years, after which payments cease. Individual long-term policies are characterized by benefit periods of more than two years, such as 5, 10, or 20 years. In some cases, a long-term policy will provide for benefits until the insured reaches age 65. The classifications of short term and long term are not necessarily the same for individual and group plans. See Unit 13 for a discussion of group disability plans.

Delayed Disability Provision

In some cases, total disability does not occur immediately after an accident, but develops some days or weeks later. Most policies allow a certain amount of time during which total disability may result from an accident and the insured still will be eligible for benefits. The amount of time allowed for a delayed disability may be 30, 60, or 90 days, for example.

Recurrent Disability Provision

It is not unusual for a person who experienced a total disability to recover and then, weeks or months later, undergo a recurrence of the same disability. Most policies provide for recurrent disabilities by specifying a period of time during which the recurrence of a disability is considered a continuation of the prior disability. If the recurrence takes place after that period, it is considered a new disability and will be subject to a new elimination period before benefits are again payable.

✓ ***For Example:*** Rachel has a short-term disability policy that stipulates a new benefit-paying period begins if the insured is disabled, recovers, returns to work for six months, and then becomes disabled again. Rachel is totally disabled and off work from January 15 to April 15, when she returns to work. She is stricken again the same year and is off work from September 1 to November 10. Rachel's policy would resume paying benefits, classifying her recurrence as a continuation of her prior disability, because her return to work did not last six months. She would not be subject to a new elimination period.

Nondisabling Injury

Frequently, a person covered by a disability income policy will suffer an injury that does not qualify for income benefits. Many such policies include a provision for a medical expense benefit that pays the actual cost of medical treatment for nondisabling injuries that result from an accident.

The benefit generally is limited to a percentage of the weekly or monthly income benefit specified in the policy. It is payable to eligible insureds in lieu of other benefits under the policy.

Quick Quiz 7.1

True or False?

_____ 1. If Susan is blind but is able to teach school, she will be considered to have a presumptive disability.

_____ 2. If Matt is injured in a sky-diving accident and as a result is unable to work, he likely will receive benefits under most disability income policies today.

_____ 3. If Paul is injured in a car accident 10 days after obtaining disability income insurance, he will be subject to a 30-day probationary period before disability benefits will be paid.

_____ 4. If Mary is injured in a train accident but does not develop back problems that prevent her from working until two weeks later, she probably will be eligible for disability benefits under most policies.

_____ 5. The percent-of-earnings approach generally is used in group disability insurance plans, while the flat-amount method is more common in individual plans.

Answers

1. ***True****.*

2. ***True****.*

3. ***False****. The probationary period in a disability income policy applies to sickness only; it does not apply to accidents. This is because while it is possible to expect a sickness-related disability, it is not possible to anticipate an accident. As a result, Paul will be entitled to disability income benefits immediately after the accident.*

4. ***True****.*

5. ***True****.*

Disability Income Policy Riders

As is true with life insurance policies, disability income policies may be purchased with riders or options that will enhance their value to the insured. Some of the more common riders are discussed below.

Waiver of Premium Rider

A waiver of premium rider generally is included with guaranteed renewable and noncancellable individual disability income policies. It is a valuable provision because it exempts the policyowner from paying the policy's premiums during periods of total disability. To qualify for the exemption, the insured must experience total disability for more than a specified period, commonly three months. In some cases, the waiver applies retroactively to the original date of disability and any premiums paid for that period are refunded. The trend is to have the waiver apply to the entire period of total disability, rather than to just the benefit period.

✓ ***Take Note:*** The waiver of premium generally does not extend past the insured's age 60 or 65. When the waiver is added, policy premiums are adjusted upward to cover the additional risk. Premiums then are reduced when the waiver is dropped due to the insured reaching the specified age limit.

Social Security Rider

The Social Security rider, sometimes called the social insurance substitute rider, provides for the payment of additional income when the insured is eligible for social insurance benefits but those benefits have not yet begun, have been denied, or have begun in an amount less than the benefit amount of the rider. Usually covered under the definition social insurance are disability benefits from Social Security, as well as state and local government programs or workers' compensation programs.

When applying for the rider, the applicant states the amount of benefit expected from Social Security and any other programs for which he might be eligible. Of course, the level of expected benefits must be realistic in light of the applicant's earnings level. When total disability strikes, the applicant must show that social insurance benefits have been applied for. After the Social Security Administration (or comparable administrative body of a state or local program) determines the benefit payable, the difference between the actual benefit and the expected benefit listed in the rider is payable as an additional disability income benefit.

Cost of Living Adjustment (COLA) Rider

The cost of living adjustment (COLA) rider links the monthly or weekly benefit payable under a disability policy to changes in the Consumer Price Index (CPI). Typically, the benefit amount is adjusted on each disability anniversary date to reflect changes in the CPI (though often a minimum CPI change, such as 4%, is required to trigger a disability income benefit increase).

✓ ***Take Note:*** When the disability ceases, the policyowner can elect to maintain the disability policy at the new (increased) benefit level by paying additional premiums or can choose to let the benefit return to the originally scheduled amount for the same premium as was paid before the disability commenced.

Guaranteed Insurability Rider

A disability income policy is the only type of health insurance policy to which a guaranteed insurability rider may be attached. This option guarantees the insured the right to purchase additional amounts of disability income coverage at predetermined times in the future without evidence of insurability. The guarantee may be contingent upon the insured meeting an earnings test prior to each purchase—a condition stipulated by the insurer to avoid overinsurance.

Most guaranteed insurability riders require the insured to exercise the option for additional coverage before reaching a specific age.

Summary

Often called the forgotten need, disability income insurance is an important part of a complete insurance program. Monthly or weekly benefits are paid when the insured is totally disabled, as determined by either the *any occupation* or the more liberal *own occupation* definition. If the policy has a partial disability provision, benefits may be payable if the insured is able to work only part-time or suffers a less-than-total disability. Another feature of disability income policies is that they define the cause of a disabling accident on an accidental means or accidental results basis.

Disability income contracts are characterized by probationary periods, which exclude pre-existing sickness from immediate coverage, and elimination periods which specify the time after the start of a disability when benefits are not payable thereby excluding very short-term disabilities from coverage. Like life insurance, disability income policies may be purchased with policy riders that can increase their value to the insured.

Disability income coverage may be purchased as individual or group policies. Its uses for businesses and business owners will be discussed in Unit 14.

Key Concepts

In preparing for their licensing examination, students should be familiar with the following concepts:

- total disability
- own occupation
- presumptive disability
- probationary period
- waiver of premium rider
- cost of living adjustment rider
- any occupation
- partial disability
- residual disability
- elimination period
- Social Security rider
- guaranteed insurability rider

Unit Exam 7

1. Assume an insurer will issue a maximum monthly disability income benefit of $5,000 of an insured's monthly income, provided the total of such benefits payable by all companies does not exceed 60% of the insured's regular monthly income. Ted earns $4,500 per month and has no existing disability income policy. The maximum monthly disability income benefit this insurer would issue to Ted is

   A. $2,500
   B. $2,700
   C. $4,500
   D. $5,000

2. Which of the following is NOT a basis for occupational suitability when determining total disability?

   A. Education
   B. Training
   C. Experience
   D. Job interest

3. Which of the following statements about elimination periods in disability income policies is NOT correct?

   A. Elimination periods apply to disabilities due to sickness and not accidents.
   B. Benefits are not payable during an elimination period, but are paid retroactively to the beginning of the period if the insured remains disabled throughout the period.
   C. An elimination period follows the start of a disability.
   D. Elimination periods help keep premiums down.

4. Which of the following riders provides for changes in the benefit payable based on changes in the consumer price index (CPI)?

   A. Guaranteed insurability
   B. Cost of living adjustment
   C. Social Security
   D. Waiver of premium

5. Benefit periods for individual short-term disability policies typically vary from

   A. 1 to 12 months
   B. 3 months to 3 years
   C. 6 months to 2 years
   D. 1 to 5 years

6. Which of the following statements about the waiver of premium in health insurance policies is NOT correct?

   A. It exempts an insured from paying premiums during periods of permanent and total disability.
   B. It may apply retroactively.
   C. It generally drops off after the insured reaches age 60 or 65.
   D. It normally applies to both medical expense and disability income policies.

7. Which of the following terms relates to disability income insurance?

   A. Service basis
   B. First-dollar
   C. Residual basis
   D. Coinsurance

8. Which of the following statements pertaining to recurrent disabilities for disability insurance is NOT correct?

   A. A recurrent disability is one that the insured experiences more than once.
   B. Recurrent disability policy provisions have no effect on the payment of benefits.
   C. A new elimination period may or may not be required for a recurrent disability.
   D. A recurrent disability may begin a new benefit period.

9. Sidney has a monthly benefit of $2,500 for total disability under a residual disability income policy. If Sidney suffers a 40% loss of his predisability income, how much will his benefit be?

   A. $0
   B. $1,000
   C. $1,500
   D. $2,500

10. What is the initial period of time specified in a disability income policy that must pass, after a policy is in force, before a loss due to sickness can be covered?

   A. Pre-existing term
   B. Probationary period
   C. Temporary interval
   D. Elimination period

Unit Exam 7 Answers & Rationale

1. **B.** The insurer will issue a disability income policy to Ted that determines the benefit using a percentage of his predisability earnings, and takes into account other sources of disability income. If it will pay no more than 60% of his regular monthly income ($4,500), the policy will provide a maximum monthly benefit of $2,700 (60% of $4,500).

2. **D.** The *any occupation* definition of total disability requires the insured to be unable to perform any occupation for which he is reasonably suited by reason of education, training, or experience in order to qualify for disability income benefits.

3. **B.** During the elimination period, benefits are not payable. This eliminates claims for short-term disabilities for which the insured can usually manage without financial hardship. If the insured remains disabled throughout the period and thereafter, benefits will not be paid retroactively.

4. **B.** A cost of living adjustment rider provides for indexing monthly or weekly disability benefits to changes in the Consumer Price Index.

5. **C.** Individual short-term disability policies typically have benefit periods ranging from 6 months to 2 years, after which payments stop. In contrast, individual long-term policies provide for benefit periods of more than 2 years.

6. **D.** A waiver of premium rider generally is included with guaranteed renewable and noncancellable individual disability income policies. It normally does not apply to medical expense policies.

7. **C.** The term *residual basis* applies to disability income insurance. The amount of benefit payable when a policy covers partial disabilities depends on whether the policy stipulates a flat amount or a residual basis. A residual amount benefit is based on the proportion of income actually lost due to the partial disability, taking into account the fact that the insured can work and earn some income.

8. **B.** Recurrent disability policy provisions affect the payment of benefits. Under most policies, a recurrence of a disability is considered a continuation of the prior disability. If the recurrence takes place after that period, it is considered a new disability and will be subject to a new elimination period before benefits become payable again.

9. **B.** Sidney's benefit under his residual disability income policy will be determined by multiplying the percentage of lost income by the stated monthly benefit for total disability. Because he suffered a 40% loss of income, the residual benefit payable would be 40% of the policy's benefit (40% × $2,500), or $1,000.

10. **B.** The probationary period is the period of time that must elapse before benefits due to sickness become payable. It is a one-time-only period that ends 15 or 30 days after the policy has been in force. Its purpose is to exclude pre-existing sicknesses from coverage.

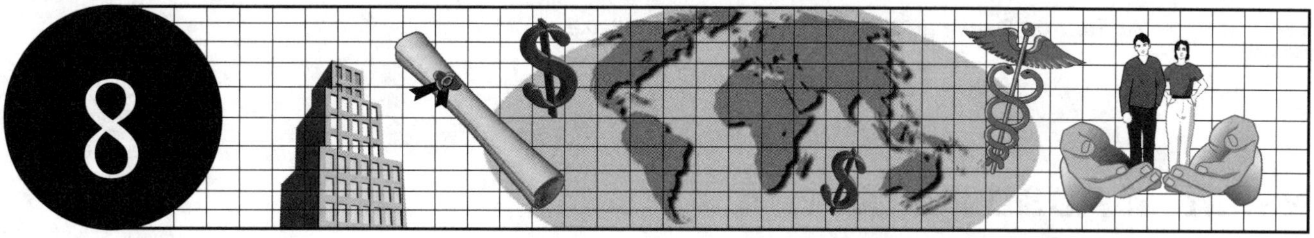

Accidental Death and Dismemberment Insurance

INTRODUCTION

The third major type of health insurance coverage is accidental death and dismemberment insurance (AD&D). It pays benefits in the event of a fatal accident or if dismemberment results from an accidental injury. Although the circumstances under which benefits are paid are somewhat limited, it is a widely used form of insurance protection and often is attached as a rider on a basic life or health insurance policy. AD&D policies are widely used in group insurance plans as well. In this unit we will examine the typical features of and benefits provided by AD&D policies and some of the other more specific forms of AD&D policies.

UNIT OBJECTIVES

When you have completed this unit, you should be able to:

- explain the purpose of accidental death and dismemberment insurance and the types of benefits that are typically payable;
- explain the difference between policies that base benefits on injuries due to accidental means versus accidental results; and
- compare and contrast limited risk policies and special risk policies, and give an example of each type of policy.

Nature of AD&D Policies

Accidental death and dismemberment insurance is the primary form of pure accident coverage. As such, it serves a somewhat limited purpose: it provides a stated lump-sum benefit in the event of accidental death or in the event of loss of body parts due to accidental injury. This latter event includes loss of hands or feet, or the loss of sight in one or both eyes. (Loss of body part is typically defined as actual severance from the body, though it may include loss of use, depending on the policy.) Separate benefits for hospital, surgical, and other medical expenses are generally not included in AD&D policies, although some may pay a medical reimbursement benefit up to a stated amount.

AD&D Benefits

Because an AD&D policy pays a specified benefit to the insured in the event of accidental death or dismemberment due to accidental injury, it is necessary for the policy to make distinctions between these two contingencies and to define the benefits accordingly. Consequently, AD&D policies make benefits payable in the form of a principal sum and a capital sum.

- **Principal Sum**. The principal sum under an AD&D policy is the amount payable as a death benefit. It is the amount of insurance purchased—$10,000, $25,000, $50,000, $100,000 or more. The principal sum represents the maximum amount the policy will pay.
- **Capital Sum**. The capital sum paid under an AD&D policy is the amount payable for the accidental loss of sight or accidental dismemberment. It is a specified amount, usually expressed as a percentage of the principal sum, that varies according to the severity of the injury. The benefit for the loss of one foot or one hand typically is 50% of the principal sum. The benefit for the loss of one arm or one leg usually is two-thirds of the principal sum. The most extreme losses, such as the loss of both feet or sight in both eyes, generally qualify for payment of the full benefit, which is 100% of the principal sum.

✓ ***For Example:*** Kevin has an accidental death and dismemberment policy that pays $50,000 for accidental loss of life and the same for accidental loss of two limbs or the sight in both eyes. Thus, $50,000 is the policy's principal sum. The same policy pays $25,000 for accidental loss of sight of one eye or dismemberment of one limb. Therefore, $25,000 is the policy's capital sum.

Some AD&D policies provide for payment of double, triple, or even quadruple the principal sum if the insured dies under specified circumstances. A double payment is referred to as double indemnity. If three times the principal sum is payable, it is called triple indemnity. However, do not let these terms confuse you. AD&D policies, because they pay a stated benefit, are valued contracts. They are not contracts of indemnity.

Accidental Means vs. Accidental Results

As we learned in the last unit, an insurance policy that provides benefits in the event of an injury due to an accident must stipulate what is considered an insurable accident. In all cases, an accident is external and violent, but accidental death and dismemberment policies (like disability income policies) make a distinction between injuries due to accidental means and those due to accidental results (or accidental bodily injury).

By way of a review, policies that base their benefit payments on accidental means require that both the cause and the result of an accident must be unintentional. Policies that use the more liberal accidental results definition stipulate that only the injury resulting from an accident must be unintentional.

✓ ***For Example:*** If Ted, the insured under an AD&D policy, intentionally jumps from the roof of his house after fixing his antenna (instead of climbing down the ladder) and so severely injures his leg that it must be amputated, he would be paid the appropriate percentage of the capital sum only if his policy used the results definition. If his policy used the means definition, no benefit would be payable because Ted intentionally performed the action that resulted in the injury.

As noted in the discussion of disability income policies, most states require that policies that provide any form of accident benefit, as do AD&D policies, base the definition of accident on the results definition, not the means definition.

Other Forms of AD&D

Accidental death and dismemberment coverage is made available in a variety of ways. It can be purchased by individuals as a single policy or it may be a part of an individual disability income policy. Typically, it is an aspect of a group insurance plan—either group life or group health—or it may in and of itself constitute a group plan. Usually, AD&D benefits are payable whether the injury resulted on or off the job.

By their very nature, AD&D policies are somewhat narrow, providing benefits only in the event of death or dismemberment due to an accident. There is another type of AD&D coverage, even more narrow in scope, that provides protection against accidental death or dismemberment only in the event of certain specified accidents. These are **limited risk policies** and **special risk policies**.

Limited Risk Policies

As noted in Unit 6, limited risk policies set forth a specific risk and provide benefits to cover death or dismemberment due to that risk. For example, an aviation policy provides benefits for accidental death or dismemberment if death or injury results from an aviation accident during a specified trip. An automobile policy provides benefits for accidental death or injury while riding in a car. Travel accident covers most kinds of travel accidents, but only for a specified period of time, such as one year.

Special Risk Policies

A distinction should be made between limited risk and special risk policies. A special risk policy covers unusual hazards normally not covered under ordinary accident and health insurance. An actress who insures her legs for $1 million or a pilot test-flying an experimental airplane who obtains a policy covering his life while flying that particular plane are both purchasing special risk policies. But a traveler who purchases an accident policy at the airport to provide coverage while he is a passenger on a commercial airlines flight is purchasing a limited risk policy.

Summary

Accidental death and dismemberment insurance (AD&D) represents the purest form of accident coverage. It provides a stated sum benefit in the event of accidental death or accidental loss of one or more body parts or accidental loss of sight. The benefit payable in the event of death is known as the principal sum. The benefit payable in the event of dismemberment or loss of sight is the capital sum.

Like all policies that provide accident benefits, AD&D policies must define the term accident on either a means basis (in which both the cause and the result of the accident must be unintentional) or on a results basis (requiring only that the injury itself be accidental). Most states stipulate the use of the results definition.

AD&D coverage may be purchased as an individual policy but is usually part of a larger group life or health plan. In some cases, it is offered as a separate group plan. Specialized forms of AD&D coverage, known as limited risk and special risk insurance, provide accident protection in the event of specified limited risks, such as travel or aviation.

Key Concepts

In preparing for their licensing examination, students should be familiar with the following concepts:

- Capital sum
- Special risk policies
- Accidental death and dismemberment coverage
- Principal sum
- Limited risk policies
- Accidental means vs. accidental results

Unit Exam 8

1. The amount payable as a death benefit in an accidental death and dismemberment policy is known as the

   A. primary amount
   B. capital sum
   C. indemnity amount
   D. principal sum

2. Theodore received a $15,000 cash benefit from his $50,000 accidental death and dismemberment policy for the accidental loss of one eye. The amount he received could be identified as the policy's

   A. principal sum
   B. secondary sum
   C. capital sum
   D. contingent amount

3. Which of the following examples about accidental death and dismemberment insurance is CORRECT?

   A. Merrill is the insured under a $50,000 AD&D policy and dies unexpectedly of a heart attack. His beneficiary will receive $50,000 as the death benefit.
   B. Linda has a $40,000 AD&D policy that pays triple indemnity. If she should be killed in a train wreck, her beneficiary would receive $120,000.
   C. Paula has an AD&D policy that pays $15,000 for the loss of one hand or foot or the sight in one eye. That benefit is called the principal sum.
   D. Eric has an AD&D policy. He is killed in an auto accident. The $30,000 his beneficiary receives as a death benefit is the policy's capital sum.

4. Agnes purchases a round-trip travel accident policy at the airport before leaving on a business trip. Her policy would be which type of insurance?

   A. Limited risk
   B. Business overhead expense
   C. Credit accident and health
   D. Industrial health

5. Paul has an accidental death and dismemberment policy that paid him $100,000 after he was injured in a skydiving accident. His policy bases its benefit payments on accidental

   A. means
   B. results
   C. methods
   D. means and methods

Unit Exam 8 Answers & Rationale

1. **D.** The principal sum under an AD&D policy is the amount payable as a death benefit. It is the amount of insurance purchased and represents the maximum amount the policy will pay.

2. **C.** The $15,000 cash benefit Theodore received for the accidental loss of one eye is the policy's capital sum. This is the amount payable for the accidental loss of sight or accidental dismemberment. It is a specified amount that usually is expressed as a percentage of the principal sum and varies according to the severity of the injury.

3. **B.** If Linda's $40,000 AD&D contract pays triple indemnity, her beneficiary will receive 3 times this amount ($120,000) if she dies in a train accident.

4. **A.** Agnes purchased a limited risk policy that sets forth a specific risk (death or dismemberment from an aviation accident) and provides benefits to cover death or dismemberment due to that risk.

5. **B.** Paul's AD&D policy bases its benefit payments on accidental results. Policies using this definition stipulate that only the injury resulting from an accident must be unintentional. If Paul's policy used the accidental means definition, it would not pay any benefits because Paul intentionally performed the action (skydiving) that resulted in injury.

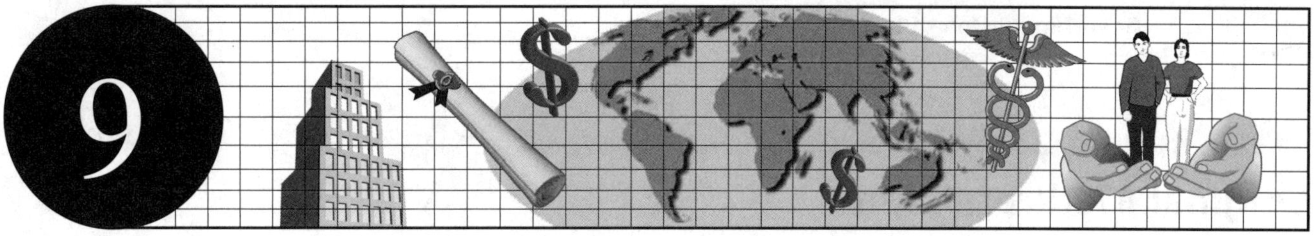

Government Health Insurance Programs

INTRODUCTION

Because of limited resources and the need for more extensive care than younger members of society, senior citizens often face special problems when paying health care bills. To help provide affordable health care for elderly Americans, the federal government enacted Medicare in 1965, which established a health insurance program for aged persons. Since its creation, Medicare has undergone numerous changes affecting its financing, its method of operation, its benefits, and its methods of cost control. Despite these changes, the basic mission of Medicare remains the same: to provide a system for the delivery and payment of medical and hospital care for people age 65 and over (and for people with certain disabilities). Today, Medicare covers around 95% of our nation's elderly population, as well as many people who are on Social Security because of disability.

We will begin our discussion in this unit with the Original Medicare Plan, and will then review Medicare+Advantage, a program designed to provide Medicare beneficiaries with a variety of health plan options. We also will look at another government program, called Medicaid, which reimburses hospitals and physicians for providing care to needy and low income people who cannot finance their own medical expenses. The unit ends with a brief discussion of state workers' compensation programs, which provide benefits for work-related injuries, illness, or death.

UNIT OBJECTIVES

When you complete this unit you should be able to:

- explain the types of coverage available under Medicare Part A and Part B;
- identify the different health plan options available under the Medicare+Advantage Program;
- explain the purpose of Medicaid and how it differs from Medicare; and
- describe the goal of state workers' compensation laws.

Original Medicare Plan

The Original Medicare Plan consists of two parts: Medicare Part A and Medicare Part B. Medicare Part A is compulsory hospitalization insurance (HI) that provides specified in-hospital and related benefits. It is compulsory in that all workers covered by Social Security finance its operation through a portion of their FICA taxes and automatically are provided with benefits once they qualify for Social Security benefits.

Medicare Part B is a voluntary program designed to provide supplementary medical insurance (SMI) to cover physician services, medical services, and supplies not covered under Part A. Those who desire the coverage must enroll and pay a monthly premium. Medicare Part B is financed by monthly premiums and by tax revenues.

Medicare Part A Coverages

Medicare Part A provides coverage for inpatient hospitalization and posthospital skilled facility care and home care. For the first 60 days of hospitalization during any one benefit period, Medicare pays for all covered services, except for an initial deductible ($876 in 2004). Covered services include a semiprivate room, nursing services, and other inpatient hospital services.

For the 61st through the 90th day of hospitalization, Medicare pays a reduced amount of the covered services. The patient is responsible for a daily copayment ($219 per day in 2004).

This 90-day hospitalization coverage is renewed with each benefit period. A benefit period starts when a patient enters the hospital and ends when the patient has been out of the hospital for 60 days. If a patient re-enters a hospital before the end of a benefit period, the deductible is not reapplied, but the 90-day hospital coverage period is not renewed. However, if the patient reenters a hospital after a benefit period ends, a new deductible is required, and the 90-day hospital coverage period is renewed.

Medicare patients also have a lifetime reserve of 60 days of hospital coverage. If a patient is hospitalized longer than 90 days in a benefit period, he can tap into the 60-day reserve. The lifetime reserve is a one-time benefit; it does not renew with a new benefit period. If a patient is hospitalized and taps into the reserve days, he is required to pay a higher copayment ($438 per day in 2004). If a patient is hospitalized beyond the 60th lifetime reserve day, thereby exhausting the reserve, he is responsible for all hospital charges.

Test Topic Alert! Medicare Part A is available when an individual turns 65 and automatically is provided when he applies for Social Security benefits.

FIGURE 9.1 What Medicare Covers

Part A	*Part B*
• Inpatient hospital services, including semiprivate room and board and nursing services	• Physicians' and surgeons' services, whether in a hospital, clinic or elsewhere
• Posthospital skilled nursing care, in an accredited care facility • Posthospital home health services, including nursing care, therapy and part-time home health aides • Hospice benefits for the care of terminally ill patients (to the exclusion of all other Medicare benefits, except for physician services) • Inpatient psychiatric care, on a limited basis	• Medical and health services, such as X-rays, diagnostic lab tests, ambulance services, medical supplies, medical equipment rental and physical and occupational therapy

✓ ***Take Note:*** Most of the people enrolled in Medicare Part A are elderly. In 1999, of the 39 million people who received Medicare Part A benefits, 34 million were over age 65. However, some individuals under age 65 also are eligible for Medicare. For instance, a person under age 65 who receives Social Security or Railroad Retirement disability checks is eligible for Medicare Part A and may enroll in Medicare Part B. Persons with permanent kidney failure who are treated with dialysis or a transplant also are eligible.

In addition, Part A provides benefits for skilled nursing facility care, hospice care, home health services and, to a limited degree, inpatient psychiatric care. In all cases, Part A covers only those services that are medically necessary and only up to amounts deemed reasonable by Medicare.

Part A covers the costs of care in a skilled nursing facility as long as the patient was first hospitalized for three consecutive days. Treatment in a skilled nursing facility is covered in full for the first 20 days. From the 21st to the 100th day, the patient must pay the daily copayment ($109.50 per day in 2004). No Medicare benefits are provided for treatment in a skilled nursing facility beyond 100 days.

✓ ***Test Topic Alert!*** Medicare Part A deductibles and copayments are applied per benefit period, not on an annual basis.

Medicare Part B Coverages

For those who desire, additional coverage is available under Medicare Part B for physician services, diagnostic tests, physical and occupational therapy, medical supplies, and the like.

✓ ***Take Note:*** Some preventive services, such as mammograms and flu shots, also are covered. However, Medicare Part B does not cover routine physical exams, eyeglasses, dental care, hearing aids, most prescription drugs, orthopedic shoes, or routine foot care.

Part B participants are required to pay a monthly premium ($58.70 in 2004) and are responsible for an annual deductible ($100 in 2004, $110 in 2005). After the deductible, Part B will pay 80% of covered expenses, subject to Medicare's standards for reasonable charges.

Test Topic Alert! Medicare Part B deductibles and copayments are applied on an annual basis. Part B is an optional coverage.

As of January 1, 2005, Medicare Part B will expand its coverage of preventative services to include the following:

- An initial preventative physical examination within the first six months after a beneficiary's initial coverage begins under Medicare Part B;
- Cardiovascular blood screening tests, including tests for cholesterol levels and other lipids or triglyceride levels; and
- Diagnostic screening tests for an individual at risk of diabetes to detect diabetes early.

Medicare Part B will also provide benefits for coordinated care of people with chronic illness.

Primary Payor and Secondary Payor

Anyone aged 65 who is eligible for Medicare and who works for an employer of 20 or more employees is entitled to the same health insurance benefits as the employer offers to younger employees. In these cases, the employer-sponsored plan is the primary payor and Medicare is the secondary payor. This means that Medicare pays only those charges that the employer-sponsored plan does not cover. This also applies to any disabled Medicare enrollee who also is covered by an employer-provided health care plan as a current employee or as a family member of an employee, but only if the employer plan covers 100 or more employees.

Medicare+Advantage Program (Medicare Part C Coverage)

While Medicare is facing many challenges, the most pressing are the financial pressures resulting from changing demographics. Today, and in the future, the number of people becoming eligible for Medicare will increase rapidly and the number of workers paying taxes to support Medicare will decrease.

In 1997, Congress passed a law to reduce the financial strain on Medicare funds and provide Medicare beneficiaries with a variety of new health plan options. The Original Medicare Plan and Medicare supplement insurance (discussed in the next unit), which is purchased from private insurance companies, still are available. However, new options are available through Medicare Part C, or what is called the Medicare+Advantage (MA) Program.

Medicare Part C Coverage

The new Medicare Part C, called Medicare Advantage (MA), includes Medicare+Choice and Medicare Medical Savings Accounts. The Medicare+Choice Program offers a variety of Medicare managed care choices, a private fee-for-service plan (PFFS), and a Medicare Medical Savings Account Plan (MSA).

A major goal of Medicare Advantage is to encourage beneficiaries to join private health plans as an alternative to the traditional fee-for-service Medicare program. These private health plans may be local Health Maintenance Organizations (HMOs) or regional Preferred Provider Organizations (PPOs).

Starting in 2004, all private plans will be reimbursed at a rate at least as high as the rate for traditional fee-for-service Medicare. These plans have the flexibility to design plans that include the drug benefit as well as overall medical benefits in an effort to reduce premiums and out-of-pocket costs to Medicare beneficiaries. A beneficiary enrolled in a Medicare Advantage plan providing qualified prescription drug coverage will have coverage through that plan and may not enroll in a prescription drug plan (PDP) under the new Medicare Part D (discussed later in this unit) with limited exceptions.

Managed Care System

Medicare's managed care system consists of a network of approved hospitals, doctors, and other health-care professionals who agree to provide services to Medicare beneficiaries for a set monthly payment from Medicare. The health care providers receive the same fee every month, regardless of the actual services provided. As a result of this arrangement, health care providers try to manage care in such a way that they achieve a balance between budgetary and health care concerns.

✓ ***Take Note:*** The options available include HMOs, PPOs, and provider sponsored organizations (PSOs). Some HMOs and all PPOs offer a point of service option (POS). With this option, beneficiaries can use providers outside the network for an additional fee.

Private Fee-for-Service Plan

Another Medicare+Advantage option is a private-fee-for-service (PFFS) plan. This type of plan offers a Medicare-approved private insurance plan. Medicare pays the plan for Medicare-covered services while the PFFS plan determines, up to a limit, how much the care recipient will pay for covered services. The Medicare beneficiary is responsible for paying the difference between the amount Medicare pays and the PFFS charges.

Medical Savings Account

Medicare beneficiaries have the most control over their health care expenditures with Medicare Medical Savings Accounts (MSAs). A Medicare+Advantage MSA consists of two parts: a high-deductible insurance policy (the policy) and a savings account (the account). The policy pays for at least all Medicare-covered items and services after an enrollee meets the annual deductible. Medicare pays the premium for the policy and deposits the difference between the premium and the fixed amount Medicare allots for each Medicare+Advantage enrollee in the individual's account. Money in the account may earn interest or dividends and can be withdrawn tax free to pay for services covered under the Medicare benefit package, as well as services listed as qualified medical expenses in the Internal Revenue Code. MSA funds can also be used to buy long-term care insurance.

Note that health care providers can charge whatever they want above what is paid by the Medicare MSA policy. Furthermore, unlike other Medicare+Advantage options, individuals who choose an MSA must enroll in the Medicare MSA Plan for at least one year, from January to December. They then can withdraw by December 15 of the following year. Although sales of MSAs have been slow, the federal government has extended the program indefinitely.

✓ ***Take Note:*** To be eligible for any Medicare+Advantage options, a Medicare beneficiary must be enrolled in both Medicare Part A and Part B. Individuals with end-stage renal disease (kidney failure) cannot enroll in most Medicare+ Advantage plans.

Health Savings Accounts

As of January 1, 2004, individuals under 65 are eligible to establish and contribute to a new type of health care savings account (HSAs) if they have a qualified health plan. The purpose of an HSA is to serve as a tax-favored way to accumulate funds to cover medical expenses. For an individual, a qualified health plan is one with a minimum deductible of $1,000 and a $5,000 cap on out-of-pocket expenses (indexed annually). For a family, a qualified health plan is one with a minimum deductible of $2,000 and a $10,000 cap on out-of-pocket expenses (indexed annually).

Annual contributions of up to 100% of an individual's health plan deductible can be made to an HSA. For 2004, the maximum annual contribution is $2,600 for self-only policies and $5,150 for family policies (indexed annually), provided the insured has a deductible at least that high. Individuals who are 55 to 65 years old can make an additional catch-up contribution. Starting in 2004, they can contribute an additional $500, an amount which they can increase by $100 a year, and by up to $1,000 per year in 2009 and thereafter.

Earnings in HSAs grow tax-free, and account beneficiaries can make tax-free withdrawals to cover current and future qualified healthcare costs. Qualified healthcare expenses include retiree health insurance premiums, Medicare expenses (but not Medigap), prescription drugs, qualified long-term care services, and COBRA coverage. Nonqualified withdrawals are subject to income taxes and a 10% penalty tax. HSAs are fully portable and assets can accumulate from year to year. Upon death, HSA ownership may be transferred to a spouse tax-free.

✓ ***Take Note:*** Employers can offer HSAs through cafeteria plans. Employer contributions are made on a pre-tax basis and are not taxable to the employee.

Medicare Part D: Prescription Drug Plan (PDP)

Beginning in 2006, a new Medicare Part D prescription drug benefit will be offered to Medicare beneficiaries. Under the standard benefit for 2006, Medicare beneficiaries will pay a projected monthly premium of $35 and a $250 annual deductible. Beneficiaries will then pay 25% of the first $2,250 of prescription drug costs, and Medicare will pay the other 75%. Coverage then stops completely. However, if a beneficiary's total drug costs are more than $5,100 after the beneficiary has spent another $2,850, then coverage starts again and beneficiaries pay copayments of $2 for generic drugs and $5 for brand name drugs, or 5% or total costs, whichever is higher. (These dollar thresholds are scheduled to increase each year.)

This benefit will be available through Prescription Drug Plans (PDPs) and the Medicare Advantage (MA) plans described below. PDPs are private plans that will contract with Medicare to provide drug coverage to people with Medicare who live in a certain area. A six-month initial enrollment period is set to commence on November 15, 2005, for both the PDPs and the MA plans.

The law provides federal subsidy payments to employers and unions that sponsor qualified retiree prescription drug plans.

Medigap Amendments. Three of the 10 standardized Medigap benefit plans include coverage for prescription drugs. The new law prohibits the sale of these Medigap policies with prescription drug coverage starting in 2006. Beneficiaries who already have Medigap-with-drug policies and do not enroll in a Part D prescription drug plan can renew their policies. If these beneficiaries choose to enroll in a Part D prescription drug plan, they can keep their current Medigap policies, but without the drug coverage and with the premium adjusted. These beneficiaries will have the option to switch to another Medigap policy offered by the same insurer, but only if they elect Part D during the initial enrollment period.

Medicare-Endorsed Prescription Drug Discount Cards

To bridge the gap between now and implementation of the new Medicare Part D prescription drug plan in 2006, Medicare-endorsed prescription drug cards will be available to Medicare beneficiaries. The cards will cost about $30 a year and will enable beneficiaries to receive discounts of between 10% and 25% off the price of prescription drugs. The discount card program begins in 2004 and expires on December 31, 2005.

Medicaid

Medicaid is a government-funded, means-tested program designed to provide health care to poor people of all ages. The goal of Medicaid is to offer medical assistance to those whose income and resources are insufficient to meet the costs of necessary medical care. Individuals claiming benefits must prove they do not have the ability or means to pay for their own medical care.

Applicants must complete a lengthy questionnaire, disclosing all assets and income. To qualify for Medicaid, a person must be poor or become poor. Such people frequently include children born to low-income parents, babies born addicted to drugs, AIDS patients, and the indigent elderly.

Individual states design and administer the Medicaid programs under broad guidelines established by the federal government. On average, the federal government contributes about 56 cents for every Medicaid dollar spent; however, the amount contributed may be lower or higher. State governments contribute the balance and the extent of coverage, and the quality of services vary widely from state to state.

Qualifying for Medicaid Nursing Home Benefits

Unlike Medicare, Medicaid does provide for custodial care or assisted care in a nursing home. However, as explained earlier, individuals claiming a need for Medicaid must prove that they cannot pay for their own nursing home care. In addition, the potential recipient must:

- be at least age 65, blind, or disabled (as defined by the recipient's state);
- be a United States citizen or permanent resident alien;
- need the type of care that is provided only in a nursing home; and
- meet certain asset and income tests.

✓ ***Take Note:*** People meeting these basic criteria usually will have their long-term nursing home care paid for by Medicaid. However, each state (and even some counties within certain states) evaluates an individual's ability to pay by looking at the nursing home resident's (and spouse's) income and assets. The specific limits for each of these sources vary by state and change annually.

Test Topic Alert! Eligibility for Medicaid is based not on an applicant's age, but on his income.

State Workers' Compensation Programs

All states have workers' compensation laws, which were enacted to provide mandatory benefits to employees for work-related injuries, illness, or death. Employers are responsible for providing workers' compensation benefits to their employees and do so by purchasing coverage through state programs, private insurers, or by self-insuring.

Workers' compensation laws are designed to help injured workers recover and return to work. They are based on the principle that work-related injuries are compensable by the employer without regard to fault. However, the amount of compensation payable is limited and fixed by law. In general, such compensation encompasses medical care costs, disability income, rehabilitation benefits, and, for certain specified injuries, specific lump-sum benefits. These benefits relieve injured workers of the burden of medical expenses, replace some of the wages lost due to the disability, and provide rehabilitation services to return the person to work. Because of the wide variation among state programs, the laws of each state must be examined to discover available coverages and benefits. See Unit 5 for a listing of common procedures, requirements, and benefits.

Summary

The Original Medicare Plan provides hospital and medical expense insurance protection to those aged 65 and older, to those of any age who suffer from chronic kidney disease, or to those who are receiving Social Security disability benefits. Medicaid is a joint federal and state program to pay health care expenses for the poor. To qualify for Medicaid benefits, an individual must meet certain asset and income limitation tests. However, even if a person qualifies for Medicaid, finding an adequate nursing home is difficult because Medicaid does not pay for the full cost of care. Medicaid patients are limited in choice regarding which nursing home they go to.

Key Concepts

In preparing for their licensing examination, students should be familiar with the following concepts:

- Medicare
- Medicaid
- benefit period
- Medicare Part A
- Medicare Part B
- lifetime reserve
- Medicare Part C
- Medicare+Advantage program
- Medicare Part D

Unit Exam 9

1. Which of the following statements pertaining to Medicare is CORRECT?
   A. Bob is covered under Medicare Part B. He submitted a total of $1,100 of approved medical charges to Medicare after paying the required deductible. Of that total, Bob must pay $880.
   B. Each individual covered by Medicare Part A is allowed one 90-day benefit period per year.
   C. For the first 90 days of hospitalization, Medicare Part A pays 100% of all covered services, except for an initial deductible.
   D. Medicare Part A is provided automatically when a qualified individual applies for Social Security benefits.

2. Under Medicare Part B, the participant must pay all of the following EXCEPT
   A. an annual deductible
   B. a per benefit deductible
   C. 20% of covered charges above the deductible
   D. a monthly premium

3. Which of the following statements about Medicare Part B is NOT correct?
   A. It is a compulsory program.
   B. It covers services and supplies not covered by Part A.
   C. It is financed by monthly premiums.
   D. It is financed by tax revenues.

4. For how many days of skilled nursing facility care will Medicare pay benefits?
   A. 25
   B. 60
   C. 75
   D. 100

5. Which of the following statements concerning workers' compensation is NOT correct?
   A. Workers' compensation laws are designed to return injured persons to work.
   B. Benefits include medical care costs and disability income.
   C. A worker receives benefits only if the work-related injury was not his fault.
   D. All states have workers' compensation laws.

Unit Exam 9 Answers & Rationale

1. **D.** When an individual turns age 65, Medicare Part A is available and is provided automatically when he applies for Social Security benefits.

2. **B.** Under Medicare Part B, a participant must pay a monthly premium and an annual deductible. Once the deductible has been met, Part B will pay 80% of covered expenses and the participant must pay the remaining 20%.

3. **A.** Medicare Part B is an optional program that provides additional coverage for physician services, diagnostic tests, physical and occupation therapy, medical supplies, and the like.

4. **D.** Medicare Part A covers the cost of care in a skilled nursing facility for 100 days. For the first 20 days, treatment is covered in full. From the 21st to the 100th day, the patient must pay a daily copayment. No Medicare benefits are provided for treatment beyond this period.

5. **C.** All states have workers' compensation laws that are designed to help injured workers recover and return to work. They are based on the principle that the employer should provide compensation for work-related injuries, regardless of who was at fault.

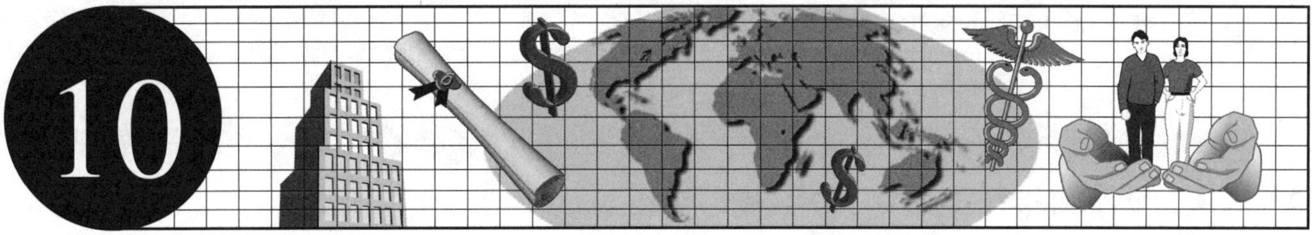

Private Insurance Plans for Seniors

INTRODUCTION

As the US population ages, individuals inevitably encounter more medical problems that require additional and costly health care services. As health care costs have increased at a dizzying rate, there has been an ever-growing concern over how to pay for these costs. Because the coverage and benefits provided by Medicare are by no means comprehensive, insurance companies have stepped in to fill these gaps in coverage by offering Medicare supplement policies. As a result, most Medicare recipients supplement their health care through a Medicare supplement policy that picks up coverage where Medicare leaves off.

As we saw in the last unit, although Medicare was designed to cover physician and hospital costs associated with acute illness and injuries, it never was intended to cover chronic conditions requiring long-term care, whether at home or in a nursing facility. To finance this level of care, many individuals purchase long-term care insurance. In this unit, we will look at typical features and benefits of long-term care policies and we also will focus on Medicare supplement policies, which are designed to protect elderly people from the high cost of health care.

UNIT OBJECTIVES

When you complete this unit you should be able to:

- explain the purpose of Medicare supplement policies and describe the types of coverage they provide;
- list and describe the different types of coverage provided under long-term care policies;
- identify the basic provisions and typical limits and exclusions found in most long-term care policies; and
- explain the tax treatment of long-term care benefits.

Medicare Supplement Policies

As is apparent from the discussion of Medicare in the previous unit, Medicare leaves many gaps in its coverage. With its structure of limited benefit periods, deductibles, copayments, and exclusions, the coverage it provides is limited at best. To help fill these gaps, private insurance companies market Medicare supplement insurance policies to consumers. Medicare supplement (or Medigap) policies are designed to pick up coverage where Medicare leaves off.

The term Medicare supplement implies that the policy should cover what Medicare does not. Unfortunately, until recently some policies did not live up to what was expected of them. To combat this, in 1990 Congress passed a far-reaching Medigap law that required the National Association of Insurance Commissioners (NAIC) to address the subject of Medicare supplement policies. Specifically, the NAIC's task was to develop a standardized model Medicare supplement policy, which would provide certain core benefits, plus as many as nine other supplement policies that would provide increasingly more comprehensive benefits. These 10 model policies then could be adopted by the states as prototype policies for their insurers. (See Figure 10.1)

Each of the 10 plans developed by the NAIC has a letter designation ranging from A (the most basic policy) to J (the most comprehensive policy). Plan A is the core benefits plan; each of the remaining nine plans incorporates these core benefits and adds various other combinations of benefits. Insurers may not alter these combinations of benefits, nor may the letter designations be changed (although insurers may add names or titles to the letter designations).

The purpose of this law was to reduce the variety of Medicare supplement policies being offered for sale and to eliminate some of the questionable marketing practices associated with these policies. It was intended that these model policies would help consumers better understand Medicare supplement policies, thereby allowing them to make more informed buying decisions by:

- standardizing coverages and benefits from one policy to the next;
- simplifying the terms used in these policies;
- facilitating policy comparisons; and
- eliminating policy provisions that may be misleading or confusing.

Qualifying for Medigap Coverage

People age 65 or older who enroll in Medicare Part B are afforded a six-month open enrollment period for purchasing a Medicare supplement

FIGURE 10.1 Standard Medicare Supplement Plans

BASIC BENEFITS: Included in All Plans
Hospitalization: Part A coinsurance plus coverage for 365 additional days after Medicare benefits end
Medical Expenses: Part B coinsurance (20% of Medicare-approved expenses)
Blood: First three pints of blood each year

A	B	C	D	E	F	G	H	I	J
Basic Benefits	Basic Benefits	Basic Benefits	Basic Benefits	Basic Benefits	Basic Benefits	Basic Benefits	Basic Benefits	Basic Benefits	Basic Benefits
		Skilled Nursing Coinsurance	Skilled Nursing Coinsurance	Skilled Nursing Coinsurance	Skilled Nursing Coinsurance	Skilled Nursing Coinsurance	Skilled Nursing Coinsurance	Skilled Nursing Coinsurance	Skilled Nursing Coinsurance
	Part A Deductible	Part A Deductible	Part A Deductible	Part A Deductible	Part A Deductible	Part A Deductible	Part A Deductible	Part A Deductible	Part A Deductible
		Part B Deductible			Part B Deductible				Part B Deductible
					Part B Excess (100%)	Part B Excess (80%)		Part B Excess (100%)	Part B Excess (100%)
		Foreign Travel Emergency	Foreign Travel Emergency	Foreign Travel Emergency	Foreign Travel Emergency	Foreign Travel Emergency	Foreign Travel Emergency	Foreign Travel Emergency	Foreign Travel Emergency
			At-Home Recovery			At-Home Recovery		At-Home Recovery	At-Home Recovery
							Basic Drugs ($1,250 Limit)	Basic Drugs ($1,250 Limit)	Basic Drugs ($3,000 Limit)
				Preventive Care					Preventive Care

Source: National Association of Insurance Commissioners.

policy. They may select any of the Medigap policies available in their state and they cannot be denied coverage because of health problems. In fact, insurers may not discriminate in the pricing of the policy or condition the issuance of the policy on good health.

✓ ***Take Note:*** An insurer may exclude certain pre-existing conditions, such as health problems treated within the six months before the policy went into effect.

In general, people under age 65, disabled and enrolled in Medicare Part B are not eligible for open enrollment unless their state mandates otherwise.

Protecting the Consumer

As stated earlier, the standardization of Medigap policies was intended to help consumers understand what these policies cover and, more importantly, what they do not cover. Consumers now are encouraged to do some comparison shopping before they purchase a Medicare supplement policy. Prospective insureds should compare benefits, the coverage limitations, the exclusions, and the premiums of several insurers before they buy a policy. In many cases, policies that provide the same coverage will not necessarily have the same premiums.

As further protection for the consumer, purchasers have the option of reviewing their policies and canceling the coverage. Consumers can receive a refund of their premium if they notify the insurer within a specified number of days after the policy is delivered. In most states, this free-look period is 30 days, but some states have shorter periods.

Test Topic Alert! Medicare supplement insurance is not social insurance. It is offered through private insurers to supplement Medicare. An additional premium is charged for this coverage under the various supplement plans.

Long-Term Care Insurance

Americans are living longer and many can expect to live a substantial portion of their lives in retirement. That's the good news. The bad news is, although statistics regarding longevity for older Americans may be improving, many individuals over age 65 still have to deal with poor health during their retirement years. As people age, they consume a larger proportion of health care services because of chronic illness, such as Alzheimer's disease, heart disease, and stroke. The cost of the extended day-in, day-out care some older people need can be staggering: as much as $50,000 each year or more for nursing home care, and upwards of $1,000 a month—or more—for aides who come to one's home.

As beneficial as Medicare and Medicare supplement insurance are to the elderly in protecting them against the costs of medical care, neither of these programs covers long-term custodial or nursing home care. Medicaid covers some of the costs associated with long-term care, but a person is ineligible for

Medicaid until she is practically destitute. How can these costs be paid? The solution for many is long-term care insurance.

What Is Long-Term Care?

You often will see nursing home care referred to as long-term care. However, long-term care (LTC) refers to a broad range of medical, personal, and environmental services designed to assist individuals who have lost their ability to remain completely independent in the community. Although care may be provided for short periods of time while a patient is recuperating from an accident or illness, LTC refers to care provided for an extended period of time, normally more than 90 days. And, depending on the severity of the impairment, assistance may be given at home, at an adult care center or in a nursing home.

Test Topic Alert! Long-term care is care rendered for an extended period of time, usually more than 90 days.

A large percentage of the elderly population will spend time in a nursing home. In fact, the Department of Health and Human Services estimated that, in 2000, expenditures on nursing home care exceeded $85.8 billion. The cost of care for elderly or disabled people who remained at home but required some type of home care exceeded $34.7 billion in 2000.

What Is Long-Term Care Insurance?

Long-term care insurance is a relatively new type of insurance product. However, more and more insurance companies are beginning to offer this coverage as the need for it grows. It is similar to most insurance plans, in that the insured, in exchange for a certain premium, receives specified benefits in the event he requires long-term care, as defined by the policy. Most LTC policies pay the insured a fixed dollar amount for each day he receives the kind of care the policy covers, regardless of what the care costs.

✓ ***For Example:*** If the daily benefit amount is $125 per day and the facility charges $110 per day, the insurance company will pay the full $125 per day. The claimant decides what to do with the remaining funds.

Insurers offer a wide range of benefit amounts, ranging from, for example, $40 each day to $200 each day for nursing home care. The daily benefit for at-home care typically is half the nursing home benefit. Many policies include an inflation rider or option to purchase additional coverage, enabling the policies to keep pace with increases in LTC costs.

Long-Term Care Coverages

As individuals age, they are likely to suffer from acute and (or) chronic illnesses or conditions. An acute illness is a serious condition, such as pneumonia or influenza, from which the body can recover fully with proper medical attention. The patient also may need some assistance with chores for short periods of time until recovery and rehabilitation from the illness are complete.

Some people will suffer from chronic conditions, such as arthritis, heart disease, or hypertension, that are treatable but not curable illnesses. When chronic conditions such as diabetes or heart disease initially manifest, many people ignore the inconvenience or pain they cause. Over time, however, a chronic condition frequently goes beyond being a nuisance and begins to inhibit a person's independence.

Typically, the need for long-term care arises when physical or mental conditions, whether acute or chronic, impair a person's ability to perform the basic activities of daily living—eating, toileting, transferring, bathing, continence, and dressing. This is the risk that long-term care insurance is designed to protect.

✓ ***Take Note:*** Activities of daily living (ADLs) provide an excellent means to assess an individual's need for nursing home care, home health care, or other health-related services. A policy should indicate what number and type of ADLs will be used to trigger benefits. When the insured cannot perform these ADLs independently, benefits will be paid to cover expenses for assistance with those activities.

The kinds of services and support associated with long-term care are provided at three levels: institutional care, home-based care, and community care. The appropriate level of care depends, of course, on the individual's medical or health care needs. Within each of these broad levels are many types of care, any or all of which may be covered by a long-term care insurance policy. Typical types of coverages are explained below.

Skilled Nursing Care

Skilled nursing care is continuous around-the-clock care provided by licensed medical professionals under the direct supervision of a physician. Skilled nursing care is usually administered in nursing homes.

Intermediate Nursing Care

Intermediate nursing care is provided by registered nurses, licensed practical nurses, and nurse's aides under the supervision of a physician. Intermediate care is provided in nursing homes for stable medical conditions that require daily, but not 24-hour, supervision.

Custodial Care

Custodial care provides assistance in meeting daily living requirements, such as bathing, dressing, getting out of bed, toileting, etc. Such care does not require specialized medical training, but it must be given under a doctor's order. Custodial care usually is provided by nursing homes but also can be given by adult day care centers, by respite centers, or at home.

Home Health Care Home health care is provided in the insured's home, usually on a part-time basis. It can include skilled care (such as nursing, rehabilitative, or physical therapy care ordered by a doctor) or unskilled care (such as help with cooking or cleaning).

Adult Day Care Adult day care is designed for those who require assistance with various activities of daily living, while their primary caregivers (usually family or friends) are absent. These day care centers offer skilled medical care in conjunction with social and personal services, but custodial care usually is their primary focus.

Respite Care Respite care is designed to provide a short rest period for a family caregiver. There are two options: either the insured is moved to a full-time care facility or a substitute care provider moves into the insured's home for a temporary period, giving the family member a rest from his caregiving activities.

Continuing Care A fairly new kind of LTC coverage, continuing care coverage, is designed to provide a benefit for elderly individuals who live in a continuing care retirement community. Retirement communities are geared to meet senior citizens' full-time needs, both medical and social, and often are sponsored by religious or nonprofit organizations. It provides independent and congregate living and personal, intermediate, and skilled nursing care, and attempts to create an environment that allows each resident to participate in the community's life to whatever degree desired.

Quick Quiz 10.1

True or False?

_____ 1. Long-term care insurance usually only covers the cost of care provided in a nursing home.

_____ 2. Jim has a long-term care policy that pays $80 per day. If his nursing home costs $60 per day, his policy most likely still will pay him $80 per day in benefits.

_____ 3. The daily benefit for at-home care under a long-term care policy usually is equal to one-third the nursing home benefit.

_____ 4. Jane is in a nursing home and receives 24-hour care. This type of care is known as skilled nursing care.

_____ 5. Medicare and Medicare supplement policies provide a significant amount of long-term care coverage.

Answers

1. ***False***. *Long-term care insurance provides a broad range of coverage for services rendered at home, at adult care centers, or in nursing homes.*
2. ***True***.
3. ***False***. *The daily benefit for at-home care under most long-term care policies typically is equal to half the nursing home benefit.*
4. ***True***.
5. ***False***. *Medicare and Medicare supplement policies are designed to protect the elderly against the costs of medical care. However, neither program covers a significant part of the costs of long-term custodial or nursing home care.*

LTC Policy Provisions and Limits

As we have stated, a number of long-term care policies are on the market today, each characterized by some distinguishing feature or benefit that sets it apart from the rest. However, there are enough similarities to allow us to discuss the basic provisions of these policies and their typical limits or exclusions.

In addition, as a result of the passage of the Health Insurance Portability and Accountability Act (HIPAA) of 1996, all LTC policies now must contain certain provisions for their benefits to qualify for tax-exempt treatment. These provisions include, for example, a definition of the types of services offered by the plan and when an individual becomes eligible for benefits under the plan. Both provisions, of course, must conform to qualifying standards under HIPAA. In addition, LTC policies also must adopt certain provisions of the NAIC's long-term care insurance model regulation. (See Figure 10.2.)

LTC Services

Qualified LTC services are defined as the necessary diagnostic, preventive, therapeutic, curing, treating, mitigating, and rehabilitative services, and maintenance or personal care services that are required by a chronically ill individual and are provided under a plan of care set forth by a licensed health care practitioner.

Qualifying for Benefits

When LTC policies first were introduced, insurers frequently required at least three days of prior hospitalization or skilled nursing home stays before the LTC policy benefits were triggered. The benefit trigger is an event or condition that must occur before policy benefits become payable. As a result of HIPAA, prior hospitalization no longer can be used as a benefit trigger; instead, the individual must be diagnosed as chronically ill.

FIGURE 10.2 NAIC Model LTC Regulations

The Health Insurance Portability and Accountability Act (HIPAA) of 1996 laid to rest concerns about how the benefits payable under a long-term care policy would be treated for tax purposes. Essentially, the question was whether such benefits were taxable. HIPAA determined that LTC policies are to be treated as other health insurance contracts—that benefits payable under LTC policies are considered reimbursement for expenses incurred for medical care—and therefore, are not taxable to the insured. However, there is an important caveat: to be treated this way, the LTC policy must be qualified. This means that the policy's provisions must conform to certain standards and guidelines as set forth by the Internal Revenue Code and HIPAA. Among the qualifying standards is the requirement to conform to the NAIC's long-term care insurance model regulations. In brief, the NAIC model addresses such things as:

- policy renewability (the policy must be guaranteed renewable)
- prohibitions on limits and exclusions
- policy replacement
- policy conversion
- prohibitions against post-claims underwriting
- the requirement to offer inflation-adjusted benefits
- proper marketing standards
- suitability and appropriateness of the recommended purchase
- a standard format for the outline of coverage

Diagnosis of chronic illness can be made on two levels: physical and/or cognitive. The physical diagnosis of a chronically ill individual is one who has been certified as being unable to perform at least two activities of daily living. A long-term care policy must take into account at least five of these ADLs. In addition, an individual would be considered chronically ill if she requires substantial supervision to protect her health or safety owing to severe cognitive impairment and this condition was certified within the previous 12 months.

Test Topic Alert! A benefit trigger in a long-term care policy is an event or condition that must occur before benefits become payable. An insured who is diagnosed as chronically ill triggers these benefits. Chronic illness can arise from a physical or cognitive illness or condition.

Benefit Limits

Almost all LTC policies set benefit limits, in terms of how long the benefits are paid or how much the dollar benefit will be for any one covered care service or a combination of services. Maximum dollar amounts vary considerably from policy to policy. Maximum coverage periods also vary.

In fact, with LTC policies, it is not unusual for one policy to include separate maximum coverage periods for nursing home care and home health care.

✓ ***Take Note:*** Maximum coverage periods extend anywhere from two to six years. Some policies offer unlimited lifetime coverage.

FIGURE 10.3 The Impairment Continuum—Activities of Daily Living

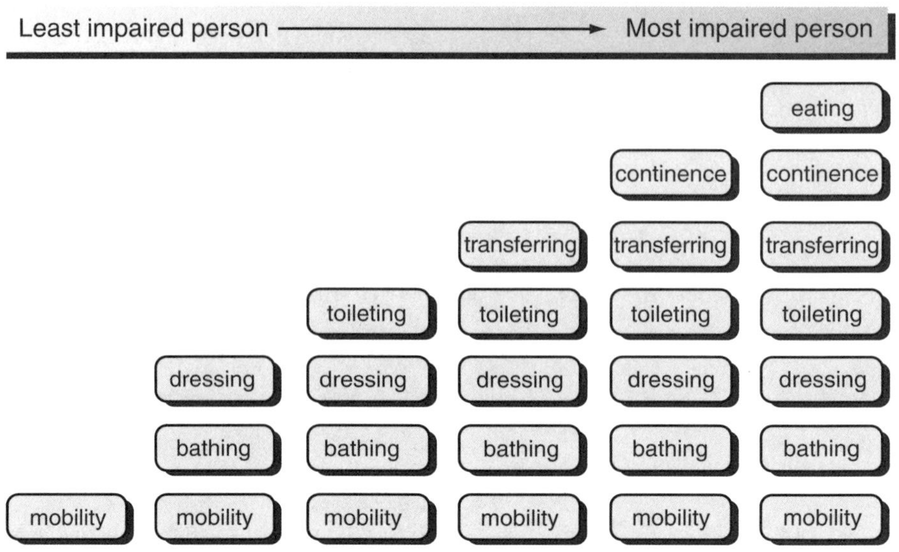

This illustration shows the progression of impairments included in the activities of daily living. Persons with a more severe impairment usually have all lesser impairments.

Age Limits LTC policies typically set age limits for issue, with an average age of about 79. However, some newer policies can be sold to people up through age 89. Many policies also set a minimum purchase age, with an average of age 50.

Renewability As a result of the 1996 HIPAA, all long-term care policies sold today must be guaranteed renewable. This means the insurance company cannot cancel the policy and must renew coverage each year, as long as premiums are paid. A guaranteed renewable policy allows the insurer to raise premiums, but only for entire classes of insureds.

Probationary Periods LTC probationary periods can range from 0 to 365 days, and many insurers give the insured the option of selecting the period that best serves her needs. The longer the deductible or probationary period, the lower the premium.

Specified Exclusions Most LTC policies exclude coverage for drug and alcohol dependency, acts of war, self-inflicted injuries, and nonorganic mental conditions. Organic cognitive disorders, such as Alzheimer's disease, senile dementia, and Parkinson's disease, almost always are included.

Premiums The cost for an LTC policy is based on a number of factors: the insured's age and health, the type and level of benefits provided, the inclusion or absence of a deductible or probationary period and the length of that period, and whether or not options or riders are included with the policy (such as the option to purchase additional coverage in the future or the inflation-adjustment rider, which increases the policy's coverage to match inflation levels automatically).

Taxation of LTC Benefits

As noted earlier, qualified LTC insurance contracts are treated in the same manner as accident and health insurance contracts. Consequently, amounts received under an LTC contract are excluded from income because they are considered amounts received for personal injuries and sickness. However, there is a limit on these amounts. The limit is $230 each day or $83,950 each year. (These amounts apply for 2004 and will be adjusted for inflation in later years.) In other words, benefits payable under LTC policies are not taxable at all to the extent that they cover incurred costs. If an LTC policy pays a benefit that exceeds actual costs, the excess above $230 a day (or $83,950 a year) is taxable to the insured.

Summary

Medicare supplement or Medigap policies are designed to make up for what Medicare doesn't cover and also are becoming increasingly popular. In 1990, the NAIC developed 10 Medicare standard supplement plans, ranging from the basic core policy, Plan A, to those with more comprehensive coverage.

As beneficial as Medicare and Medicare supplement insurance are to the elderly in protecting them against the costs of medical care, long-term care insurance still is needed to offer a broad range of medical and personal services to individuals who need assistance with daily activities for an extended period of time.

Key Concepts

In preparing for their licensing examination, students should be familiar with the following concepts:

- Medicare supplement policies
- long-term care policies
- chronically ill
- skilled nursing care
- custodial care
- adult day care
- continuing care
- acute illness
- activities of daily living (ADLs)
- intermediate nursing care
- home health care
- respite care

Unit Exam 10

1. The core policy (Plan A) developed by the NAIC as a standard Medicare supplement policy includes all of the following EXCEPT
   A. the Medicare Part A deductible
   B. Part A coinsurance amounts
   C. the first 3 pints of blood each year
   D. the 20% Part B coinsurance amounts for Medicare-approved services

2. Which of the following is a serious condition from which a patient can fully recover with proper medical attention?
   A. Chronic illness
   B. Long-term illness
   C. Acute illness
   D. Terminal illness

3. Skilled nursing care differs from intermediate care in which of the following ways?
   A. It must be performed by skilled medical professionals, whereas intermediate care does not require medical training
   B. It must be available 24 hours a day, while intermediate care is daily, but not 24-hour care
   C. It typically is given in a nursing home, while intermediate care usually is given at home
   D. It encompasses rehabilitation, while intermediate care is for meeting daily personal needs, such as bathing and dressing

4. All of the following conditions typically are covered in a long-term care insurance policy EXCEPT
   A. Alzheimer's disease
   B. senile dementia
   C. alcohol dependency
   D. Parkinson's disease

5. Which of the following statements about long-term care policies is NOT correct?
   A. Maximum coverage periods generally extend from 2 to 6 years.
   B. Long-term care policies sold today must be guaranteed renewable.
   C. A long-term care policy with a long probationary period will have a lower premium than one with a shorter probationary period.
   D. Premiums for a long-term care policy are based solely on the insured's age, the insured's health, and the type of benefits provided.

Unit Exam 10 Answers & Rationale

1. **A.** Plan A covers the Medicare Part A coinsurance amounts, the first 3 pints of blood each year and the 20% Part B coinsurance amounts. It does not cover the Medicare Part A deductible.

2. **C.** An acute illness is a serious condition from which a person can fully recover with proper medical attention. In contrast, a chronic illness is one that is treatable but not curable.

3. **B.** Skilled nursing care involves continuous around-the-clock care while intermediate care is provided in nursing homes for stable medical conditions that require daily, but not 24-hour, supervision.

4. **C.** Most long-term care policies exclude coverage for drug and alcohol dependency. Organic cognitive disorders, such as Alzheimer's disease, senile dementia, and Parkinson's disease almost always are included.

5. **D.** The cost of a long-term care policy is based on a number of factors, including the insured's age and health, the type and level of benefits provided, the inclusion or absence of a deductible or probationary period and the length of that period, and whether or not riders or options are included with the policy.

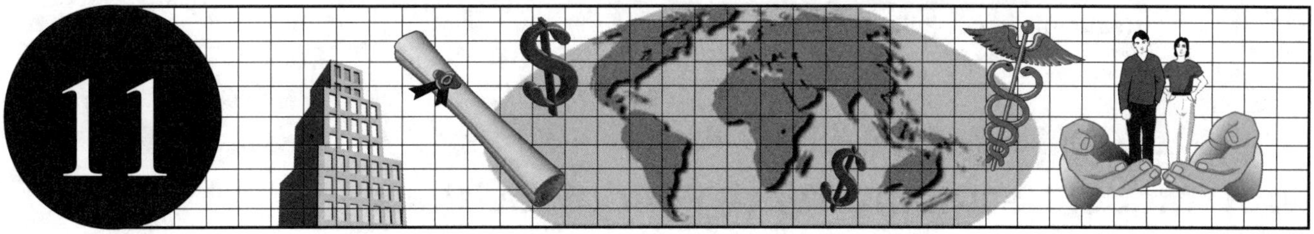

Health Insurance Policy Provisions

INTRODUCTION

Health insurance is characterized by a number of mandatory provisions that must be included in the contract. These provisions were developed by the National Association of Insurance Commissioners (NAIC) to protect the rights of individual health insurance policyholders. In this unit, we will review the 12 mandatory provisions and 11 optional provisions that the NAIC developed to add uniformity to health insurance contracts. This unit also will discuss more common exclusions and restrictions found in health policies as well as typical renewability provisions that allow the insurer to continue or discontinue coverage. (It might be helpful to review the sample health policy in the Appendix as you read this unit.)

UNIT OBJECTIVES

When you complete this unit you should be able to:

- list and describe the 12 mandatory policy provisions for individual health insurance contracts;
- list and describe the 11 option policy provisions for individual health insurance contracts;
- explain the purpose of the insuring clause, consideration clause, conversion privilege for dependents, and free-look provision in a health insurance contract;
- identify the typical exclusions that are not covered by health insurance policies; and
- list and describe the five types of renewability provisions found in health insurance policies.

NAIC Model Health Insurance Policy Provisions

In 1950, the National Association of Insurance Commissioners (NAIC) developed a model Uniform Individual Accident and Sickness Policy Provisions Law. Almost all states have adopted this model law or similar legislation or regulations.

The purpose of the NAIC law was to establish uniform or model terms, provisions, and wording standards for inclusion in all individual health insurance contracts or all contracts that provide insurance against loss resulting from sickness or from bodily injury or death by accident or both. The result was 12 mandatory policy provisions and 11 optional policy provisions.

✓ ***Take Note:*** Because these provisions are to be followed in substance, insurers may employ different wording from that of the law, as long as the protection is provided and is no less favorable to the insured than the law stipulates.

A health insurance contract obligates the insurer to pay the insured (or a beneficiary) a stipulated benefit under circumstances specified in the contract. The specifics of the benefit and the requisite circumstances are set forth in the contract's provisions. Let's take a look at these provisions.

Mandatory Policy Provisions

In accordance with the NAIC model law, there are 12 mandatory provisions that must be in all health insurance contracts. These are as follows:

Entire Contract The entire contract provision in a health insurance policy protects the policyowner in two ways. First, it states that nothing outside of the contract—which includes the signed application and any attached policy riders—can be considered part of the contract; that is, nothing can be incorporated by reference. Second, it assures the policyowner that no changes will be made to the contract after it has been issued, even if the insurer makes policy changes that affect all policy sales in the future.

Time Limit on Certain Defenses Under the time limit on certain defense provisions, the policy is incontestable after it has been in force for at least two years. A fraudulent statement on a health insurance application is grounds for contest at any time, unless the policy is guaranteed renewable, in which case it cannot be contested for any reason after the contestable period expires.

Another part of this provision concerns any pre-existing conditions an insured may have. Under the provision, the insurance company cannot deny a claim on the basis of a pre-existing condition after expiration of the stated contestable period—unless the pre-existing condition has been excluded specifically from the policy by name or description.

Grace Period

Per the grace period provision, the policyowner is given a number of days after the premium due date during which time the premium payment may be delayed without penalty and the policy continues in force.

✓ ***Take Note:*** Depending on the state, the minimum grace periods that may be specified typically are seven days for policies with weekly premium payments (i.e., industrial policies), 10 days for policies with premiums payable on a monthly basis, and 31 days for other policies. Some states, however, require a standard grace period of 31 days, regardless of the frequency of premium payment or policy term.

Reinstatement

Under certain conditions, a policy that has lapsed may be reinstated. Reinstatement is automatic if the delinquent premium is accepted by the company or its authorized agent and the company does not require an application for reinstatement.

If a company does require such an application, it may or may not approve the application. If it takes no action on the application for 45 days, the policy is reinstated automatically. To protect the company against adverse selection, losses resulting from sickness are covered only if the sickness occurs at least 10 days after the reinstatement date.

Test Topic Alert!

The probationary period may apply when a new application is required. The probationary period excludes claims arising from illness within 10 days of the policy's reinstatement. Losses arising from accidents are covered immediately.

Notice of Claim

The notice of claim provision describes the policyowner's obligation to the insurer to provide notification of loss within a reasonable period of time. Typically, this period is 20 days after the occurrence or a commencement of the loss, or as soon thereafter as is reasonably possible. If the loss involves disability income payments that are payable for two or more years, the disabled claimant must submit proof of loss every six months. Such proof may be submitted to either the company or an authorized agent of the company.

Claim Forms

It is the company's responsibility to supply a claim form to an insured within 15 days after receiving notice of claim. If it fails to do so within the time limit, the claimant may submit proof of loss in any form, explaining the occurrence, the character, and the extent of the loss for which the claim is submitted.

Proof of Loss

After a loss occurs, or after the company becomes liable for periodic payments (for example, disability income benefits), the claimant has 90 days in which to submit proof of loss. The claim will not be affected in any way, however, if it is not reasonably possible for the claimant to comply with the 90-day provision.

There is a time limit for submitting proof of loss—whether or not it is reasonably possible to do so—and that is one year after the company becomes liable for the loss. The only exception to the one-year limit is if the claimant does not have the legal capacity to comply.

Test Topic Alert!

The proof of loss, or claim form, must be submitted within 90 days of the date of loss, unless it is not reasonably possible to do so.

Time of Payment of Claims

The time of payment of claims provision provides for immediate payment of the claim after the insurer receives notification and proof of loss. If the claim involves disability income payments, they must be paid at least monthly, if not at more frequent intervals specified in the policy. In some states, the time of payment of claims is 60 days; in other states, it is 30 days.

Payment of Claims

The payment of claims provision in a health insurance contract specifies how and to whom claim payments are to be made. Payments for loss of life are to be made to the designated beneficiary. If no beneficiary has been named, death proceeds are to be paid to the deceased insured's estate. Claims other than death benefits are to be paid to the insured.

✓ ***Take Note:*** In accordance with this required provision are two optional provisions that insurers may add. One gives the insurer the right to expedite payment of urgently needed claim funds and pay up to $1,000 in benefits to a relative or individual who is considered to be equitably entitled to payment. The other optional provision allows the insured to have medical benefits assigned—or paid directly—to the hospital or physician rendering the covered services.

Physical Exam and Autopsy

The physical exam and autopsy provision entitles a company, at its own expense, to make physical examinations of the insured at reasonable intervals during the period of a claim. In the case of death, the insurer has the right to conduct an autopsy on the body of the insured, provided it is not forbidden by state law.

Legal Actions

The insured cannot take legal action against the company in a claim dispute until after 60 days from the time the insured submits proof of loss. The same rule applies to beneficiaries. Also, if legal action is to be taken against the company, it must be done within a certain time after proof of loss is submitted (usually two or three years).

FIGURE 11.1 NAIC Uniform Health Insurance Policy Provisions

Mandatory Provisions	*Optional Provisions*
1. Entire Contract	1. Change of Occupation
2. Time Limit on Certain Defenses	2. Misstatement of Age
3. Grace Period	3. Other Insurance in This Insurer
4. Reinstatement	4. Insurance with Other Insurer
5. Notice of Claims	5. Insurance with Other Insurers
6. Claims Forms	6. Relation of Earnings to Insurance
7. Proof of Loss	7. Unpaid Premiums
8. Time of Payment of Claims	8. Cancellation
9. Payment of Claims	9. Conformity with State Statutes
10. Physical Exam and Autopsy	10. Illegal Occupation
11. Legal Actions	11. Intoxicants and Narcotics
12. Change of Beneficiary	

Change of Beneficiary

The insured, as policyowner, may change the beneficiary designation at any time, unless a beneficiary has been named irrevocably. So long as the insured reserves the right to change beneficiaries, he also may surrender or assign the policy without obtaining the consent of the beneficiary.

Optional Provisions

There are 11 optional health policy provisions, and companies may ignore them or use only those that are needed in their policy forms. The provisions pertaining to other insurance in this insurer, insurance with other insurers, and relation of earnings to insurance seldom are used. They were intended to deal with the problem of overinsurance but generally proved to be ineffective.

Change of Occupation

The change of occupation provision sets forth the changes that may be made to premium rates or benefits payable should the insured change occupations. Many insurers include this provision in their disability income policies because an individual's occupation has a direct bearing on her risk profile, and one's risk profile has a direct bearing on premium charges. Consequently, this provision allows the insurer to reduce the maximum benefit payable under the policy if the insured switches to a more hazardous occupation, or to reduce the premium rate charged if the insured changes to a less hazardous occupation.

✓ ***Take Note:*** These benefit and premium changes take effect at the time the insured changes occupations. If a change in jobs is discovered after a disability begins, the changes are made retroactively.

Misstatement of Age The misstatement of age provision allows the insurer to adjust the benefit payable if the age of the insured was misstated when application for the policy was made. Benefit amounts payable in such cases will be what the premiums paid would have purchased at the correct age. The older the applicant is, the higher the premium would be; therefore, if the insured was older at the time of application than is shown in the policy, benefits would be reduced accordingly. The reverse would be true if the insured was younger than as listed in the application.

Other Insurance in This Insurer The purpose of the other insurance in this insurer provision is to limit the company's risk with any insured individual. Under this provision, the total amount of coverage to be underwritten by a company for one person is restricted to a specified maximum amount, regardless of the number of policies issued. Premiums that apply to any such excess of coverage must be returned to the insured or the insured's estate.

Insurance With Other Insurer In attempting to deal with the potential problem of overinsurance, the insurance with other insurer provision states that benefits payable for "expenses incurred" will be prorated in cases where the company accepted the risk without being notified of other existing coverage for the same risk. When premiums are paid that exceed the amount needed to cover what the company determines it will pay, the excess premiums must be refunded to the policyowner.

Insurance With Other Insurers Similar to the above, the insurance with other insurers provision calls for the pro-rating of benefits that are payable on any basis other than "expenses incurred." It also provides for a return of premiums that exceed the amount needed to pay for the company's portion of pro-rated benefits.

Relation of Earnings to Insurance If disability income benefits from all disability income policies for the same loss exceed the insured's monthly earnings at the time of disability (or the average monthly earnings for two years preceding disability), the relation of earnings provision states that the insurer is liable only for that proportionate amount of benefits as the insured's earnings bear to the total benefits under all such coverage.

✓ ***Take Note:*** Total indemnities payable to the insured may not be reduced below $200 or the sum total benefits under all applicable coverage, whichever is less. Any premiums paid for the excess coverage are refunded.

Unpaid Premiums If there is an unpaid premium at the time a claim becomes payable, the amount of the premium is to be deducted from the sum payable to the insured or beneficiary. Or, if the premium is covered by a note when a claim is submitted, the note payment will be subtracted from the amount payable for the claim.

Cancellation Though prohibited in a number of states, the provision for cancellation gives the company the right to cancel the policy at any time with five days' written notice to the insured. It also provides that the insured may cancel the policy anytime after the policy's original term has expired. Any unearned premium is to be refunded to the insured. If a claim is pending at the time of cancellation, the claim cannot be affected by the cancellation. (See also *Renewability Provisions,* later in this unit.)

Conformity with State Statutes Any policy provision that conflicts with state statutes in the state where the insured lives at the time the policy is issued automatically is amended to conform with the minimum statutory requirements.

Illegal Occupation The illegal occupation provision specifies that the insurer is not liable for losses attributed to the insured's commission of, or being connected with, a felony or participation in any illegal occupation.

Intoxicants and Narcotics The insurer is not liable for any loss attributed to the insured while intoxicated or under the influence of narcotics, unless such drugs were administered on the advice of a physician.

Other Health Insurance Policy Provisions

The 12 mandatory provisions and 11 optional provisions just described comprise the substantive elements of individual health insurance policies. However, a number of other very important clauses and provisions should be noted.

Insuring Clause Generally, the insuring clause is a broad statement on the first page of the health policy, stipulating conditions under which benefits are to be paid. While these critical provisions vary considerably in health insurance contracts, they basically represent a company's promise to pay benefits for specific kinds of losses resulting from sickness or accidents. They usually specify that benefits are subject to all provisions and exclusions stated in the policy.

Consideration Clause The consideration clause states the amount and frequency of premium payments. If the first premium has not been paid—even though the application has been completed and signed by the applicant—the necessary consideration is partially lacking.

✓ ***Take Note:*** As is the case with life insurance, the legal consideration for a health policy consists of the application and payment of the initial premium. A copy of the application is attached to the policy.

Frequently, the consideration clause also lists the effective date of the contract and defines the initial term of the policy. In addition, it may specify the insured's right to renew the policy.

Conversion Privilege for Dependents A single health policy may insure one person, or more than one if the applicant is an adult family member and the others to be covered are members of her family. Thus, additional persons who may be insured include the husband, wife, dependent children, or others dependent on the adult applicant. To be eligible, children must meet certain age requirements.

Generally, children of the insured are eligible for coverage under a family policy until they attain a specified age, usually age 19 or, if they are in school full time, age 23. Adopted children, stepchildren, and foster children usually are eligible for coverage. As long as a policy is in force, coverage for a child generally continues until the child marries or reaches the limiting age. However, a number of states have enacted special laws that require insurers to retain as insureds under the parent's individual health policy any child who reaches the limiting age but is dependent on the insured and incapable of self-support because of mental or physical impairment.

Attaining a minimum age, such as 14 days, may be required for coverage. However, legislation in some states mandates that health policies insuring family members also provide coverage for newborn children from the date of birth. Typically, such legislation permits the insurer to require that notice of the child's birth be given and an application and additional premium be submitted within a specified period.

If the insurance on a covered individual is terminated because he no longer fits the policy definition of a family member, that person has a right to take out a conversion policy without evidence of insurability.

✓ ***For Example:*** Faye divorces Stanley and thus no longer can be covered under his family policy. She has a right to obtain a conversion policy. When their children reach the limiting age for children's coverage, they also will be eligible for a conversion policy.

Free Look Provision

Most states mandate that their health insurance policies contain a free-look provision permitting policyowners either 10 or 20 days in which to examine their new policies at no obligation. If they decide not to keep their policies, they may return them within the prescribed time limit and receive full refunds of premiums paid.

Test Topic Alert!

The state may require that policies sold to seniors have a free-look period that is longer than 20 days.

Common Exclusions or Restrictions

Health insurance policies frequently cite a number of exclusions or conditions that are not covered. The common ones are injuries due to war or an act of war, self-inflicted injuries, and those incurred while the insured is serving as a pilot or crew member of an aircraft.

Other exclusions are losses resulting from suicide, hernia (as an accidental injury), riots, or the use of drugs or narcotics. Losses due to injuries sustained while committing a felony, or attempting to do so, also may be excluded. Foreign travel may not be excluded in every instance, but extended stays overseas or foreign residence may cause a loss of benefits.

Maternity Benefits

Maternity benefits generally are handled differently in individual health policies than in group health policies. When available for individual policies, a maternity provision may provide a fixed amount for childbirth or a benefit based upon a specified multiple of the daily hospital room benefit.

Test Topic Alert! Individual health policies often offer the maternity benefit only as an added benefit for an additional premium.

Maternity coverage in group health plans is discussed in Unit 13.

Pre-existing Conditions

As we have learned, medical expense and disability income policies usually exclude paying benefits for losses due to pre-existing conditions pertaining to illness, disease, or other physical impairments. For purposes of issuing individual health policies, insurers consider a pre-existing condition to be one that the insured contracted (or one that was manifested) before the policy's effective date. Consequently, in the event the insured did not cite the condition on the application specifically and the insurer did not exclude the condition from coverage expressly, the pre-existing condition provision would serve to exclude the condition nonetheless. However, such exclusions are subject to the time limit on certain defenses provision.

✓ ***Take Note:*** Any pre-existing condition that the insured has disclosed clearly in the application usually is not excluded or, if it is, the condition is named specifically in an excluding waiver or rider.

The treatment of pre-existing conditions under group health plans is a little different and is discussed in Unit 13.

Waivers for Impairments

The majority of health policies are standard and are issued as applied for. However, a few people have an existing impairment that increases the risk and so are required to pay an extra premium. A few people are uninsurable and must be declined. Others, however, fall in between and would not be able to obtain health insurance if waivers were not in use. Waivers usually are stated in simple language. For example: "This policy does not cover or extend to any disability resulting directly or indirectly from . . ." A waiver is dated and bears the signature of an officer of the company and, in many cases, the applicant. This usually is called an impairment rider.

If the insured's condition improves, the company may be willing to remove the waiver. Meanwhile, the person at least has health protection from other hazards that she otherwise could not obtain.

✓ ***Test Topic Alert!*** The impairment rider allows for coverage despite a preexisting condition, when such coverage might not otherwise be available to the insured, or only at prohibitive cost.

Quick Quiz 11.1 True or False?

_____ 1. The time of payment of claims provision in a health policy provides that if a claim involves disability income payments they must be paid at least monthly.

_____ 2. If an insurer fails to take action on an application for reinstatement within 30 days, the policy will be reinstated automatically.

_____ 3. If Jane names her brother as revocable beneficiary under her health policy, she may surrender the policy at any time without first obtaining her brother's consent.

_____ 4. Adopted children, stepchildren, and foster children usually are eligible for health insurance coverage under a family policy.

_____ 5. Once Jan's son Bill reaches age 19 and no longer is eligible for family health coverage, he can take out a conversion policy but first must provide evidence of insurability.

Answers

1. ***True***.
2. ***False***. *If an application is required for reinstatement and an insurer takes no action on the application for 45 days, the policy will be reinstated automatically.*
3. ***True***.
4. ***True***.
5. ***False***. *Once Bill reaches the limiting age for children's coverage under his family's health policy, he may take out a conversion policy without evidence of insurability.*

Renewability Provisions

One distinguishing feature of health insurance policies is the provisions they contain that allow the insurer to continue or discontinue coverage. Known as renewability provisions, they vary from policy to policy. Generally, the more favorable the renewability provision is to the insured policyholder, the higher the premium.

Cancellable Policies

The renewability provision in a cancellable policy allows the insurer to cancel or terminate the policy at any time, simply by providing written notification to the insured and refunding any advance premium that has been paid. Cancellable policies also allow the insurer to increase premiums.

Optionally Renewable Policies

The renewability provision in an optionally renewable policy gives the insurer the option to terminate the policy on a date specified in the contract. Furthermore, this provision allows the insurer to increase the premium for any class of optionally renewable insureds.* The insurer can also increase the premium on an individual policy. Usually termination or premium increases take place on policy anniversary dates or premium due dates.

Conditionally Renewable Policies

A conditionally renewable policy allows an insurer to terminate the coverage, but only in the event of one or more conditions stated in the contract. These conditions cannot apply to the insured's health; most frequently, they are related to the insured reaching a certain age or losing gainful employment. Usually, the premium for conditionally renewable policies may be increased, if such an increase applies to an entire class of policies.

---

* A class of insureds includes all insureds of policies of a particular kind or all insureds of a specific group. For example, a class of insureds may be those of a particular age or in a specific geographic region.

Guaranteed Renewable Policies

The renewal provision in a guaranteed renewable policy specifies that the policy must be renewed, as long as premiums are paid, until the insured reaches a specified age, such as 60 or 65. Premium increases may be applied, but only for the entire class of insureds; they cannot be assessed to individual insureds.

Noncancellable Policies

A noncancellable, or noncan, policy cannot be cancelled nor can its premium rates be increased under any circumstances; these rates are specified in the policy. The term of most noncancellable policies is to the insured's age 65. Noncan provisions most commonly are found in disability income policies; they rarely are used in medical expense policies. A noncancellable and guaranteed renewable policy is synonymous with a noncancellable policy.

Test Topic Alert! Applicants for guaranteed renewable policies and noncancellable policies are subject to the most stringent underwriting qualifications.

Summary

To protect the rights of individual health insurance policyholders, the NAIC developed a set of 12 mandatory and 11 optional policy provisions. These provisions help assure consumers that the health policies they buy will meet at least a minimum level of standards. Other provisions, though not categorized as required or optional, are equally important. Of special note are the renewability provisions—absent from life insurance policies, but an essential feature of health policies.

Key Concepts

In preparing for their licensing examination, students should be familiar with the following concepts:

- entire contract
- grace period
- notice of claims
- proof of loss
- payment of claims
- legal actions
- change of occupation
- other insurance in this insurer
- insurance with other insurer(s)
- unpaid premiums
- conformity with state statutes
- intoxicants and narcotics
- consideration clause
- free look
- pre-existing conditions
- optionally renewable
- guaranteed renewable
- time limit on certain defenses
- reinstatement
- claims forms
- time of payment of claims
- physical examination and autopsy
- change of beneficiary
- misstatement of age
- relation of earnings to insurance
- cancellation
- illegal occupation
- insuring clause
- conversion privilege
- exclusions and waivers
- cancelable
- conditionally renewable
- noncancelable

Unit Exam 11

1. A company may change the wording of a uniform policy provision in its health insurance policies only if the
   A. company's board of directors approves the change
   B. modified provision is not less favorable to the insurer
   C. applicant directs that it be changed
   D. modified provision is not less favorable to the insured

2. Children of the insured are eligible for health insurance coverage until they reach age 19 or, if they remain in school full time, age
   A. 20
   B. 21
   C. 22
   D. 23

3. Which of the following statements about the grace period and reinstatement provisions in health insurance policies is NOT correct?
   A. Craig's health policy has a grace period of 31 days. He had a premium due June 15, while he was on vacation. He returned home July 7, mailed his premium the next day and the insurer received it July 10. His policy would have remained in force.
   B. Warren's medical expense policy was reinstated on September 30 and he became ill and entered the hospital on October 5. His hospital expense will not be paid by the insurer.
   C. Under a health policy's reinstatement terms, insured losses from accidental injuries and sickness are covered immediately after reinstatement.
   D. States may require grace periods of 7, 10, or 31 days, depending on the mode of premium payment or term of insurance; however, many states require a 31-day grace period in any case.

4. Which of the following is the usual grace period for a semiannual premium policy?
   A. 7 days
   B. 20 days
   C. 31 days
   D. 60 days

5. Diana, the beneficiary under her husband's AD&D policy, submits an accidental death claim on May 1, 2004, following his death. However, the company denies the claim on the basis that death was due to natural causes. She decides to talk to her attorney. When is the earliest she could bring legal action against the insurer?
   A. May 2, 2004
   B. June 1, 2004
   C. July 1, 2004
   D. May 1, 2005

6. All of the following are required uniform provisions in individual health insurance policies EXCEPT

   A. change of occupation
   B. grace period
   C. entire contract changes
   D. reinstatement

7. Under the misstatement of age provision in a health insurance policy, what can a company do if it discovers that an insured gave a wrong age at the time of application?

   A. Cancel the policy
   B. Increase the premium
   C. Adjust the benefits
   D. Assess a penalty

8. The conformity with a state statutes provision in a health insurance policy stipulates that any policy provision that conflicts with the statutes of the state where the insured resides is

   A. to be submitted to the insurance commissioner for approval
   B. cause for the insured's policy to be voided
   C. automatically amended to conform to the minimum requirements of the state's statutes
   D. to be rewritten if the policy is returned to the company

9. Which section of a health insurance policy specifies the conditions, times, and circumstances under which the insured is NOT covered by the policy?

   A. Coinsurance provision
   B. Coverages
   C. Insuring clause
   D. Exclusions

10. Which kind of health insurance policy assures renewability up to a specific age of the insured, although the company reserves the right to change the premium rate on a class basis?

    A. Noncancellable
    B. Guaranteed renewable
    C. Optionally renewable
    D. Cancellable

11. According to the notice of claims provision in a health insurance policy, a claimant normally must notify the insurance company of loss within how many days after the loss occurs?

    A. 10
    B. 20
    C. 40
    D. 60

12. Which of the following types of health insurance policies prevents the company from changing the premium rate or modifying the coverage in any way?

    A. Optionally renewable
    B. Noncancellable
    C. Guaranteed renewable
    D. Cancellable

13. After an insurer receives a notice of claim, it must supply a claim form to the insured within how many days?

    A. 10
    B. 15
    C. 20
    D. 30

14. A cancellation provision gives an insurer the right to cancel a policy at any time after giving how many days' notice to the insured?

    A. 5
    B. 10
    C. 15
    D. 30

15. Which of the following statements about the insuring clause in a health insurance policy is NOT correct?

    A. It is found on the first page of a health policy.
    B. It represents an insurer's promise to pay benefits.
    C. It specifies that benefits will be subject to the exclusions stated in the policy.
    D. It is one of the 11 NAIC optional provisions.

Unit Exam 11 Answers & Rationale

1. **D.** An insurer need not use the exact wording contained in the 12 mandatory provisions. Instead, it may use different wording as long as the same protection is provided and is no less favorable to the insured than the law stipulates.

2. **D.** Generally, an insured's children are eligible for health insurance coverage under a family policy until they attain a certain age, usually age 19 or, if they are in school full time, age 23.

3. **C.** A policy that has lapsed may be reinstated. However, to protect the insurer against adverse selection, losses resulting from sickness are covered only if the sickness occurs at least 10 days after the reinstatement date.

4. **C.** A semiannual premium policy usually has a 31-day grace period in which the policyowner can pay the premium due. For policies with weekly premium payments, the grace period is 7 days, and policies with monthly premiums have 10-day grace periods.

5. **C.** Diana cannot take legal action against the insurer until after 60 days from the date she submitted an accidental death claim. She submitted a claim on May 1 and will have to wait 60 days until July 1 to bring a legal action against the insurer.

6. **A.** The grace period, entire contract changes, and reinstatement provisions are mandatory uniform provisions. The change of occupation provision sets forth the changes that may be made to premium rates or benefits payable if the insured changes occupations. This provision is optional.

7. **C.** The mis-statement of age provision allows the insurer to adjust the benefit payable if the insured's age was misstated when the policy application was made. The benefit amounts payable in such cases equals what the premiums paid would have purchased at the correct age.

8. **C.** Any policy provision that conflicts with the statutes of the state where the insured resides will be amended automatically to conform with the minimum statutory requirements.

9. **D.** The exclusions section of a health insurance policy specifies the conditions, times, and circumstances under which the insured is not covered by the policy. Common exclusions include injuries due to war and self-inflicted injuries.

10. **B.** In a guaranteed renewable policy, the renewal provision states that the policy must be renewed, as long as premiums are paid, until the insured reaches a specified age, such as 60 or 65. Premiums may be increased, but only for the entire class of insureds.

11. **B.** A policyowner typically must notify the insurer within 20 days after a loss has occurred.

12. **B.** A noncancellable policy prevents the insurance company from cancelling or modifying the coverage or changing the premium rate.

13. **B.** After an insurer receives a notice of claim, it must supply a claim form to the insured within 15 days. If it fails to do so, the claimant may submit proof of loss in any form, explaining the occurrence, character, and extent of the loss for which the claim is submitted.

14. **A.** A cancellation provision gives an insurer the right to cancel a policy at any time by giving 5 days' written notice to the insured. It also allows the insured to cancel the policy any time after the policy's original term has expired.

15. **D.** The insuring clause in a health insurance policy is not one of the 11 optional provisions developed by the NAIC. It is a broad statement found on a policy's first page that stipulates the conditions under which benefits are to be paid. It also usually specifies that benefits are subject to all provisions and exclusions stated in the policy.

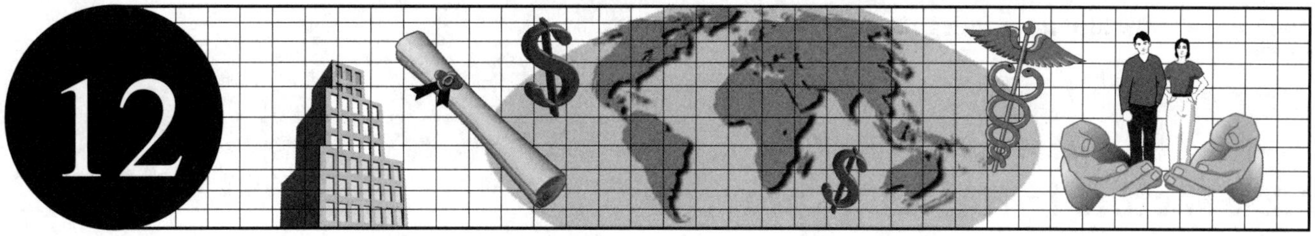

Health Insurance Underwriting and Premiums

INTRODUCTION

Health insurers often are faced with balancing two conflicting demands: charging adequate premiums to cover the increasingly high cost of health insurance claims, while keeping rates as low as possible in response to consumer sentiment and competition within the industry. Health insurers have done this by tightening their underwriting requirements, becoming more selective in the risks they will accept and controlling claims through innovative measures. In this unit, we will examine how the underwriting process works in the health insurance arena, including the factors that influence the premiums charged. We also will take a look at the important topic of health insurance taxation, that is, how premiums and benefits are taxed under individual and group policies as well as the rules that apply to self-employed individuals. Finally, we will review some of the methods that managed care uses to contain rising health care costs.

UNIT OBJECTIVES

When you complete this unit you should be able to:

- explain how a person's lifestyle, occupation, and physical condition affect the underwriting of a health insurance policy;
- list and describe the four risk categories in which health insurance applicants may be classified;
- explain how morbidity, interest, and expenses affect health insurance premiums and identify the other factors influencing premium rates;
- explain the tax treatment of health insurance premiums and benefits; and
- list and describe the common techniques that managed care organizations use to contain health care costs.

Risk Factors in Health Insurance

While most underwriting factors that apply to life insurance also apply to health insurance, they take on greater significance in the context of health risks. With life insurance, there is only one death claim per insured. But with health insurance, multiple claims per insured is the rule rather than the exception. Thus, the classification of health insurance risks is critically important. Data accumulated over the years by insurance companies in underwriting health insurance serves as the primary basis for classifying risks.

Classifying risks for health insurance is more complex than simply deciding whether a risk is acceptable or not acceptable. The degree of risk is highly important when considering the probable future health of an individual applicant and the amount of premium to be charged. So home office underwriters are charged with the responsibility of scrutinizing health insurance applications with special care.

Many factors are reviewed in underwriting health insurance policies. Three of the most important factors are physical condition, moral hazards, and occupation.

Physical Condition

An applicant's present physical condition is of primary importance when evaluating health risks. The underwriter must know whether the individual has been treated for any chronic conditions, and any physical impairments of the applicant are checked out carefully. Hernias or ulcers, for example, may require surgical correction or treatment in the future and, thereby, represent an additional risk. Persons with an unusual body build, including obesity or extreme height, also represent higher risks to the insurer.

Moral Hazards

The habits or lifestyles of applicants also can flash warning signals that there may be additional risk for the insurer. Personalities and attitudes may draw attention in the underwriting process. Excessive drinking and the use of drugs represent serious moral hazards. Applicants who are seen as accident-prone or potential malingerers (feigning a continuing disability in order to collect benefits) likewise might be heavy risks, particularly those applying for disability income insurance. Other signals of high moral hazard can be a poor credit rating or dishonest business practices.

Occupation

A third significant factor involved with health insurance risks is the applicant's occupation. This is because occupation has a direct bearing on both the probability of disability and the average severity of disability.

Experience shows that disability benefit costs for insurers can vary considerably from occupation to occupation. Little physical risk is associated with professional persons, office managers or office workers, but occupations involving heavy machinery, strong chemicals or high electrical voltage, for example, represent a high degree of risk for the insurer.

Jobs requiring manual labor also can influence the length of recuperation periods for disabled workers and how soon they can return to work. Further, the sporadic nature of employment in certain occupations can have a bearing on claim costs because the number and size of such claims tend to rise when insureds are unemployed.

Some occupations involve irregular hours, uncertain earnings and, in some cases, not even a definite place of business—all of which contribute to higher risks for insurers. Examples are entertainers and authors, who generally do not have regular business hours. In addition, disability benefit costs to insurers also can be influenced by the social and economic character of persons in some occupational classifications.

✓ ***Take Note:*** For underwriting purposes, many insurers divide occupations into five classes: AAA, AA, A, B, and C. The five classes range from the top classification (AAA), which includes professional and office workers, to more hazardous occupations in the lower (B and C) classes. Persons in a few occupations, such as steeplejacks, airplane test pilots, or stunt flyers, usually are uninsurable.

The applicant's occupation and the renewability factor of a policy also are connected from an underwriting standpoint. According to the change of occupation provision, if the insured changes to a less hazardous job, the insurer will return any excess unearned premium; however, if the change is to a more hazardous occupation, the benefits are reduced proportionately and the premium remains the same. The occupation change clause generally is not included in guaranteed renewable policies, especially long-term disability income policies. Noncancellable policies are sold only to individuals in the higher occupational classes in which change of occupation seldom is a factor. Limited and industrial health policies usually are available at standard rates for all occupations, except those excluded by specific policy provisions.

Other Risk Factors

Additional health insurance risk factors include the applicant's age, sex, medical and family history, and avocations.

- **Age**. Generally, the older the applicant, the higher the risk he represents. Most individual health insurance policies limit the coverage to a specified age such as 60 or 65 (although some lifetime coverages are available).
- **Sex**. An applicant's sex also is an underwriting consideration. Men show a lower rate of disability than women, except at the upper ages.
- **History**. An applicant's medical history may point to the possibility of a recurrence of a certain health condition. Likewise, an applicant's family history may reflect a tendency she has toward certain medical conditions or health impairments.
- **Avocations**. Certain hobbies an applicant may have—such as skydiving or mountain climbing—may increase his risk to the insurer. An applicant's avocations are evaluated carefully.

Insurable Interest

Finally, when evaluating health insurance risks, the underwriter must determine whether an insurable interest exists between the applicant and the individual to be insured. In health insurance, an insurable interest exists if the applicant is in a position to suffer a loss should the insured incur medical expenses or be unable to work due to a disability. As with life insurance, insurable interest is a prerequisite for issuing a health insurance policy.

Classification of Applicants

Once an underwriter has reviewed the various risk factors associated with an individual applicant and has measured them against the company's underwriting standards, there are four ways to classify the applicant and her request for health coverage: as a standard risk, a preferred risk, an uninsurable risk, or a substandard risk.

Standard risk applicants usually are issued a policy at standard terms and rates. Preferred risks generally receive lower rates than standard risks, reflecting the fact that people in this class have a better-than-standard risk profile. Uninsurable applicants usually are rejected and denied coverage. Substandard risk applicants—those who pose a higher-than-average risk for one or more reasons—are treated differently. Substandard applicants may represent a very low risk on moral and occupational considerations and still pose a high risk because of their physical condition. Other substandard applicants may be in top physical condition, but work at a hazardous occupation. Besides outright rejection, three techniques commonly are used by insurers in issuing health insurance policies to substandard risks:

- attaching an exclusion (or impairment) rider or waiver to a policy;
- charging an extra premium; or
- limiting the type of policy.

Exclusion or impairment riders rule out coverage for losses resulting from chronic conditions or physical impairments. With the questionable risks excluded, policies then are issued at standard rates. When some occupational hazard exists, applicants may be charged an extra premium to compensate for the additional risk. The same may be true when applicants are overweight or show signs of high blood pressure, etc. Extra premiums may be charged for only a few years or on a permanent basis.

When applicants represent a substandard risk, the type of policy requested may be modified in some manner. For example, a policy may exclude all sickness or a specific kind of sickness, but cover all losses from accidental injuries. In other cases, a policy may provide protection for a lower amount than requested or provide a shorter benefit period. Or a provision may be inserted calling for a longer waiting period than indicated in the application.

✓ ***Take Note:*** Only a small percentage of applicants are classified as substandard risks. And, with years of experience to guide them, insurers today reject a smaller percentage of applicants for health insurance than in the past.

Health Insurance Premium Factors

Rate making is more complex for health insurance policies than for life insurance, primarily because it involves more than one type of benefit. The average frequency of covered health insurance losses further complicates premium computations. There are a number of variables—primary and secondary—all insurers take into account when determining the premium rate for a particular health insurance product.

Primary Premium Factors

At the base level, three primary factors affect health insurance premiums: morbidity, interest, and expenses. Note how closely these correspond to basic life insurance premium factors, except that morbidity is substituted for mortality.

Morbidity Whereas mortality rates show the average number of persons within a larger group of people who can be expected to die within a given year at a given age, morbidity rates indicate the average number at various ages who can be expected to become disabled each year due to accident or sickness. Morbidity statistics also reveal the average duration of disability, so insurers can approximate not only how many in a large group will become disabled, but how long the disabilities can be expected to last.

Morbidity statistics, which are available to companies offering health insurance, have been collected over many years and reflect the disabilities of hundreds of thousands of people. They are compiled into morbidity tables.

Test Topic Alert! Morbidity statistics serve the same purpose for health insurance that mortality statistics do for life insurance.

Interest Just as with life insurance, interest is a major element in establishing health insurance premiums. A large portion of every premium received is invested to earn interest. The interest earnings reduce the premium amount that otherwise would be required from policyowners.

Expenses Every business has expenses that must be paid, and the insurance business is no different. Each health insurance policy an insurer issues must carry its proportionate share of the costs for employees' salaries, agents' commissions, utilities, rent or mortgage payments, maintenance costs, supplies, and other administrative expenses.

Secondary Premium Factors

In addition to these three primary factors, the actual rate assigned to a specific health policy by the underwriter depends on several other factors, including the benefits provided under the policy, past claims experience, the age and sex of the insured, and the insured's occupation and hobbies.

Benefits A health insurance policy may offer a specific type of benefit or a variety of benefits. For example, a hospital expense-only policy offers benefits to cover just hospitalization expenses while a comprehensive major medical policy covers a much broader range of medical expenses. The number and kinds of benefits provided by a policy affect the premium rate.

Another aspect is that, while two policies may provide identical types of benefits, the amount of protection or benefits in one policy may be higher than in another. So, the greater the benefits, the higher the premium, or, to state it another way, the greater the risk to the company, the higher the premium.

Claims Experience Before realistic premium rates can be established for health insurance, the insurer must know what can be expected as to the dollar amount of the future claims. The most practical way to estimate the cost of future claims is to rely on claims tables based on past claims experience. For instance, experience tables have been constructed for hospital expenses based on the amounts paid out in the past for the same types of expenses. Such tables, along with an added factor to account for rising hospital costs, enable companies to estimate the average amounts of future hospital expenses. Similarly, experience tables have been developed for surgical benefits, covering various kinds of surgery based on past experience. The same procedure is followed to estimate average claims expected in the future for other medical expenses. Such tables must be adjusted periodically, of course, to reflect more recent experience.

Age and Sex of the Insured

As discussed earlier, experience has shown that health insurance claims costs tend to increase as the age of the insured increases. For any given coverage, the older the insured, the higher the applicable premium rate.

Also, disabilities among women under age 55, on the average, have a greater frequency and longer duration than among men, so female premium rates for certain coverages are higher than the premium rates for males. At the older ages, however, that generally is not true.

Occupation and Hobbies

Because some types of work are more hazardous than others, the premium rates for a person's health insurance policy may be affected by her occupation. If an insured's occupation indicates a higher than normal risk to the company, the policy may carry an extra premium charge. (Insurers establish their own occupational classifications, which represent another element in the premium structure.) The same holds true for any dangerous hobbies in which the insured may participate.

✓ ***For Example:*** Jim is a certified scuba diver and dives almost every weekend, and his best friend Tom golfs in his free time. All other things being equal, an insurance company may sell health insurance policies to both men, but probably will add a surcharge to Jim's premiums because of his high-risk hobby.

Tax Treatment of Health Insurance Premiums and Benefits

The tax treatment of health insurance premiums and benefits depends, to a large degree, on the type of insurance in question.

Taxation of Disability Income Insurance

Premiums paid for personal disability income insurance are not deductible by the individual insured, but the disability benefits are tax free to the recipient.

When a group disability income insurance plan is paid for entirely by the employer and benefits are paid directly to individual employees who qualify, the premiums are deductible by the employer. The benefits, in turn, are taxable to the recipient. On the other hand, if an employee contributes to any portion of the premium, her benefit will be received tax free in proportion to the premium contributed.

✓ ***For Example:*** An employee pays 40% of the premium and the employer pays 60%. Forty percent of the benefit is tax free to the employee and 60% is taxable.

Also in 2004 and later years, a self-employed individual may deduct 100% of amounts paid for health insurance covering the individual, spouse, and dependents.* The deduction cannot exceed self-employment net earnings and is not available where the individual or spouse is eligible to participate on a subsidized basis in an employer-sponsored health plan.

Persons under age 65 who are retired on permanent and total disability may be eligible for a tax credit on their disability income. The credit is equal to 15% of an initial base amount ($5,000 if married with one spouse eligible or unmarried), less:

- amounts received under pensions, annuities, or Social Security disability benefits; and
- one-half the excess of the individual's adjusted gross income over specified amounts (for example, $10,000 if married and filing a joint return or $7,500 if single).

Test Topic Alert!

Premiums paid for personal disability income insurance are not deductible by the insured, but the disability benefits are received tax free. Employers who pay the premium for a group disability income insurance plan can deduct the premium payments, but employees are taxed on the benefits. If employees pay part of the premium, they receive benefits tax free in proportion to the amount of the premium they pay.

---

*When this deduction first was introduced, it included an expiration date, after which the deduction would not be allowed. This expiration date consistently has been extended through various pieces of legislation, the latest being the Revenue Reconciliation Act of 1993.

Taxation of Medical Expense Insurance

Incurred medical expenses that are reimbursed by insurance may not be deducted from an individual's federal income tax. Furthermore, incurred medical expenses that are not reimbursed by insurance may only be deducted to the extent they exceed 7.5% of the insured's adjusted gross income. For example, an individual who has an adjusted gross income of $35,000 would be able to deduct only the amount of unreimbursed medical expenses over $2,625.

For purposes of figuring any deductible medical expenses, prescription drugs, insulin, hospital expenses, physician and surgeon fees, nursing care, dental care, rehabilitative treatments, and medical insurance premiums (including long-term care insurance premiums, within limits) all can be considered.

Benefits received by an insured under a medical expense policy are not included in her gross income, because they are paid to offset losses she incurred. However, medical expense insurance benefits must be included in gross income to the extent that reimbursement is received for medical expenses deducted in a prior year.

For self-employed individuals and their families, the rules are slightly different. They may deduct all amounts paid for medical care (including insurance premiums).

Quick Quiz 12.1

1. Jim is self-employed. In 2004, what percentage of his costs for medical expense insurance can he deduct?

   A. 25
   B. 50
   C. 75
   D. 100

2. Insurers commonly will use all of the following techniques when issuing health insurance policies to substandard risks EXCEPT

   A. attaching an impairment rider to a policy
   B. charging an extra premium
   C. limiting the type of policy
   D. requiring additional collateral to pay for extraordinary claims

3. Which of the following statements about the taxation of medical expense insurance is CORRECT?

   A. An individual may not take an income tax deduction for medical expenses that are reimbursed by insurance.
   B. An individual cannot take an income tax deduction for the cost of prescription drugs, dental care, and rehabilitative treatments.
   C. Reimbursed medical expenses may be deducted only if they exceed 7.5% of an insured's adjusted gross income.
   D. Benefits that an insured receives under a medical expense policy must be included in gross income.

4. Which of the following statements about health insurance premiums is NOT correct?

   A. The older the insured, the higher the premium rate.
   B. A person's hobbies may affect her health insurance premium rates.
   C. The age and sex of the insured are considered primary factors that affect health insurance premium rates.
   D. Women under age 55 will pay a higher premium for disability income insurance than men of the same age, all other things being equal.

Answers

1. ***D.*** *In 2004 and thereafter, Jim can deduct 100% of his costs for medical expense insurance.*

2. ***D.*** *When issuing health insurance policies to substandard risks, insurers commonly will attach an impairment rider to the policy, charge an extra premium, or limit the type of policy benefits. They will not require the applicant to pay additional collateral to pay for extraordinary claims.*

3. ***A.*** *An individual may not take an income tax deduction for medical expenses that are reimbursed by insurance. Only unreimbursed expenses, to the extent they exceed 7.5% of a person's adjusted gross income, may be deducted.*

4. ***C.*** *The age and sex of the insured are considered secondary rather than primary factors that affect health insurance premium rates. The 3 primary factors are morbidity, interest, and expenses.*

Managed Care

With the support and involvement of government, business, and the insurance industry, managed care has become the key strategy for containing rising health care costs that were threatening the country's competitive position in global markets. The success of this strategy was revealed in a recent survey conducted by benefit consultants Foster Higgins. The survey found that managed care costs grew at a consistently slower pace than traditional indemnity costs into the late 1990s. Indemnity plan costs for active and retired employees of private- and public-sector employers with 10 or more employees rose a cumulative 29% from 1993 through 1996, while for the same period the costs of preferred provider organizations (PPO) rose 8% and the costs of health maintenance organizations (HMO) rose only 3%. (However, by 2000, HMO costs actually exceeded costs for all other product types.) PPOs and HMOs exemplify methods or systems of managed care; indemnity plans do not.

Managed care organizations (MCOs) achieve these results because they integrate the financing and delivery of health care services to contain and control costs and to provide health care and services as efficiently as possible.

✓ ***Take Note:*** Common techniques MCOs use to achieve their objectives include: selectively contracting with efficient and effective health care professionals and organizations; establishing financial incentives for members to use providers and procedures sanctioned by the plan; controlling expensive hospital admissions and lengths of stay; using utilization management tools such as utilization review, standardized medical practices guidelines, and clinical pathways to achieve better outcomes and case management; and emphasizing disease prevention and health promotion programs.

These characteristics are typical of HMOs, PPOs, and exclusive provider organizations (EPOs), which were discussed in Unit 5.

Other important and related actions insurers are taking to contain health care costs address policy design and medical cost management techniques. The medical cost management techniques discussed below are common practices in managed care organizations.

Policy Design

The design or structure of a policy and its provisions will greatly affect an insurer's cost containment efforts. A higher deductible will help limit claims, for instance, and, in fact, the average deductible has increased in recent years. Whereas the typical deductible was $100 for an individual and $300 for a family just a few years ago, it is more common now to find deductibles in the $300 to $500 range for an individual and $900 or higher for a family. Coinsurance is another important means of sharing the cost of medical care between the insured and the insurer. Shortened benefit periods also can prove beneficial from a cost containment standpoint in that they can reduce the tendency some people have to seek medical attention for a condition that has long since been resolved.

Medical Cost Management

Medical cost management is being recognized widely and applauded as the most promising means of controlling claims expenses. Basically, it is the process of controlling how policyowners utilize their policies. Insurers use four general approaches for cost management: mandatory second opinions, precertification review, ambulatory surgery, and case management.

Mandatory Second Opinions

In an effort to reduce unnecessary surgical operations, many health policies today contain a provision requiring the insured to obtain a second opinion before receiving non-life-threatening surgery. Benefits often are reduced if a second opinion is not obtained.

Precertification Review

To control hospital claims, many policies today require policyowners to obtain approval from the insurer before entering a hospital on a nonemergency basis. Even if the admission was on an emergency basis, most policies with this type of provision require the insured to notify the insurer within a short period of time (usually 24 hours) after being admitted. The insurer then will determine how much of the hospital stay it will cover, depending on the reason for the admission. If the insured wants to stay longer, the additional expense will be the responsibility of the insured, not the insurer.

Ambulatory Surgery

The advances in medicine now permit many surgical procedures to be performed on an outpatient basis where once an overnight hospital stay was required. To encourage insureds to utilize less expensive outpatient care, many policies offer some sort of inducement. For instance, a policy may waive the deductible or coinsurance if the policyowner elects to be treated on an outpatient basis rather than as an admitted patient.

Case Management

Case management, as referred to here, involves a specialist within the insurance company, such as a registered nurse, who reviews a potentially large claim as it develops to discuss treatment alternatives with the insured.

✓ ***For Example:*** The insured's policy might state that treatment for a kidney ailment can only be performed in a hospital or registered hemodialysis center. However, if it makes economic sense to the insurer—and practical sense to the insured—to have treatments conducted at the insured's home, the case manager might negotiate with the insured to allow treatment to be performed at home as long as certain conditions are met.

The purpose of case management is to let the insurer take an active role in the management of what potentially could become a very expensive claim.

Summary

The escalating cost of medical care makes it imperative that insurers exercise precaution in their underwriting. A number of important factors come together during the health underwriting process. Pre-existing medical conditions as well as circumstances that may affect future medical losses are reviewed carefully by health underwriters. Health insurance premium rates are affected not only by the three primary factors of morbidity, interest, and expenses, but also by secondary factors, including the particular benefits provided by the policy and characteristics of the insured. As is true with all aspects of life and health insurance, the tax treatment of health insurance premiums and benefits is an important consideration from a personal financial standpoint. Typically, premiums paid for personal health insurance are not deductible and benefits received are not taxable. The exception is self-employed individuals, whose insurance is regarded partly as employer-sponsored. These individuals may deduct the cost of medical care up to certain limits.

In an effort to control health claims expenses, many insurers exercise some form of cost management, from requiring second surgical opinions to instituting full case management.

Key Concepts

In preparing for their licensing examination, students should be familiar with the following concepts:

- health insurance risk factors
- health insurance premium factors
- cost containment measures
- substandard risks
- tax treatment of premiums and benefits

Unit Exam 12

1. Susan is covered under her employer-sponsored disability group plan. The premium is $50 a month: Susan pays $10 and the employer pays $40. Assuming Susan were to become disabled and receive monthly disability benefits of $700 from the plan, how much, if any, of the monthly benefit would be taxable income?

   A. $0
   B. $70
   C. $140
   D. $560

2. Assume the following individuals are issued health insurance policies with varying renewability provisions. All other factors being equal, who would pay the highest premium?

   A. Dan—cancellable
   B. Jim—optionally renewable
   C. Henry—conditionally renewable
   D. Jack—noncancellable

3. Which of the following is the purpose of medical cost management?

   A. To influence hospital charges and doctors' fees
   B. To discourage individuals from utilizing health care services
   C. To control health claims expenses
   D. To encourage individuals to seek medical help only as a last resort

4. All of the following are primary risk factors in underwriting individual health insurance policies EXCEPT

   A. geographical location
   B. moral hazard
   C. occupation
   D. physical condition

5. Which of the following statements most aptly describes health insurance benefits?

   A. Each policy offers a single type of benefit.
   B. Claims, not benefits, affect premium rates.
   C. Policyowners who have policies with identical benefits pay the same premiums.
   D. The greater the benefits, the higher the premium.

6. Which of the following probably would NOT be considered in underwriting a health insurance risk?

   A. Personal habits
   B. Credit rating
   C. Medical history
   D. Marital status

7. All of the following factors would affect a health policy's premium rate EXCEPT

   A. age of the insured
   B. occupation of the insured
   C. type of benefit provided
   D. location of the insured's residence

8. Rick, who has no health insurance, experienced $3,000 in medical expenses this year. Assuming his adjusted gross income was $29,000, how much of those medical expenses can he deduct from his income taxes, if any?

   A. $0
   B. $825
   C. $2,175
   D. $3,000

9. What kind of table reflects the average number of disabilities due to sickness or accidents at various ages?

   A. Mortality
   B. Morbidity
   C. Claims underwriting
   D. Underwriting

10. What is the effect of an impairment rider attached to a health insurance policy?

    A. To increase the premium rate charged
    B. To decrease the amount of benefits provided
    C. To exclude from coverage losses resulting from specified conditions
    D. To increase the policy's waiting period

Unit Exam 12 Answers & Rationale

1. **D.** Susan will receive part of her disability benefit tax free in proportion to the premium she contributed. Because Susan contributed 20% of the total premium ($10 of $50), she will receive 20% of the benefit tax free (20% of $700 = $140). The remaining amount ($560) will constitute taxable income.

2. **D.** In general, the more favorable the renewability provision is to the insured policyholder, the higher the premium. Dan's cancellable policy, therefore, will have the lowest premium while Jack's noncancellable policy will have the highest premium.

3. **C.** The purpose of medical cost management is to control health claims expenses. Four approaches are used: mandatory second opinions, precertification review, ambulatory surgery, and case management.

4. **A.** The 3 primary risk factors affecting individual health insurance underwriting are moral hazards, occupation, and physical condition.

5. **D.** The more benefits that a health insurance policy offers, the higher the premiums. Because the insurer is taking on more risk, it will charge a higher premium.

6. **D.** When underwriting a health insurance policy, an insurer will consider a person's personal habits or lifestyle, her credit rating and medical history. However, a person's marital status probably will not be considered.

7. **D.** The insured's age and sex will affect the premium rate, as will the amount of protection provided under the policy. For example, the older the insured, the higher the premium. Similarly, premiums will increase as more benefits are provided. Also, premiums will be higher if a person is employed in a hazardous occupation. Where a person lives will not affect the premium she is charged.

8. **B.** Rick can take a deduction for medical expenses that exceed 7.5% of his adjusted gross income. Because he earned $29,000 this year, he could take a deduction for any expenses exceeding $2,175 (7.5% of $29,000). Therefore, he could therefore deduct $825.

9. **B.** Morbidity tables show the average number of disabilities due to sickness or accidents at various ages. Mortality tables, on the other hand, show the average number of persons within a larger group of people who can be expected to die within a given year at a given age.

10. **C.** If an impairment rider is attached to a health insurance policy, coverage will not be provided for losses resulting from chronic conditions or physical impairments. With the questionable risks excluded, policies then can be issued at standard rates.

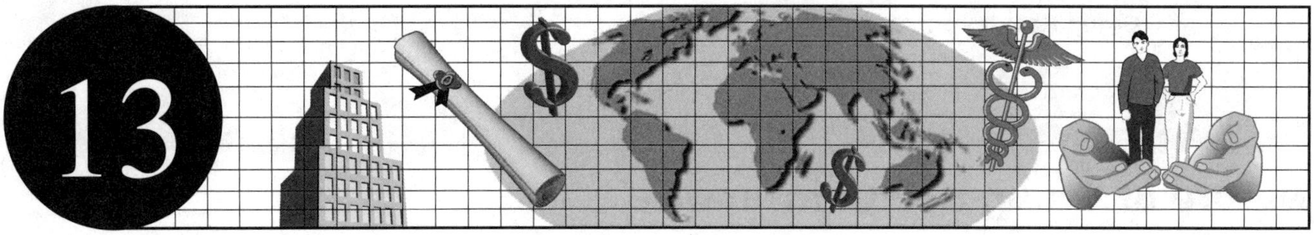

Group Health Insurance

INTRODUCTION

Most of our discussion of health and accident insurance so far has focused on individual coverage. However, because of the high cost of purchasing insurance, many people are unable to purchase individual coverage. As a result, most Americans rely on employer-sponsored plans as their sole source of health insurance.

Group health insurance, like individual health insurance coverage, can be tailored to meet the employer's needs. By its very nature, however, group insurance has several features that set it apart from individual plans, including the nature of the contract, the cost of the plan, the form of premium payments, and eligibility requirements. In this unit, we will examine the characteristics of this type of insurance protection and review the favorable tax treatment given to group plans.

UNIT OBJECTIVES

When you complete this unit you should be able to:

- list and describe the principal characteristics of group health insurance;
- explain the general underwriting factors that are considered when issuing a group health insurance policy;
- compare and contrast group and individual medical expense, disability income, and AD&D insurance;
- explain the rights given to terminated employees under COBRA; and
- explain the tax treatment of group health premiums and benefits.

Nature of Group Health Insurance

Group health insurance is a plan of insurance that an employer (or other eligible group sponsor) provides for its employees. The contract for coverage is between the insurance company and the employer, and a master policy is issued to the employer. The individual insureds covered by the policy are not given separate policies; instead, they receive certificates of insurance and an outline or booklet that describes their benefits. Generally, the benefits provided under a group health plan are more extensive than those provided under an individual health plan. Group health plans typically have higher benefit maximums and lower deductibles.

Characteristics of Group Health Insurance

The characteristics of group health insurance are similar to those of group life. These include eligibility standards for groups and for individuals within the groups, method of premium payments (contributory vs. noncontributory), lower cost, predetermined benefits, underwriting practices, conversion privileges, and pre-existing conditions provisions. Let's briefly review each.

Eligible Groups

To qualify for group health coverage, the group must be a natural group. This means that it must have been formed for some reason other than to obtain insurance. Qualifying groups include employers, labor unions, trade associations, creditor-debtor groups, multiple employer trusts, lodges, and the like.

State laws specify the minimum number of persons to be covered under a group policy. One state may stipulate 15 persons as a minimum number, while another state may require a minimum of 10.

✓ ***Take Note:*** Group policies must typically cover a minimum of 10 people.

Individual Eligibility

Group health plans commonly impose a set of eligibility requirements that must be met before an individual member is eligible to participate in the group plan. It is common to find the following requirements:

- minimum of one to three months employment service; and
- full-time employment status

Contributory vs. Noncontributory

Group health plans may be contributory or noncontributory. If the employer pays the entire premium, the plan is noncontributory; if the employees share a portion of the premium, it is contributory. Almost universally, noncontributory group health plans require 100% participation by eligible members, whereas contributory group health plans require participation by 75% of eligible members. The reason for these minimum participation requirements is to protect the insurer against adverse selection and to keep administrative expenses in line with coverage units.

Lower Cost

Benefit for benefit, the cost of insuring an individual under a group health plan is less than the cost of insurance under an individual plan. This is because the administrative and selling expenses involved with group plans are far less.

Predetermined Benefits

Another characteristic of group health plans is that the benefits provided to individual insureds are predetermined by the employer in conjunction with the insurer's benefit schedules and coverage limits. For example, group disability benefits are tied to a position or earnings schedule, as are accidental death and dismemberment benefits.

Underwriting Practices

Generally, the approach in underwriting group health plans is the same as underwriting group life plans: the insurer evaluates the group as a whole, rather than individuals within the group. Based on the group's risk profile, which is measured against the insurer's selection standards, the group is either accepted or rejected.

However, there are some changes taking place with regard to underwriting group medical expenses plans, especially for small groups. Whereas for large group medical plans it is common to accept all currently eligible members and new members coming into the group, this is not necessarily true for smaller groups. In smaller groups the presence of even one bad risk can have a significant impact on the claims experience of the group. Consequently, most insurers today reserve the right to engage in individual underwriting to some degree with groups they insure.

As the term implies, individual underwriting is the process of reviewing a group member's individual risk profile. This is done most commonly on two occasions: when a group first is taken on by an insurer and when a group member (for example, an employee) tries to enter the plan after initially electing not to participate. In the latter case, the underwriter's objective is to reduce the risk of adverse selection. In the former case, individual underwriting is done only on members for whom the initial application indicates a potential risk problem (such as a pre-existing condition). If the member is found to represent too great a risk, the insurer often retains the right to reject the member from participating in the plan, or at least charge an increased premium (or exclude coverage for the specified condition). It is important to note that if an insurer does reserve this right of individual underwriting, most states require the insurer to explain, in the policy, how it will exercise this right.

FIGURE 13.1 General Group Underwriting Considerations

In spite of the many differences between types of groups, certain general underwriting considerations apply to all or most types of groups:

- the reason for the group's existence (purchasing group insurance must be incidental to the group's formation, not the reason for it)
- the stability of the group (underwriters want to see a group of stable workers without an excessive amount of turnover)
- the persistency of the group (groups that change insurers every year do not represent a good risk)
- the method of determining benefits (it must be by a schedule or method that prevents individual selection of benefits)
- how eligibility is determined (insurers want to see a sickness-related probationary period, for example, to reduce adverse selection)
- the source of premium payments, whether contributory or noncontributory (noncontributory plans are preferred because they require 100 percent participation, which helps spread the risk and reduces adverse selection)
- the prior claims experience of the group
- the size and composition of the group
- the industry or business with which the group is associated (hazardous industries are typified by higher-than-standard mortality and morbidity rates)

✓ ***Take Note:*** An entire group rarely is rejected on the basis of one bad risk, unless the group is very small. The underwriter reviews a number of factors to determine whether or not the group should be accepted. (See Figure 13.1.)

Conversion Privilege

Group health plans that provide medical expense coverage universally contain a conversion privilege for individual insureds, which allows them to convert their group certificate to an individual medical expense policy with the same insurer, if and when they leave their employment. Insurers are permitted to evaluate the individual and charge the appropriate premium, be it a standard rate or substandard rate; however, an individual cannot be denied coverage, even if she has become uninsurable.

The conversion must be exercised within a given period of time, usually 30 or 31 days, depending on the state. During this time, the individual remains insured under the group plan, whether or not a conversion ultimately takes place. Conversion privileges generally are reserved for those who were active in the group plan during the preceding three months.

Test Topic Alert! The conversion privilege is exercised when the insured no longer is eligible for coverage under the group plan. The insured converts the group certificate of coverage to an individual medical expense policy with the same insurer.

Pre-Existing Conditions

In the past, group health insurance plans typically excluded a person from coverage because of pre-existing conditions. A pre-existing condition generally was defined as any condition for which a participant received treatment at any time during the three months before the effective date of the group coverage. Group plans also specified when a condition would stop being considered pre-existing.

However, the Health Insurance Portability and Accountability Act (HIPAA) has changed the rules governing pre-existing conditions for group health plans. HIPAA limited the ability of employer-sponsored groups and insurers to exclude individuals on the basis of pre-existing medical conditions. The exclusion for pre-existing conditions now is limited to conditions for which medical advice or treatment was recommended or received within the six-month period ending on the enrollment date. However, the exclusion can extend for no more than 12 months (18 months for late enrollees).

✓ ***Take Note:*** This exclusion period must be reduced by one month for every two months that the employee was covered at a previous job. For example, if an employee had prior group health coverage for eight months, he would be subject to only a four-month exclusion period when he changes jobs. Thereafter, the employee's new plan must cover all of his medical problems. In contrast, if the employee was covered by a group health plan for 12 straight months, the new plan could not invoke the pre-existing condition exclusion at all. It must cover the new employee's medical problems as soon as he enrolls in the plan.

Group Health Insurance Coverages

All types of health insurance coverages discussed in this text—medical expense, disability income, and accidental death and dismemberment—are available for group plans. Rather than repeat the discussion of these policies—their purpose and functions are the same for group and individual products—let's focus on the features of these coverages when they are part of a group plan.

FIGURE 13.2 Dental and Vision Care—Popular Group Benefits

Relatively new to the array of health care benefits offered to groups are coverages for *dental care* and *vision care.*

Dental care coverage is designed to cover the costs associated with normal dental maintenance as well as oral surgery, root canal therapy and orthodontia. The coverage may be on a reasonable and customary charge basis or on a dollar-per-service schedule approach. Deductible and coinsurance features are typical (although some policies will cover routine cleaning and exams at 100 percent), as are maximum yearly benefit amounts, such as $1,000 or $2,000.

Vision care coverage usually pays for reasonable and customary charges incurred during eye exams by opthalmologists and optometrists. Expenses for the fitting or cost of contact lenses or eyeglasses often are excluded.

Group Basic Medical Expense

The three standard forms of basic medical expense insurance—hospital, surgical, and physicians' expenses—are available for group insurance. In addition, a number of newer coverages have been developed in recent years, including dental and vision care, prescription drugs, home health care, extended care facilities, diagnostic x-rays, and laboratory services. In fact, some of these specified coverages, such as vision and dental care, are available only on a group basis.

A group basic medical expense plan can combine two or more of these coverages or it may consist of only one type of coverage, such as hospital expense only.

Dental Insurance

Dental expense insurance helps pay for routine dental care as well as injuries caused by accidents. Although dental insurance can be provided through an individual policy, it is usually available through group insurance plans. Employers often offer it as an employment benefit. Policies typically cover oral exams, x-rays, fillings, cleaning, extractions, bridgework, dentures, oral surgery, root canals, and related services. Coverage is usually subject to a deductible. The patient must typically also make a copayment of 20% to 50% of the cost.

Dental insurance encourages the insured to obtain routine preventive care because most dental disease can be prevented. Dental examinations and proper care are usually enough to keep the insured in good dental health. Therefore, this coverage is designed to ensure that the insured receives regular examinations and care to prevent dental disease.

✓ ***Take Note:*** Dental plans commonly cover the costs of regular teeth cleaning procedures and dental examinations. A general practitioner will usually render these services, though treatment from a specialist may be necessary in some cases.

With the insured playing such an important part in preventing dental disease, dental plans usually require the insured to pay a greater portion of the cost of treatment for dental disease than for preventive treatment.

Three types of entities can arrange for an insured's dental benefits:

1. Dental service corporations are not-for-profit entities that negotiate and administer contracts for treatment of individuals or groups of insureds. Blue Cross/Blue Shield is an example of this type of entity.
2. Insurance companies provide coverage for dental services by offering a variety of dental benefits packages that can include fee-for-service and managed care plans.
3. Self-funded insurers are employers that have the assets necessary to underwrite the expense of giving dental care to their employees.

Types of Dental Plans

Dental insurance carriers control costs by negotiating fees with dentists. The degree of the patient's ability to choose a dentist can directly affect the premium. In general, plans that allow the patient to choose any dentist will cost more than one in which the patient must select a dentist from a group with rates set by agreement with the insurer.

Open Panel Open panel plans permit insureds to receive dental care from any dentist. Dentists may accept or refuse to treat insureds enrolled in the plan.

Closed Panel Closed panel plans limit insureds to receiving dental care from dentists who have contracted with the insurer to participate in the plan. These dentists are usually located within a specified geographic area. There are two types of closed panel plans: PPO and EPO.

Preferred Provider Organization (PPO)

A Preferred Provider Organization (PPO) offers dental care through a panel of dentists who have agreed, by contract, to treat a group of insureds. In contracting to render their services, these dentists agree to charge less than their usual fees when treating members of this group. These negotiated rates save money for the insurance carrier. Insureds are therefore encouraged to seek treatment from participating dentists. If an insured chooses to obtain treatment from a dentist who does not participate in the panel, the insurance carrier will usually require the insured to pay a greater portion of the cost.

Exclusive Provider Organization (EPO)

Somewhat similar to a PPO in the manner in which fees are established among participating dentists, an exclusive provider organization (EPO) goes further to limit the insured's choice of dentists. Coverage is limited to treatment from participating dentists. Therefore, if an insured receives treatment from a dentist who has not contracted to provide services for the group members at reduced rates, the insurance carrier will not pay for the cost of the services. Many dentists prefer not to participate in EPOs because of the substantially-reduced rates that they are compelled to charge for their services. In fact, some plans make the dentists salaried employees of the EPO. Insureds may be restricted from receiving specialized care, and the EPO may also limit the number of services that insureds can receive in a calendar year.

Forms of Dental Plans

Dental plans take several forms. Each form differs on the basis of treatment and method of payment for services. State insurance departments regulate insurers that sell indemnity plans, capitation plans, and plans with PPOs.

Indemnity Plans

An indemnity plan pays the dentist on a traditional fee-for-service basis. The insurer uses the monthly premium to pay the dentist directly for services rendered. This is done after the insured pays the deductible. The insurer usually pays 50% to 80% of the dentist's fees for covered services, and the insured pays the balance. These plans often have a predetermined or set deductible amount that differs among plans. These plans may limit the amount of services that are covered within a year.

Capitation Plans

A capitation plan, also known as a Dental Health Maintenance Organization (DHMO), offers comprehensive dental care to patients through specified dentists. It operates in a manner similar to medical HMOs. Dentists are paid on a per capita (or per person) basis instead of the usual fee-for-service basis. Participating dentists are paid a fixed monthly fee based on the number of patients assigned to them. Insureds pay a premium and may also pay a copayment for each visit.

Preferred Provider Organizations A Preferred Provider Organization (PPO) allows a group of insureds to obtain dental care from a group of participating dentists. These dentists agree to charge fees that are lower than usual when treating patients in this group. Insureds who choose a dentist who is not a "preferred provider" may need to pay a greater portion of the fee for any services. Unlike a DHMO, a dental PPO provides some benefit even if the insured seeks treatment from a dentist who does not participate in the PPO.

Direct Reimbursement Plans A direct reimbursement plan is a self-funded benefit plan and is not insurance. An employer or sponsor pays for dental care with its own funds. No premiums are paid to an insurer or third-party administrator. The patient selects any dentist, pays for services rendered, and obtains a receipt showing services performed and payments made. The patient presents this receipt to the employer, who reimburses the patient for all or part of the costs. Although the plan does not limit the services available, it may limit the amount of money a patient can spend on this care within one year. Most plans limit benefits at $500 to $2,000 each year.

Dental Discounts A dental discount is offered by local dental offices that have agreed to set prices for specific dental procedures that are lower than the regular American Dental Association pricing code. These discounts can be as much as 70%. Unlike traditional dental insurance plans, dental discounts do not exclude pre-existing conditions. A patient can obtain immediate coverage for treatment without satisfying any waiting period requirements. Dental discounts are not true insurance.

Forms of Payment

There are four common payment schedules under the various dental plans.

Capitation Plans that offer a predefined level of benefits use a capitation fee schedule. A capitation fee schedule makes the patient responsible for paying the costs of treatment that the plan does not cover. This means that the cost of the care may exceed the benefit paid and the patient's copayment. The result is that the patient may settle for a level of care that is the most affordable but not necessarily the best. If the benefit payment and the copayment are not sufficient to cover the cost of treatment, the patient may also decide to postpone treatment.

Schedule of Allowances Plans using a table of scheduled allowances to calculate benefits set a maximum dollar limit for every covered procedure without regard to the actual charge. If the charge is greater than this limit, the patient must pay the difference. An important consideration for patients in these plans is the frequency with which the insurer adjusts the table for inflation or to accommodate changes in dental procedures.

Direct Reimbursement

A direct reimbursement plan is a self-funded plan in which the patient pays the dentist for services rendered. The plan sponsor (usually the insured patient's employer) then reimburses the patient (usually an employee) for a predetermined percentage of the cost. Because the patient bears the burden of covering the cost for services, the patient is more likely to seek productive and economical treatment.

Usual, Customary, and Reasonable (UCR)

The Usual, Customary, and Reasonable payment schedule is found in most indemnity (fee-for-service) plans. Patients can choose their own dentists. This schedule pays benefits on the basis of a fixed percentage of either the dentist's fee; or the fee that the insurer considers to be usual, customary, or reasonable for the community in which the service is rendered.

✓ ***Take Note:*** Because the UCR fees can differ widely between communities, the UCR payment schedule is controversial, especially when the insurer sets the UCR percentage too low in relation to the community's usual fees for dental services. Patients are then compelled to pay more of the expense themselves. Although the insurer usually pays the dentist, it may pay the beneficiary instead.

Controlling Costs of Dental Treatment

Most dental insurance plans control costs by one of the following means:

- limiting the dollar limit on the amount of benefits an insured can receive in one year; or
- limiting the number or type of services that the plan will cover.

Predetermination of Costs

A plan may request that the dentist or the patient propose a course of treatment to the plan administrator before treatment begins. This process is known as predetermination of costs, preauthorization, prior authorization, precertification, or pretreatment review. The administrator then determines the patient's eligibility, the eligibility period, the services to be covered, the patient's copayment, and the maximum limitation of benefits. In some cases, the plan may require predetermination of costs for treatment that exceeds a certain dollar amount.

Annual Benefits Limitations

A plan may control costs by limiting the number of procedures provided in one year, the dollar amount of benefits paid, or both.

Dispute Resolution Through Peer Review

Some plans offer a peer review process through which disputes between third parties, patients, and dentists can be resolved. This process can eliminate the costs of litigating claims. Peer review helps to ensure fairness, consideration of each case on its own merits, and a complete examination of records, treatment procedures, and the results obtained.

Premium Adjustment and Reevaluation Insureds and plan sponsors can request periodic reviews of premium levels to be sure that UCR or payment schedules continue to fairly address the costs of dental services.

Coordination of Benefits Insureds who are covered by two dental benefits plans should notify the administrator or insurer of their primary plan. Coordination of benefits protects the insured's rights and maximizes the benefits to which she is entitled. Coordination can ensure full coverage where plans overlap and provide coverage under one plan when the other excludes it.

Types of Dental Care Services

As noted above, dental plans vary in the services they provide and in the manner in which they control costs. Most plans cover certain diagnostic services, preventive, and emergency treatment.

Routine Services The following services are usually covered without a deductible or copayment:

- initial oral examinations (once per dentist);
- recall examinations (twice per year);
- complete x-ray surveys (once every three years);
- bite-wing x-rays to locate cavities (once per year);
- prophylaxis or teeth cleaning (twice each year);
- topical fluoride treatment (twice per year); and
- sealants (for insureds under 18 years of age).

Although preventive care reduces the chance that the insured will need more extensive treatment, additional treatment may be necessary to maintain health. Such treatment can encompass a wide variety of procedures with plans covering 70% to 80% of the treatment. The insured pays the balance of the cost.

Routine care includes the following services:

- restorative care: amalgam and composite resin fillings and stainless steel crowns on primary teeth;
- endodontics: treatment of root canals and removal of nerves from teeth;
- oral surgery: removal of teeth, tissue biopsies, drainage of minor oral infections, and other minor surgical procedures;
- periodontics: treatment of uncomplicated periodontal disease including scaling, root planing, and care of acute infections or lesions; and

- prosthodontics: repair, realignment, or reseating of dentures and bridges.

Major Services Dental plans encourage insureds to take advantage of preventive services that are available at relatively little or no cost under the plans. These preventive services can eliminate the need for major dental work. Therefore, when major dental treatment becomes necessary, most plans cover less than half of the cost. Benefits can be limited to a certain number of procedures and a dollar amount per year.

Major care includes the following services:

- restorative care: gold restorations and individual crowns;
- oral surgery: extraction of impacted teeth and complex oral surgery;
- periodontics: treatment of complicated periodontal disease that necessitates surgical procedures involving bone, underlying tissues, or grafts;
- orthodontics: treatment including retainers, braces, or diagnostic materials;
- dental implants: surgical replacement or restoration of implants; and
- prosthodontics: fixed bridges and partial, removable, or fixed dentures.

Referral to Specialists

Some plans may limit visits to specialists. They may require that the dentist refer the patient to a specialist before covering any treatment by a specialist. These specialists contract with the insurer to provide services at a specific rate. Some plans may also require approval from the plan administrator before a specialist can treat the patient. The cost of specialized treatment causes some plans to discourage the use of specialists.

Group Major Medical Plans

Like individual major medical plans, group major medical plans may be offered as a single, extensive plan (comprehensive major medical) or superimposed over a group basic plan (supplemental major medical). Participants usually are required to satisfy an initial deductible with comprehensive plans and either a corridor or an integrated deductible with supplemental plans.

Benefits provided by group major medical plans usually are more extensive than those of individual plans. For example, it is not uncommon to find group plans that offer individual benefit maximums of $1 million; still others do not set any maximum benefit limits. Also, deductibles usually are lower for group plans, typically ranging from $100 to $250, whereas deductibles for individual policies can be $500 or more.

Two other characteristics of group medical expense plans distinguish them from individual plans. These are the coordination of benefits provision and the treatment of maternity benefits.

Coordination of Benefits

The purpose of the coordination of benefits (COB) provision, found only in group health plans, is to avoid duplication of benefit payments and overinsurance when an individual is covered under more than one group health plan. The provision limits the total amount of claims paid from all insurers covering the patient to no more than the total allowable medical expenses.

✓ ***For Example:*** An individual who incurs $700 in allowable medical expenses would not be able to collect any more than $700, no matter how many group plans she is covered by.

The COB provision establishes the primary plan, that is, the plan that is responsible for providing the full benefit amounts as it specifies. Once the primary plan has paid its full promised benefit, the insured may submit the claim to the secondary provider for any additional benefits payable. In no case, however, will the total amount the insured receives exceed the costs incurred, or the total maximum benefits available under all plans. Coordinating benefits is appropriate for married couples, when each is covered by an employer group plan.

✓ ***For Example:*** John and Cindy, a married couple, are participants in separate health plans and also are covered as dependents under each other's plan. John's plan specifies that it is the primary plan for John; Cindy's plan is his secondary plan. Likewise, Cindy's plan specifies that it is the primary plan for Cindy; John's plan is her secondary plan.

Maternity Benefits

Whereas it is common for individual health plans to exclude routine maternity care from coverage, group medical expense plans must provide maternity benefits. This is the result of a 1979 amendment to the Civil Rights Act, which requires plans covering 15 or more people to treat pregnancy-related claims no differently than any other allowable medical expense.

However, the Act does not compel insurers to pay for expenses arising from abortion except when the mother's life would be endangered if the fetus were carried to term, or where medical complications have arisen from an abortion.

Test Topic Alert! Although individual health plans commonly exclude coverage for routine maternity care, group medical expense plans must provide maternity benefits.

Age Discrimination in Employment Act

This Act prohibits employers from discriminating against or giving preference to employees who are 40 years old or older. For instance, an employer may not reject a job applicant solely on the basis of age if the applicant is at least 40 years old. Similar prohibitions protect workers of this age from discrimination in group health insurance coverage.

Cost comparisons and adjustments for group health insurance plans must be made on a benefit-by-benefit basis or on a benefit package basis.

Benefit-by-Benefit Basis

Adjustments made on a benefit-by-benefit basis must be made in the amount or level of a specific benefit for a specific occurrence or event.

✓ ***For Example:*** The higher group insurance costs associated with coverage for older workers would justify a corresponding reduction in the amount of group insurance coverage for these workers on the basis of age.

However, a benefit-by-benefit approach would not justify substitution of one benefit for another, even though both benefits are designed for the same occurrence.

Benefit Package Basis

Cost comparisons and adjustments for group health insurance plans may also be made on a limited benefit package basis. Under this approach, cost comparisons and adjustments can be made in the aggregate. This basis offers greater flexibility than a benefit-by-benefit basis in order to carry out the intent of the act, which is to help employers and workers find ways of meeting problems arising from the impact of age on employment.

Cost Data—Five-Year Maximum Basis

Cost comparisons and adjustments for group health insurance plans may be made on the basis of age brackets of up to five years. A particular benefit may be reduced for older employees by an amount that can be justified by the additional cost to give them the same level of the benefit as younger employees within a specified five-year age group immediately preceding theirs.

✓ ***For Example:*** Suppose an employer chooses to provide unreduced group insurance benefits until age 60. Benefits for employees who are between 60 and 65 years old may be reduced only to the extent necessary to achieve approximate equivalency in costs with employees who are 55 to 60 years old. Similarly, any reductions in benefit levels for 65- to-70- year-old employees cannot exceed an amount which is proportional to the additional costs for their coverage over 60- to-65- year-old employees.

Employee Contributions in Support of Employee Benefit Plans

An older employee may not be required as a condition of employment to make greater contributions than a younger employee in support of an employee benefit plan. This would amount to a mandatory reduction in the older employee's take-home pay.

However, an older employee may be required as a condition of participation in a voluntary employee benefit plan to make a greater contribution than a younger employee only if the older employee is not required to bear a greater proportion of the total premium cost (employer-paid and employee-paid) than the younger employee. Otherwise the requirement would discriminate against the older employee by making compensation in the form of an employer contribution available on less favorable terms than for the younger employee and denying that compensation to an older employee who is unwilling or unable to make the greater contribution.

The increased contribution need not be mandatory, of course; an older employee may be given the option to make the additional contribution necessary to receive the same level of benefits as a younger employee.

Any benefit reduction greater than would be justified under a benefit-by-benefit approach must be offset by another benefit available to the same employees. No employees may be deprived of one benefit because of age unless they are given another benefit to make up for it.

COBRA Continuation of Benefits

Participants in group medical expense plans are protected by a federal law that guarantees a continuation of their group coverage if their employment is terminated for reasons other than gross misconduct. Practically, the law protects employees who are laid-off, but not those who are fired for cause. (The circumstances that qualify for this continued coverage are noted in Figure 13.3.)

This law, known as the Consolidated Omnibus Budget Reconciliation Act of 1985 (or COBRA), requires employers with 20 or more employees to continue group medical expense coverage for terminated workers (as well as their spouses, divorced spouses, and dependent children) for up to 18 months (or 36 months, in some situations) following termination.

FIGURE 13.3 COBRA Continued Coverage for Former Employees

The following events would qualify for extended medical expense coverage under COBRA for a terminated employee:

- Employment is terminated (for other than gross misconduct):
  18 months of continued coverage (or up to 29 months if disabled).
- Employee's hours are reduced (resulting in termination from the plan):
  18 months of continued coverage (or up to 29 months if disabled).
- Employee dies:
  36 months of continued coverage for dependents.
- Dependent child no longer qualifies as dependent child under the plan:
  36 months of continued coverage.
- Employee becomes eligible for Medicare:
  36 months of continued coverage.
- Employee divorces or legally separates:
  36 months of continued coverage for former spouse.

✓ ***Take Note:*** COBRA is not the same as the policy conversion privilege by which an employee may convert a group certificate to an individual policy. COBRA permits the terminated employee to continue his group coverage.

The law does not require the employer to pay the cost of the continued group coverage; the terminated employee can be required to pay the premium, which may be up to 102% of the premium that otherwise would be charged. (The additional 2% is allowed to cover the insurer's administrative expenses.) The schedule of benefits will be the same during the continuation period as under the group plan.

Test Topic Alert! COBRA is a continuation of benefits formerly provided under the group plan. The insured may have to pay up to 102% of the premium that would otherwise be charged.

Group Disability Income Plans

Group disability income plans differ from individual plans in a number of ways. Individual plans usually specify a flat income amount, based on the person's earnings, determined at the time the policy is purchased. In contrast, group plans usually specify benefits in terms of a percentage of the individual's earnings.

Like individual plans, group disability can include short-term plans or long-term plans. The definitions of short term and long term, however, are different for group and individual.

Group short-term disability plans are characterized by maximum benefit periods of rather short duration, such as 13 or 26 weeks. Benefits typically are paid weekly and range from 50% to 100% of the individual's income.

✓ ***Take Note:*** A group short-term disability policy typically will pay benefits from the first day of a disability, resulting from an accident, but will impose a waiting period from one to seven days for a disability due to sickness.

Group long-term disability plans provide for maximum benefit periods of more than two years, occasionally extending to the insured's retirement age. Benefit amounts usually are limited to about 60% of the participant's income.

If an employer provides both a short-term plan and a long-term plan, the long-term plan typically begins paying benefits only after the short-term benefits cease. Often, long-term plans use an own occupation definition of total disability for the first year or two of disability and then switch to an any occupation definition.

Most group disability plans require the employee to have a minimum period of service, such as 30 to 90 days, before she is eligible for coverage. In addition, most group plans include provisions making their benefits supplemental to workers' compensation benefits, so that total benefits received do not exceed a specified percentage of regular earnings. In some cases, group disability plans actually limit coverage to nonoccupational disabilities, because occupational disabilities normally qualify for workers' compensation benefits.

✓ ***Take Note:*** Group disability plans also contain specific exclusions under which benefits will not be paid, even if the definition of disability is otherwise met. For example, common exclusions include self-inflicted injuries, disabilities during periods when the employee is not under a physician's care, disabilities resulting from war, and those beginning before the employee was eligible for plan coverage.

Group AD&D

Accidental death and dismemberment insurance is a very popular type of group coverage, frequently offered in conjunction with group life insurance plans. It also may be provided as a separate policy, in which case it normally is paid for entirely by the employee. Such employee-pay-all plans are called voluntary group AD&D, because plan participation is voluntary. Benefits may be provided for both occupational and nonoccupational losses, or for nonoccupational losses only. Voluntary group AD&D typically provides benefits for both types of losses.

Like individual AD&D, group AD&D pays a principal sum upon the insured's accidental death (or loss of any two body members). A capital sum is payable upon the accidental loss of one body member. Some group AD&D plans specify a higher death benefit if the insured dies while on company business.

✓ ***Take Note:*** Group AD&D, unlike group life and group medical, normally does not include a conversion privilege.

Other Types of Group Health Plans

In addition to the typical group health insurance plan—as would be utilized by an employer, for instance—are four plan types worth noting: blanket health insurance, franchise (or wholesale) health insurance, credit accident and health insurance, and medical savings accounts.

Blanket Health Plans

Blanket health insurance is issued to cover a group that may be exposed to the same risks, but the composition of the group—the individuals within the group—is constantly changing. A blanket health plan may be issued to an airline or a bus company to cover its passengers or to a school to cover its students.

Franchise Health Plans

Franchise health plans, sometimes called wholesale plans, provide health insurance coverage to members of an association or professional society. Individual policies are issued to individual members; the association or society simply serves as the sponsor for the plan. Premium rates usually are discounted for franchise plans.

Credit Accident and Health Plans

Like credit life plans, credit accident and health plans are designed to help the insured pay off a loan in the event she is disabled due to an accident or sickness. If the insured becomes disabled, the policy provides for monthly benefit payments equal to the monthly loan payments due.

Medical Savings Accounts

Medical savings accounts (MSAs) are intended to help employees of small businesses and the self-employed to pay for health care expenses. Available since January 1, 1997, they are designed for self-employed individuals or companies that have 50 or fewer employees.

The purpose of the MSA is to enable individuals to set aside funds on a tax-advantaged basis to help defray health care costs. In general, neither contributions to the MSA nor distributions from the MSA are taxable to the MSA owner, as long as distributions are used to cover qualified medical expenses for the individual, a spouse, or dependents. Distributions used for other purposes will be taxed and also could incur a 15% penalty. MSA funds belong to the insured and, if they are not spent, they accumulate to fund future health care expenses.

MSAs are designed to cover routine medical expenses; they are not meant to provide catastrophic coverage. Consequently, participation in an MSA is conditioned on being covered by a high-deductible contribution plan. The minimum and maximum deductibles for these plans must be $1,500 and $2,250 for individual coverage and $3,000 and $4,500 for family coverage. These deductibles provide a measuring rod for the amount of contribution that can be made to an account. For instance, with individual coverage, the annual MSA contribution is limited to 65% of the deductible; with family coverage, the contribution is limited to 75% of the deductible.

✓ ***For Example:*** Bob is single and self-employed. The deductible for his health insurance plan is $2,000. He can contribute $1,300 to his MSA this year (65% of $2,000).

Quick Quiz 13.1

True or False?

______ 1. XRT Company wants to help its 55 employees pay for health care expenses. To do this, it could create medical savings accounts for the employees.

______ 2. John, an attorney, obtains health insurance coverage through the local bar association. The type of health plan sponsored by the bar association is called a franchise health plan.

______ 3. Most group disability plans contain provisions making their benefits supplemental to workers' compensation benefits.

______ 4. Maria is covered by a group medical plan with a $250 deductible. If she purchases individual medical coverage instead, the deductible probably will be lower.

______ 5. Vision and dental care insurance generally are available only on a group basis.

Answers

1. ***False.*** *Only self-employed individuals or companies with 50 or fewer employees can establish medical savings accounts. Because XRT Company has 55 employees, it is not eligible for the MSA program.*
2. ***True.***
3. ***True.***
4. ***False.*** *Deductibles usually are lower for group plans than for individual health plans. As a result, the deductible for Maria's group plan probably will be less than if she purchased an individual plan.*
5. ***True.***

Tax Treatment of Group Health Plans

As an incentive for employers to provide health insurance benefits to their employees, the federal government grants favorable tax treatment to group plans. Let's briefly review this treatment.

Taxation of Group Health Premiums

Employers are entitled to take a tax deduction for premium contributions they make to a group health plan, as long as the contributions represent an ordinary and necessary business expense. By the same token, individual participants do not include employer contributions made on their behalf as part of their taxable income.

As a general rule, individual premium contributions to a group health plan are not tax deductible. Only when unreimbursed medical expenses—expenses that can include any individual contributions to a group medical plan—exceed 7.5% of an individual's adjusted gross income can a tax deduction be taken. The deduction is limited to the amount exceeding 7.5% of adjusted gross income.

✓ ***Take Note:*** Any premiums the individual contributes for group disability or group AD&D coverage are not considered qualifying medical expenses when determining this excess.

Taxation of Group Health Benefits

Any benefits an individual receives under a medical expense plan are not considered taxable income because they are provided to cover losses the individual incurred. It is a somewhat different story with disability income plans, however. Disability benefit payments that are attributed to employee contributions are not taxable, but benefit payments that are attributed to employer contributions are taxable.

✓ ***For Example:*** Anne is a participant in a contributory group disability income plan in which her employer pays two-thirds of the premium and Anne pays one-third. Her employer qualifies for a tax deduction for its share of the premium and, as is true with employer contributions to all group health plans, Anne is not taxed on those contributions. The premium portion that Anne pays does not qualify for a tax deduction for her.

Now assume Anne becomes disabled and receives disability income benefits of $900 a month. One-third of the monthly benefit—$300—would be tax free, because it is attributed to the premium she paid; the remaining two-thirds of the payment—$600—would be taxable income, because it is attributed to the premium her employer paid.

Summary

Group health insurance—like group life insurance—is evidenced by one master contract that covers multiple lives. Virtually any health insurance product available as an individual contract also is available under the group umbrella. Thus, medical expense insurance, disability income insurance, and accidental death and dismemberment insurance all are common group plans. In addition, there are a number of coverages, like vision and dental care, that are available only to groups.

Of utmost concern to insurance regulators is that employees be protected from loss of their insurance coverage if their job is terminated. Accordingly, nearly all states have provisions in their insurance laws that require group life and medical expense policies to provide a conversion option to terminating participants. The federal government also has exercised its regulatory prerogative by passing laws, like COBRA, that protect terminated employees and that guarantee maternity cases will be treated the same as any other medical condition.

Key Concepts

In preparing for their licensing examination, students should be familiar with the following concepts:

- master policy
- contributory vs. noncontributory plans
- group major medical expense
- group AD&D
- conversion privilege
- COBRA
- MSA
- certificate of insurance
- group basic medical expense
- group disability income
- group health underwriting
- pre-existing conditions
- taxation of group health insurance

Unit Exam 13

1. Which of the following statements about group health insurance is CORRECT?
   A. The insurer, not the employer, stipulates the minimum number of persons that must be covered under a group plan.
   B. Group health plans provide more extensive benefits than individual health plans.
   C. If a group plan provides medical expense benefits, it must be with a comprehensive policy.
   D. COBRA requirements are directed at employers with 20 or fewer employees.

2. Which type of group health coverage typically does NOT contain a conversion privilege?
   A. Basic medical expense
   B. Comprehensive medical expense
   C. Disability income
   D. Accidental death and dismemberment

3. Which of the following can an individual include as *qualifying expenses* for purposes of determining a medical tax deduction?
   A. Premium contributions paid by the employer to a group medical expense plan
   B. Premium contributions paid by the employer to a group disability plan
   C. Premium contributions paid by the individual to a group medical expense plan
   D. Premium contributions paid by the individual to a group disability plan

4. An individual purchased group credit accident and health insurance to cover a car loan. Following an accident 2 months later, the individual was disabled for 8 months. Which of the following benefits were paid under the policy?
   A. Monthly income benefits to the insured
   B. An amount equal to 8 months of the loan payment to the insured's creditor
   C. An amount equal to 10 months of the loan payment to the insured's creditor
   D. Monthly income benefits to the insured and an amount equal to 8 months of the loan payment to the insured's creditor

5. Dan is a participant in his company's group health plan. One of the plan's provisions specifies that, in the event he is eligible for benefits under another policy, his group plan will serve as the primary plan. What is this provision called?
   A. Excess coverage
   B. Coordination of benefits
   C. Other insurance with this insurer
   D. Double indemnity

6. A vacation cruise line that wants group health coverage for its passengers would purchase what kind of insurance?
   A. Franchise health
   B. Wholesale health
   C. Blanket health
   D. Credit health

7. The purpose of COBRA requirements concerns
   A. coordination of health benefits
   B. continuation of health insurance
   C. Medicare supplement coverage
   D. nondiscrimination in group health plans

8. Sally is covered by her employer's noncontributory group disability income plan, the premium for which is $50 a month. If she were to become disabled and receive $1,000 a month, how much of each benefit payment would be taxable income to her?

   A. $0
   B. $50
   C. $950
   D. $1,000

9. Which of the following statements regarding group disability income plans is NOT correct?

   A. Benefits are specified in terms of a percentage of the participant's earnings.
   B. Benefits paid under the group plan are supplemental to workers' compensation benefits.
   C. Employees covered under both a short-term and long-term plan collect benefits from each simultaneously.
   D. A minimum length of service may be required before an employee is eligible to participate in the plan.

10. Which of the following statements about COBRA is CORRECT?

   A. The premium for continued group medical coverage may be up to 102% of the premium that otherwise would be charged.
   B. The employer must pay the cost of the continued group coverage.
   C. The schedule of benefits during the continuation period may be different than those provided under the group plan.
   D. COBRA permits an employee to convert a group certificate to an individual policy.

Unit Exam 13 Answers & Rationale

1. **B.** Group health plans generally provide more extensive benefits than individual plans. For example, some group plans offer individual benefit maximums of $1 million; others do not set any maximum benefit limits.

2. **D.** Group basic medical expense, comprehensive medical expense, and disability income insurance all typically contain a conversion privilege that allows the insureds to convert their group certificate to an individual policy when they leave their employment. Group AD&D policies do not contain conversion privileges.

3. **C.** Individual premium contributions to a group medical expense plan are deductible only when they and other unreimbursed medical expenses exceed 7.5% of an individual's adjusted gross income. Premium contributions made by the employer and those made by an employee for group disability coverage cannot be considered for purposes of determining a medical tax deduction.

4. **B.** A group credit accident and health plan is designed to help an insured pay off a loan if he or she becomes disabled. In this case, if the insured is disabled for 8 months, the policy will pay an amount equal to eight months of the loan payment to the insured's creditor.

5. **B.** A coordination of benefits provision establishes which plan is the primary plan when an insured is covered by another health plan.

6. **C.** A vacation cruise line would purchase blanket health insurance to provide group health insurance coverage for its passengers. This type of insurance is issued to cover a group that may be exposed to the same risks, but whose members are changing constantly.

7. **B.** COBRA requires employers to continue group medical expense coverage for terminated workers (and their families) for up to 36 months after termination.

8. **D.** Because Sally does not contribute toward the cost of the premium for the group disability income plan, all of the benefits she receives will be attributed to the premium her employer paid. As a result, she will have to report all of her monthly benefits ($1,000) as taxable income.

9. **C.** If an employer provides both a short-term and long-term disability plan, the long-term plan typically begins paying benefits only after the short-term benefits cease. Employees would not collect benefits from each plan simultaneously.

10. **A.** COBRA does not require the employer to pay for the cost of continued group coverage. The terminated employee can be required to pay the premium, which may be up to 102% of the premium that otherwise would be charged.

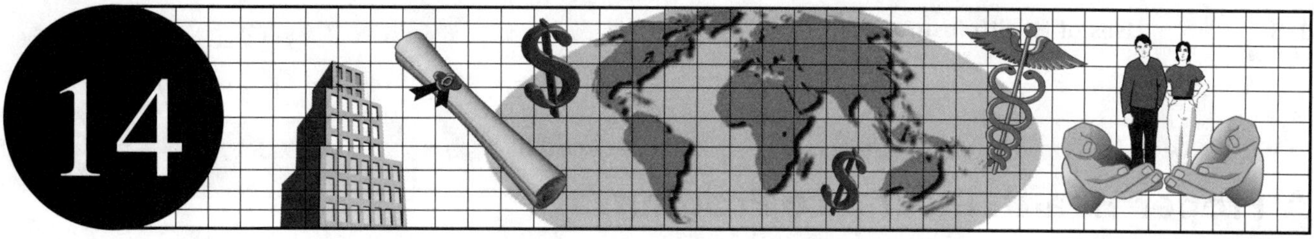

Uses of Health Insurance

INTRODUCTION

At first glance, it might seem that the uses of health insurance are self-explanatory: a person buys health insurance to protect against the cost of health care—or, more accurately, health insurance provides protection against the costs associated with losing one's health. However, health insurance plans can be used in a variety of ways to meet an individual's or business' unique needs. Individuals, for example, need to have a comprehensive health insurance plan in place to insure against the financial consequences of illness or disability. Similarly, health insurance also is necessary to protect a business against the risks it faces, including losses due to a key employee's death or disability. Businesses also commonly offer health insurance as part of an employee benefits program. In this unit, we will take a closer look at ways in which individuals and businesses use health insurance.

UNIT OBJECTIVES

When you complete this unit you should be able to:

- describe the importance of medical expense insurance and disability income insurance in an individual's total health insurance plan;
- explain how group health and disability insurance differ from individual coverage;
- list the advantages of offering health insurance as part of an employee benefits plan; and
- explain how business overhead expense insurance, health insurance, and disability buy-out plans are used to help businesses continue if an owner becomes disabled or injured.

A Proper Health Insurance Program

In order to design the proper health insurance program, several questions must be addressed. First, who is to be covered? The insurance needs of individuals, families, and businesses vary widely, as do the insurance products available to each. Second, is the needed coverage currently provided by a group plan or social insurance program? Third, how much responsibility for medical care expenses is the policyowner able (and willing) to assume through policy deductibles and coinsurance in exchange for reduced premiums? Only through a careful consideration of these and other questions can an insurance producer develop an insurance program that satisfies the distinctive needs of business, family, and individual clients.

Individual Needs for Health Insurance

At one time it was acceptable to expect one's family to provide support when illness or disability struck. Those days are now long past; today, we all must prepare for and assume the responsibility of covering the cost of medical care for ourselves. However, unless one is independently wealthy, the prospect of covering costs out-of-pocket is not an attractive one; indeed, it can be downright terrifying.

The loss of one's health can have wide-ranging consequences. Not only does the cost of medical care come with a high price tag, but the loss of income that often accompanies a disabling illness or injury can compound the devastating effects of the health loss. Current demographics, which show that both parents in most families are working, emphasize the importance of considering both parents' income needs when designing a complete health insurance program.

Medical Expense Insurance Needs

While it is difficult to measure the importance of one type of insurance over another, it is fair to presume that a health insurance program must begin with an adequate amount of medical expense insurance. Without proper protection devoted to these potential costs, even the most basic medical care can exhaust an individual's savings quickly; a catastrophic claim can spell financial disaster.

At one time, most medical policies were the basic medical expense type. However, today it is more common to find most Americans covered under some form of a major medical policy or a service plan such as Blue Cross/Blue Shield or an HMO. If the policyowner can afford the cost, an ideal policy is a combination plan in which a basic plan is enhanced by a supplementary major medical plan. Under this approach, the insured obtains the first dollar benefits of the basic plan and also has the expansive protection offered by the major medical plan.

Most policyowners, of course, are concerned with the cost of their health insurance and find that some financial sacrifice may be required. For example, an individual major medical plan with a $100 individual deductible is going to cost more than a comparable plan with a $500 deductible. A plan with an 80/20 coinsurance provision will cost more than a comparable plan with a 75/25 coinsurance provision. The question the policyowner must answer is: Am I willing to assume more of the cost risk of possible future claims in exchange for the definite cost savings offered by a plan with a higher deductible or coinsurance limit?

Group vs. Individual Coverage

More Americans are protected under group medical expense policies than individual policies. The benefit to the group member, even assuming the plan is contributory, is the significantly reduced out-of-pocket cost compared to an individual plan. The group plan participant can take comfort in knowing that even if he should terminate employment, continued coverage is guaranteed through the conversion privilege built into every group health policy.

Disability Income Insurance Needs

The importance of protecting one's earnings sometimes is overlooked in the insurance needs analysis process—a regrettable fact for the many people who become disabled every year. Americans too often assume that Social Security will provide the income necessary to survive if disability strikes. This is an unfortunate assumption; not only is the definition of disabled to qualify for Social Security benefits extremely narrow, but no assurance exists that the benefits will meet the disabled person's needs.

✓ ***Take Note:*** Social Security disability income should be viewed as a possible source of income to augment a personal plan. Whether the personal plan is based on a group policy or an individual policy, it should be regarded as the primary source of income if earnings are lost due to disability.

Policyowners can control the premium cost of a disability income plan by electing a longer elimination period than might otherwise be desired. The length of the benefit period also has a direct impact on the premium.

Because of the favorable tax treatment given to individually funded disability income policies, a plan that provides about 60% of predisability gross earnings can be considered sufficient. This is because disability income benefits are income tax free if the individual insured paid the premiums.

✓ ***For Example:*** An individual who earns $3,000 each month may only take home $2,000 after taxes. Consequently, a disability plan that provides a monthly tax-free benefit of $1,800 likely would be sufficient.

In the case of group disability income plans, the group member has little choice as to the level of benefits provided; the plan document must have a schedule of benefits that identifies what the participant will receive if she is disabled. On the other hand, the group member benefits to the extent the employer contributes to the disability income premiums.

If both parents in a family are employed, then disability income must be considered for each. If each parent's income is indispensable for the financial support of the family, then it is safe to assume that the loss of either income would present a financial problem.

Business Needs for Health Insurance

Many health insurance producers have found a niche servicing the business market. There is a good, practical reason for this—the health insurance needs of the business market are as great as the needs of individuals.

Business uses of health insurance can be divided broadly into two categories: employee benefit plans and business continuation plans.

Employee Benefit Plans

Although any given employee benefit plan can offer a wide variety of benefits—life insurance, a pension or profit-sharing plan, vacation pay, deferred compensation arrangements, funeral leave, sick time—such plans almost always include some kind of provision for health insurance or health benefits. The large and rapid increases in the cost of health care likely are the primary reasons for the popularity of employer-sponsored health plans, and many people rely on these plans as their sole source of health insurance.

Group Health Insurance

As we have learned, a group health plan can consist of medical insurance, disability income insurance, and accidental death and dismemberment insurance alone or in any combination. In fact, it is not uncommon to find all of these coverages included in a single group insurance plan.

✓ ***Take Note:*** By providing its employees with a plan for health insurance, an employer derives a number of benefits:

- The plan contributes to employee morale and productivity.
- The plan enables the employer to provide a needed benefit that employees otherwise would have to pay for with personal after-tax dollars (this helps minimize demands for wage increases).
- The plan places the employer in a competitive position for hiring and retaining employees.
- The employer can obtain a tax deduction for the cost of contributing to the plan.
- The plan enhances the employer's image in both public and employee relations.

Cafeteria Plans

Many times, employer-provided health insurance benefits are part of a cafeteria plan. As the name implies, cafeteria plans (also known as Section 125 plans) are benefit arrangements in which employees can pick and choose from a menu of benefits, thus tailoring their benefits package to their specific needs. Employees can select the benefits they value or need and forgo those of lesser importance to them. The employer allocates a certain amount of money to each employee to purchase the benefits he desires. If the cost of the benefits exceeds the allocation, the employee may contribute the balance.

The types of flexible benefits usually available under a cafeteria plan include medical coverage, accidental death and dismemberment insurance, short-term and long-term disability, life insurance, and dependent care. Some plans provide for choices within the choices: an employee may have the option of selecting from levels of medical plans or choosing from a variety of HMOs, for instance.

Business Continuation Plans

Just as life insurance provides a way to help a business continue in the event an owner or key employee dies, health insurance also serves continuation purposes in the event of a disabling sickness or injury. It does so through the following plans.

Business Overhead Expense Insurance

Business overhead expense insurance is designed to reimburse a business for overhead expenses in the event a business owner becomes disabled. It is sold on an individual basis to professionals in private practice, self-employed business owners, partners, and occasionally close corporations.

Test Topic Alert! Business overhead expense insurance does not cover the lost income of the disabled business owner.

Overhead expenses include rent or mortgage payments, utilities, telephones, leased equipment, employees' salaries, and the like—all the expenses that must be paid regardless of the owner's disability.

✓ ***Take Note:*** Business overhead expense policies do not include any compensation for the disabled owner. They are designed to help the day-to-day operations of her business during the period of disability.

The benefits payable under these kinds of policies are limited to the covered expenses incurred or the maximum that is stated in the policy.

✓ ***For Example:*** Dr. Miller is the insured under a business overhead expense policy that pays maximum monthly benefits of $4,500. If Dr. Miller became disabled and actual monthly expenses were $3,950, the monthly benefits paid would be $3,950. If Dr. Miller's actual expenses were $4,700, the benefits payable would be $4,500.

The premium for business overhead insurance is a legitimate, tax-deductible business expense. The benefits when paid, however, are treated as taxable income.

Business Health Insurance

Business health insurance is available to indemnify a business for the loss of the services of a key employee, a partner, or an owner should disability strike. In the event of a disability, this insurance provides the business with funds to bridge the period necessary to secure and train a worthy successor.

Determining the precise economic loss a business will face if a key individual becomes disabled is somewhat difficult; the cost of securing an experienced, competent replacement or the income the employee or owner currently earns are two common approaches to making this determination.

Disability Buy-Outs

A disability buy-sell agreement operates in much the same way as a life insurance buy-sell agreement. However, in this case, the plan sets forth the terms for selling and buying a partner's or stock owner's share of a business in the event she becomes disabled and is unable to participate in the business. It is a legal, binding arrangement, funded with a disability income policy.

Unlike typical disability income insurance plans that pay benefits in the form of periodic payments, the buy-out plan usually contains a provision allowing for a lump-sum payment of the benefit (also called an elective indemnity), thereby facilitating the buy-out of the disabled's interest. However, if the owners desire, the plan often permits the buy-out to occur through the use of periodic income payments.

Disability buy-out plans are characterized by lengthy elimination periods, often as long as two years. The reason for this is simple: because the plan involves the sale of a disabled partner's or owner's interest in the business, it is important to be quite sure that the disabled person will not be able to return to the business.

Considering the fact that a disabled partner can represent a double liability—the remaining partners must not only take up the slack left by the disabled partner's absence but usually must pay him an income as well—it is understandable that the disability buy-out plan is popular with business owners.

Summary

The uses of health insurance—notably medical expense and disability income—are as varied as the need for it is vital. Both the personal market and the business market have many uses for these important insurance products. Often the insured's concern is not whether she needs it, but whether she can afford it. Fortunately, every type of health insurance plan offers some way for the owner to reduce premium costs, including increasing the deductible or lengthening the elimination period.

Key Concepts

In preparing for their licensing examination, students should be familiar with the following concepts:

- individual vs. group health insurance
- business overhead expense insurance
- disability buy-out insurance
- employee benefit plans
- business health insurance

Unit Exam 14

1. All of the following are methods of keeping premium costs to a minimum in a health policy EXCEPT
   A. modifying benefit amounts
   B. increasing the deductible
   C. waiving the right to receive benefit payments when due
   D. extending the elimination period

2. Fred owns a small hardware store and is covered under a business overhead expense policy. If he becomes disabled, he can expect all the following expenses to be covered EXCEPT
   A. his employees' salaries
   B. his salary
   C. utility bills
   D. property and liability insurance premiums

3. Which of the following characteristics is associated with disability buy-out plans?
   A. A short elimination period
   B. The option to elect a lump-sum payment
   C. Provisions to cover the business' overhead expenses
   D. Irrevocable agreements

4. What is the income tax consequence if Marie's employer pays for her group disability income coverage?
   A. The premium payments are taxable income to her.
   B. The premium payments are tax deductible by her.
   C. The employer receives the disability income benefits tax free.
   D. The employer can take a tax deduction for the cost of premiums it pays.

5. With regard to health insurance policies, which of the following statements is CORRECT?
   A. A major medical plan with a $100 deductible is less expensive than one with a $500 deductible.
   B. More Americans are covered by an individual medical expense policy than by a group policy.
   C. The appropriate benefit payable under a disability income policy should equal the insured's monthly gross income.
   D. A disability policy with a 6-month elimination period is less expensive than one with a 60-day elimination period, all other factors being equal.

Unit Exam 14 Answers & Rationale

1. **C.** A person can minimize premium costs by modifying benefit amounts, increasing the deductible, and extending the elimination period. Waiving the right to receive benefit payments when due will not minimize premium expenses.

2. **B.** Business overhead expense insurance is designed to help a business' day-to-day operations continue during the owner's disability. As a result, Fred's policy would cover his employees' salaries, the utility bills, and the store's property and liability insurance premiums. His policy would not, however, cover his own compensation.

3. **B.** A disability buy-sell plan usually contains a provision allowing for benefits to be paid in a lump sum. However, if the owners desire, a plan may permit the buy-out to occur through using periodic income payments.

4. **D.** If Mary's employer pays for her group disability income coverage, it can take a tax deduction equal to the cost of its premiums. The premium payments will not constitute taxable income to Mary, nor will she be able to take a tax deduction for them.

5. **D.** Policyowners can control the premium cost of a disability income plan by electing a longer elimination period. As a result, a disability policy with a 6-month elimination period will be less expensive than one with only a 60-day period, all other factors being equal.

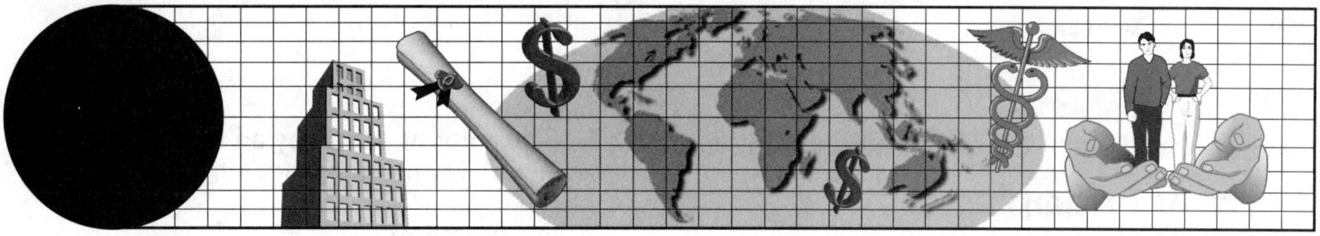

Final Exam

Remember to read the entire question before selecting an answer. Some responses may seem correct, but a careful reading may prove otherwise. Words like "all," "may," "shall," "not," and "except" can change the answer. All questions have a single correct response and are based on information found in this text.

General Principles

1. In the insurance business, risk can best be defined as

   A. sharing the possibility of a loss
   B. uncertainty regarding the future
   C. uncertainty regarding financial loss
   D. uncertainty regarding when death will occur

2. Which of the following risks is insurable?

   A. Pure
   B. Gambling
   C. Speculative
   D. Investing

3. Buying insurance is one of the most effective ways of

   A. avoiding risk
   B. transferring risk
   C. reducing risk
   D. retaining risk

4. Which of the following best describes the function of insurance?

   A. It is a form of legalized gambling.
   B. It spreads financial risk over a large group to minimize the loss to any one individual.
   C. It protects against living too long.
   D. It creates and protects risks.

5. Which of the following statements about insurable risk is NOT correct?

   A. The loss must be due to chance.
   B. The loss must be predictable.
   C. The loss must be catastrophic.
   D. The loss must have a determinable value.

6. The amount of money an insurer sets aside to pay future claims is called the

   A. premium
   B. reserve
   C. dividend
   D. accumulated interest

7. Which of the following constitutes an insurable interest?

   A. The policyowner must expect to benefit from the insured's death.
   B. The policyowner must expect to suffer a loss when the insured dies or becomes disabled.
   C. The beneficiary, by definition, has an insurable interest in the insured.
   D. The insured must have a personal or business relationship with the beneficiary.

8. Which of the following statements describes the parol evidence rule?

   A. A written contract cannot be changed once it is signed.
   B. An oral contract cannot be modified by written evidence.
   C. A written contract cannot be changed by oral evidence.
   D. An oral contract takes precedence over any earlier written contracts.

9. Which of the following factors determines whether policy dividends will be paid on a participating policy?

   A. Reserves and experience
   B. Expenses and claims costs
   C. Interest and benefits
   D. Premiums and renewability

10. Whom does a licensed agent legally represent?

    A. The insurer
    B. The applicant/insured
    C. The state insurance department
    D. Himself or herself

11. Which of the following statements regarding policy replacement is NOT correct?

    A. Replacement involves convincing a policyholder to lapse or terminate an existing policy and purchase another.
    B. Interrupting one cash value insurance plan to begin another could cause serious financial problems for the policyowner.
    C. Even if the customer wants to replace his existing policy, an agent can effect a policy replacement only by following the replacement regulations in his state.
    D. Premiums for replacement policies are lower generally than premiums for the existing policies they replace.

12. With regard to insurable risks, which of the following statements is NOT correct?

    A. Only pure risks are insurable.
    B. An insurable risk must involve loss that is within the insured's control.
    C. Insurers will not insure risks that are catastrophic in nature.
    D. An insurable risk must be measurable.

13. On August 9, Albert made an application for life insurance that his agent submitted a day later without a premium payment. On August 21, the insurer issued the policy as applied for, and on August 24, the agent delivered the policy and collected the initial premium. On what day was the contract offer made?

    A. August 9
    B. August 10
    C. August 21
    D. August 24

14. All statements made by an applicant in an application for life insurance are considered to be

    A. warranties
    B. affirmations
    C. representations
    D. declarations

15. Which of the following legal terms indicates that a life insurance contract contains the enforceable promises of only 1 party?

    A. Adhesion
    B. Unilateral
    C. Conditional
    D. Aleatory

16. Which of the following types of agent authority is specifically set forth in writing in the agent's contract?

    A. Express
    B. Implied
    C. Apparent
    D. Personal

17. If a home catches fire after it is struck by lightning and the fire destroys its structure and contents, by insurance definition, the fire is the

    A. risk
    B. hazard
    C. peril
    D. proximate cause

18. What constitutes consideration for a life insurance policy?

    A. Application and initial premium
    B. Agent's commission
    C. Adhesion feature of the contract
    D. Policy's benefits

19. Statements made by an applicant for life insurance that are guaranteed to be true are

    A. warranties
    B. material statements
    C. representations
    D. declarations

20. Which of the following types of insurance company is owned by its policyholders?

    A. Service insurer
    B. Stock insurer
    C. Reinsurer
    D. Mutual insurer

Principles of Health Insurance

21. On August 1, Roger completed an application for a major medical policy, gave his agent a check for the initial premium and received an insurability receipt from the agent. No medical examination was required. On August 3, the agent submitted Roger's application and premium to the insurance company. On August 6, Roger was involved in an accident and admitted to a hospital. On August 12, the agent received Roger's policy from the insurance company. Which of the following statements concerning this situation is CORRECT?

    A. Roger's coverage will begin when he receives the policy from the agent.
    B. Roger's coverage began when he received the insurability receipt.
    C. Roger's coverage began the day the insurance company received the application and premium from the agent.
    D. Roger's coverage began the day the agent sent the application and premium to the insurance company.

22. Beth's health insurance policy contains a provision that allows her to renew coverage up to age 65. However, the policy also states that should Beth lose her job, the insurance company will cancel the policy, regardless of Beth's age. In terms of renewability, what type of policy does Beth have?

    A. Cancellable
    B. Optionally renewable
    C. Guaranteed renewable
    D. Conditionally renewable

23. HMOs are known for stressing which of the following?

    A. Preventive care
    B. Health care and services on a fee-for-services-rendered basis
    C. Health care and services in hospital settings
    D. Health care and services to government employees

24. Which of the following statements is NOT true of PPOs?

    A. A PPO is a group of health care providers, such as doctors, hospitals, and ambulatory health care organizations, that contracts with a group to provide their services.
    B. PPOs operate on a prepaid basis.
    C. PPO members select from among the preferred providers for needed services.
    D. Groups that contract with PPOs are employers, insurance companies, or other health insurance benefits providers.

25. All of the following benefits are available under Social Security EXCEPT

    A. welfare
    B. death
    C. old age or retirement
    D. disability

26. Which of the following kinds of assistance is provided by Medicaid?

    A. Funds to states for the provision of medical care to the aged
    B. Funds to states to assist their medical public assistance programs
    C. Funds to charitable organizations for providing medical benefits to poor people
    D. Medical benefits to those who contributed to its funding through payroll taxes

27. Mr. Ritchie, a taxidermist, is insured under a business overhead expense policy that pays maximum monthly benefits of $2,000. His actual monthly expenses are $2,700. If Mr. Ritchie becomes disabled, the monthly benefit payable under his policy will be

    A. $1,300
    B. $2,000
    C. $2,350
    D. $2,700

28. Which of the following statements about Medicare supplement (Medigap) policies is NOT correct?

    A. Medigap policies supplement Medicare benefits.
    B. Medigap policies cover the cost of extended nursing home care.
    C. Medigap policies pay most, if not all, Medicare deductibles and copayments.
    D. Medigap policies pay for some health care services not covered by Medicare.

29. Which of the following is NOT a typical type of long-term care coverage?

    A. Skilled nursing
    B. Home health
    C. Hospice
    D. Residential

30. All of the following are mandatory provisions in health insurance policies EXCEPT

    A. proof of loss
    B. entire contract
    C. change of beneficiary
    D. misstatement of age

31. Under the notice of claims provision of a health insurance policy, a policyowner must provide notification of loss within a reasonable period of time, usually how long?

    A. 10 days after an occurrence or a commencement of a loss
    B. 20 days after an occurrence or a commencement of a loss
    C. 1 month after an occurrence or a commencement of a loss
    D. No later than three months after an occurrence or a commencement of a loss

32. Paul is hospitalized with a back injury and, upon checking his disability income policy, learns that he will not be eligible for benefits for at least 60 days. This would indicate that his policy probably has a 60-day

    A. elimination period
    B. probationary period
    C. disability period
    D. blackout period

33. Major risk factors in health insurance underwriting include all of the following EXCEPT

    A. physical condition
    B. habits or lifestyle
    C. marital status
    D. occupation

34. Which of the following is known for stressing preventive health care?

    A. Administrative-services-only providers
    B. Blue Cross/Blue Shield
    C. HMOs
    D. Commercial insurers

35. Leonard owns a major medical health policy which requires him to pay the first $200 of covered expenses each year before the policy pays its benefits. The $200 is the policy's

A. coinsurance amount
B. deductible
C. stop-loss amount
D. annual premium

36. Basic hospital expense insurance provides coverage for all of the following EXCEPT

A. hospital room and board
B. anesthesia and use of the operating room and supplies
C. physician services
D. drugs and x-rays

37. All of the following approaches are used by insurers to determine benefits payable under basic surgical expense insurance EXCEPT

A. relative value scale approach
B. traditional net cost method
C. reasonable and customary approach
D. surgical schedule method

38. Basic surgical expense policies generally provide coverage for all of the following EXCEPT

A. anesthesiologist services
B. surgeon services
C. postoperative care
D. miscellaneous expenses, such as lab fees and x-rays

39. A waiver of premium provision may be included with which kind of health insurance policy?

A. Hospital indemnity
B. Major medical
C. Disability income
D. Basic medical

40. The minimum number of persons to be insured under a group health insurance plan is established by

A. the NAIC
B. state law
C. federal law
D. the employer

41. Alice has a major medical policy with a $500 deductible and an 80/20 coinsurance provision. If she receives a hospital bill for $7,500 of covered expenses, how much of that bill will she have to pay?

A. $1,400
B. $1,900
C. $2,000
D. $2,400

42. Which of the following reimburses its insureds for covered medical expenses?

A. HMOs
B. PPOs
C. Commercial insurers
D. Blue Cross/Blue Shield

43. Individual health insurance policies are typically written on which basis?

A. Participating
B. Nonparticipating
C. Experience-rated
D. Claims-rated

44. Workers' compensation covers income loss resulting from

A. work-related disabilities
B. plant and office closings
C. job layoffs
D. job terminations

45. As it pertains to group health insurance, COBRA stipulates that

    A. retiring employees must be allowed to convert their group coverage to individual policies
    B. terminated employees must be allowed to convert their group coverage to individual policies
    C. group coverage must be extended for terminated employees up to a certain period of time at the employee's expense
    D. group coverage must be extended for terminated employees up to a certain period of time at the employer's expense

46. Which of the following statements regarding morbidity tables is CORRECT?

    A. They indicate the average number of individuals from a given group who will die in a given year.
    B. They indicate the average number of individuals from a given group who will become disabled.
    C. They indicate the sex and number of individuals from a given group who will die in a given year.
    D. They indicate the sex and number of individuals from a given group who will become disabled in a given year.

47. All of the following are primary health insurance premium factors EXCEPT

    A. interest
    B. expense
    C. policy benefits
    D. morbidity

48. When a group disability insurance plan is paid entirely by the employer, benefits paid to disabled employees are

    A. taxable income to the employee
    B. deductible income to the employee
    C. deductible business expenses to the employer
    D. taxable income to the employer

49. Harry, the owner of a convenience store, is the insured under a business overhead policy. Were Harry to become disabled, the policy would cover all of the following EXCEPT

    A. his salary
    B. the store manager's salary
    C. the rent
    D. utility bills

50. All of the following are mandatory health insurance policy provisions EXCEPT

    A. change of occupation
    B. entire contract
    C. grace period
    D. reinstatement

51. Which renewability provision allows an insurer to terminate a health insurance policy on any date specified in the policy and to increase the premium for any class of insureds?

    A. Conditionally renewable
    B. Optionally renewable
    C. Guaranteed renewable
    D. Cancellable

52. What does the time of payment of claims provision require?

    A. Claims must be paid after the insurer is notified of a loss.
    B. Claims must be paid after the insurer is notified and receives proof of loss.
    C. The insured must submit proof of loss within a specified time, or the claim may be denied.
    D. The insured must periodically submit proof of loss in order to receive the claim.

53. By most insurers' definitions, *partial disability* is the

    A. loss of one or more limbs
    B. ability of a disabled insured to work at any job for which he is reasonably suited
    C. inability of the insured to work at his own job
    D. inability of the insured to perform certain important duties of his job

54. What is the period of time immediately following a disability during which benefits are not payable?

    A. Elimination period
    B. Probationary period
    C. Residual period
    D. Short-term disability period

55. All of the following are characteristics of group health insurance plans EXCEPT

    A. their benefits are more extensive than those under individual plans
    B. the parties to a group health contract are the employer and the employees
    C. employers may require employees to contribute to the premium payments
    D. the cost of insuring an individual is less than what would be charged for comparable benefits under an individual plan

56. Bill's medical expense policy states that it will pay him a flat $50 a day for each day he is hospitalized. The policy pays benefits on which basis?

    A. Reimbursement
    B. Indemnity
    C. Service
    D. Partial

57. After a week in the hospital, Lola receives a bill for $9,000 of covered expenses. Her major medical policy has a $250 deductible and a 75/25 coinsurance feature. How much of the total expense will Lola's policy cover?

    A. $2,063
    B. $6,063
    C. $6,563
    D. $8,753

58. A basic surgical expense policy that covers surgeons' fees on a schedule approach

    A. bases its benefits on what is customary for a particular area
    B. assigns a set of points to each surgical procedure
    C. assigns a dollar amount to each surgical procedure
    D. bases its benefits on a percentage of hospital room and board expenses

59. A stop-loss feature in a major medical policy specifies the maximum

A. benefit amount the policy provides each year
B. benefit amount the policy provides in a lifetime
C. amount the insured must pay in premiums
D. amount the insured must pay toward covered expenses

60. Which of the following is a standard optional provision for health policies?

A. Grace period
B. Physical exam and autopsy
C. Change of beneficiary
D. Misstatement of age

General Principles Answers & Rationale

1. **C.** The concept of insurance developed from the need to minimize the adverse effects of risk associated with the probability of financial loss.

2. **A.** Only pure risks are insurable because they involve merely the chance of loss. They are pure in the sense that they do not mix both profits and losses. Insurance is concerned with the economic problems created by pure risks.

3. **B.** Buying insurance is one of the most effective ways of transferring risk. Through the insurance contract, the burden of carrying the risk and indemnifying the financial loss is transferred from the individual to the insurance company.

4. **B.** The function of insurance is to safeguard against financial loss by having the losses of the few paid by the contributions of the many who are exposed to the same risk.

5. **C.** One qualifier for an insurable risk is that it not be catastrophic. A principle of insurance holds that only a small portion of a given group will experience loss at any one time. Risks that would adversely affect large numbers of people or large amounts of property—wars or floods, for example—typically are not insurable.

6. **B.** Reserves can be defined as the amounts set aside to fulfill the insurance company's obligation to pay future claims. The reserve is compiled from past premium payments and interest.

7. **B.** Insurable interest requires the policyowner to benefit from the insured's continued life or good health or to suffer a loss from the insured's death or disability.

8. **C.** The parol evidence rule states that when parties put their agreement in writing, all previous verbal statements come together in that writing, and a written contract cannot be changed or modified by parol (oral) evidence.

9. **B.** If expenses and claims costs are less than expected, dividends are likely to be paid.

10. **A.** An agent is an individual who has been authorized by an insurer to be its representative to the public and to offer for sale its goods and services.

11. **D.** The new policy will probably be at a higher premium rate because it will be based on the insured's then-attained age.

12. **B.** To be insurable, a risk must involve a chance of loss that is fortuitous and outside the insured's control.

13. **C.** If an applicant does not submit an initial premium with the application, he is inviting the insurance company to make a contract offer. The insurer can respond by issuing a policy (the offer) that the applicant can accept by paying the premium when the policy is delivered.

14. **C.** Most states require that life insurance policies contain a provision which stipulates that all statements made in the application be deemed representations, not warranties. A representation is a statement made by the applicant that he believes to be true. A warranty is a statement made by the applicant that is guaranteed to be true. If an insurance company rejects a claim on the basis of a representation, the company bears the burden of proving materiality.

15. **B.** Insurance contracts are unilateral in that only 1 party—the insurer—makes any kind of enforceable promise.

16. **A.** Express authority is the authority a principal gives to its agent. It is granted by means of the agent's contract, which is the principal's appointment of the agent to act on its behalf.

17. **C.** A peril is the immediate specific event causing loss and giving rise to risk. When a building burns, fire is the peril.

18. **A**. Consideration is the value given in exchange for the promises sought. In an insurance contract, consideration is given by the applicant in exchange for the insurer's promise to pay benefits and it consists of the application and the initial premium.

19. **A**. A warranty in insurance is a statement made by the applicant that is guaranteed to be true. It becomes part of the contract and, if found to be untrue, can be grounds for revoking the contract. Warranties are presumed to be material because they affect the insurer's decision to accept or reject an applicant.

20. **D**. Mutual insurers are owned by the policyholders. Anyone purchasing insurance from a mutual insurer is both a customer and an owner.

Principles of Health Insurance Answers & Rationale

21. **B.** The insurability type of conditional receipt provides that when an applicant pays the initial premium, coverage is effective—on the condition that the applicant proves to be insurable—either on the date the application was signed or the date of the medical examination, if one is required.

22. **D.** A conditionally renewable policy allows an insurer to terminate the coverage, but only in the event of one or more conditions stated in the contract. These conditions cannot apply to the insured's health. Most frequently, they are related to the insured reaching a certain age or losing gainful employment.

23. **A.** HMOs stress preventive care to reduce the number of unnecessary hospital admissions and duplication of services.

24. **B.** Unlike HMOs, PPOs usually operate on a fee-for-service-rendered basis, not a prepaid basis.

25. **A.** Social Security provides death benefits, old age or retirement benefits, and disability benefits to eligible workers. Social Security is an entitlement program, not a welfare program.

26. **B.** Medicaid provides matching federal funds to states for their medical public assistance programs to help needy persons, regardless of age.

27. **B.** Business overhead expense insurance reimburses business for the covered expenses incurred or the maximum that is stated in the policy. If Mr. Ritchie's monthly expenses were $1,700, his plan would have paid a monthly benefit of $1,700. However, because Mr. Ritchie's expenses exceeded his maximum coverage, the policy pays the maximum benefit stated in the policy, $2,000.

28. **B.** Medigap policies do not cover the cost of extended nursing home care.

29. **C.** Long-term care services are designed for senior citizens, and hospice services are for terminally ill persons and their families.

30. **D.** Mis-statement of age is an optional provision of health insurance policies.

31. **B.** Under the notice of claims provision, an insured must provide notification of loss 20 days after an occurrence or a commencement of a loss.

32. **A.** Similar in concept to a deductible, the elimination period is the time immediately following the start of a disability when benefits are not payable.

33. **C.** Physical condition, habits, or lifestyle (moral hazards), and occupation are major risk factors in health insurance. Marital status is not a risk factor.

34. **C.** Health maintenance organizations stress preventive care to promote patient health and to control the use of health care resources, particularly expensive resources like hospitals.

35. **B.** A deductible is a stated initial dollar amount that the individual insured is required to pay before insurance benefits are paid.

36. **C.** Physicians' services are not covered under a basic hospital expense policy, even in the case of surgery. The cost for a physician is covered under a basic surgical expense or basic physician's (nonsurgical) expense policy.

37. **B.** The traditional net cost method is a way of comparing costs of similar policies.

38. **D.** Miscellaneous expenses are covered under basic hospital expense policies. These extras include drugs, x-rays, anesthesia, lab fees, dressings, use of the operating room, and supplies.

39. **C.** A waiver of premium rider generally is included with guaranteed renewable and noncancellable individual disability income policies. It is a valuable provision because it exempts the policyowner from paying the policy's premiums during periods of total disability.

40. **B.** State laws specify the minimum number of persons to be covered under a group policy. One state may stipulate 15 persons as a minimum number, while another state may require a minimum of 10. (Ten is a typical minimum requirement.)

41. **B.** Alice's responsibility for payment is calculated in the following manner:

Total expenses	$ 7,500
Deductible Alice pays	– 500
Basis for insurer's payment	$ 7,000
	× .80
Amount insurer pays	$ 5,600
Coinsurance amount Alice pays	$ 1,400
Deductible	+ 500
Total Alice pays	$ 1,900

42. **C.** Commercial insurance companies function on the reimbursement approach. Policyowners obtain medical treatment from whatever source they feel is most appropriate and, per the terms of their policy, submit their charges to their insurer for reimbursement.

43. **B.** Most individual health insurance is issued on a nonparticipating basis.

44. **A.** All states have workers' compensation laws, which were enacted to provide mandatory benefits to employees for work-related injuries, illness, or death.

45. **C.** COBRA requires employers with 20 or more employees to continue group medical expense coverage for terminated workers (as well as their spouses, divorced spouses, and dependent children) for up to 18 months (or 36 months, in some situations) following termination. However, the terminated employee can be required to pay the premium, which may be up to 102% of the premium that would otherwise be charged.

46. **B.** Whereas mortality rates show the average number of persons within a larger group of people who can be expected to die within a given year at a given age, morbidity tables indicate the average number of individuals at various ages who can be expected to become disabled each year due to accident or sickness. They also reveal the average duration of disability.

47. **C.** There are 3 primary factors that affect health insurance premiums: morbidity, interest, and expenses.

48. **A.** Disability benefit payments that are attributed to employee contributions are not taxable, but benefit payments that are attributed to employer contributions are taxable.

49. **A.** Business overhead expense policies do not include any compensation for the disabled owner.

50. **A.** Change of occupation is an optional provision.

51. **B.** The renewability provision in an optionally renewable policy gives the insurer the option to terminate the policy on the date specified in the contract. Furthermore, this provision allows the insurer to increase the premium for any class of optionally renewable insureds.

52. **B.** The time of payment of claims provision provides for immediate payment of the claim after the insurer receives notification and proof of loss.

53. **D.** By most definitions, partial disability is the inability of the insured to perform one or more important duties of his job.

54. **A.** The elimination period is the time immediately following the start of a disability when benefits are not payable. Elimination periods eliminate claims for short-term disabilities for which the insured can usually manage without financial hardship and save the insurance

company from the expense of processing and settling small claims.

55. **B.** The contract for coverage is between the insurance company and the employer, and a master policy is issued to the employer.

56. **B.** Indemnity medical expense policies do not pay expenses or bills; they merely provide the insured with a stated benefit amount for each day he is confined to a hospital as an in-patient. The money may be used by the insured for any purpose.

57. **C.** Lola's responsibility for payment is calculated in the following manner:

Total expenses	$ 9,000
Deductible Lola pays	– 250
Basis for insurer's payment	$ 8,750
	× .75
Amount insurer pays	$ 6,563
Coinsurance Lola pays	$ 2,187

58. **C.** Under the surgical schedule method, every surgical procedure is assigned a dollar amount by the insurer. When a claim is submitted to the insurer, the claims examiner reviews the policy to determine what amount is payable; if the surgeon's bill is more than the allowed charge set by the insurer, it is up to the insured to pay the surgeon the difference. If the surgeon's bill is less than the allowed charge, the insurer will pay only the full amount billed; the claim payment will never exceed the amount charged.

59. **D.** To provide a safeguard for insureds, many major medical policies contain a stop-loss feature that limits the insured's out-of-pocket expenses. This means that once the insured has paid a specified amount toward her covered expenses—usually $1,000 to $2,000—the company pays 100% of covered expenses after that point.

60. **D.** Misstatement of age is one of 11 optional policy provisions. Companies may ignore them or use them in their policy forms.

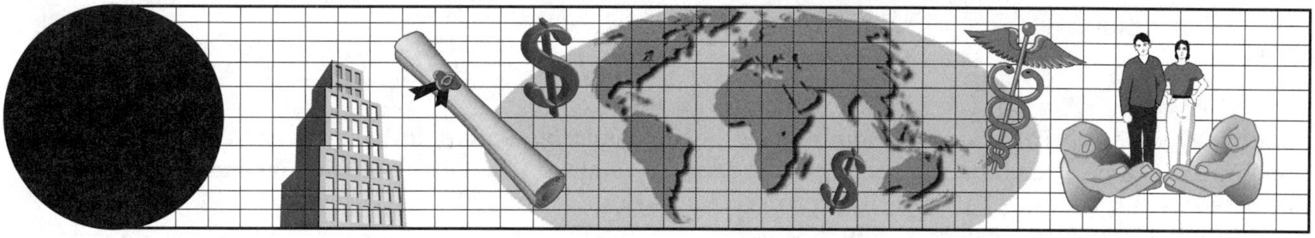

Glossary

A

absolute assignment A policy assignment under which the assignee (person to whom the policy is assigned) receives full control over the policy and also full rights to its benefits. Generally, when a policy is assigned to secure a debt, the owner retains all rights in the policy in excess of the debt, even though the assignment is absolute in form. *See also* assignee; assignment; assignor.

accelerated benefits rider A life insurance rider that allows for the early payment of some portion of the policy's face amount should the insured suffer from a terminal illness or injury.

acceptance One party's agreement to the purchase offer of another party, such that a legal contract is formed and both parties are contractually bound. With an insurance contract, acceptance generally takes place when the agent binds coverage or the policy is issued. *See also* offer and acceptance.

accidental bodily injury provision A disability income or accident policy provision that requires that the injury be accidental in order for benefits to be payable.

accidental death and dismemberment (AD&D) This is insurance that provides payment if the insured's death results from an accident, if the insured accidentally severs a limb above the wrist or ankle joints, or totally and irreversibly loses his or her eyesight.

accidental death benefit rider A life insurance policy rider that provides for payment of an additional benefit related to the face amount of the base policy when death occurs by accidental means.

accidental dismemberment Often defined as the severance of limbs at or above the wrists or ankle joints, or the entire irrevocable loss of sight. Loss of use in itself may or may not be considered dismemberment.

accidental means provision The unforeseen, unexpected or unintended cause of an accident; requirement of an accident-based policy that the cause of the mishap be accidental for any claim to be payable.

accident and health insurance An insurance policy under which benefits are payable in case of disease, accidental injury, or accidental death. Also called health insurance, personal health insurance, and sickness and accident insurance.

accumulation unit The premiums an annuitant pays into a variable annuity are credited as accumulation units. At the end of the accumulation period, accumulation units are converted to annuity units.

acquired immune deficiency syndrome (AIDS) A life-threatening condition brought on by the human immunodeficiency virus; insurers must adhere to strict underwriting and claims guidelines in regard to AIDS risks and AIDS-related conditions.

acute illness A serious condition, such as pneumonia, from which the body can fully recover with proper medical attention.

adhesion A life insurance policy is a contract of adhesion because buyers must adhere to the terms of the contract already in existence. They have no opportunity to negotiate terms, rates, or values, etc.

adjustable life insurance This products combines features of both term and whole life coverage and has adjustable lengths of coverage and amounts of accumulated cash value. Premiums may be increased or decreased to fit specific needs. Such adjustments are not retroactive and apply only to the future.

administrative-services-only (ASO) plan An arrangement under which an insurance company or an independent organization, for a fee, handles the administration of claims, benefits, and other administrative functions for a self-insured group.

admitted insurer An insurance company that has met the legal and financial requirements for operation within a given state.

adult day care A type of care offered in care centers (usually custodial) designed for individuals who require assistance with various activities of daily living while their primary caregivers are absent.

adverse selection The tendency of insureds who present a higher probability of loss to purchase or renew insurance more often than those who present a lower probability; selection against the best interests of the insurance company (e.g., people near rivers purchasing flood insurance); tendency of policyowners to take advantage of favorable options in insurance contracts.

advertising code The rules established by the National Association of Insurance Commissioners (NAIC) to regulate insurance advertising.

agency The legal principle that allows an individual or organization to represent another individual or organization.

agent A person licensed by the state insurance authority to sell insurance products. The agent represents the insurance company in all transactions. *See also* broker; producer.

agent's report The section of an insurance application where the agent reports their personal observations about the applicant.

aleatory A kind of contract in which one party may obtain greater value under the agreement than the other party and in which payment depends upon a fortuitous event. An insurance contract is an aleatory contract.

alien insurer An insurance company incorporated and organized under the laws of a foreign nation, state, province, or territory, rather than under the laws of the United States.

ambulatory surgery Surgery performed on an outpatient basis.

Amicable Society for a Perpetual Assistance Office England's first successful life insurance company; founded in 1705.

amount at risk The difference between the face amount of the policy and the reserve or policy value at a given time. In other words, the dollar amount over what the policyowner has contributed of cash value toward payment of his own claim. Because the cash value increases every year, the net amount at risk decreases until it finally reaches zero, at which time the cash value or reserve becomes the face amount.

annually renewable term (ART) A form of renewable term insurance that provides coverage for one year and allows the policyowner to renew his or her coverage each year without evidence of insurability. Also called yearly renewable term (YRT).

annuitant A person to whom an annuity is payable, or upon the continuance of whose life further payment depends.

annuity A contract that provides a stipulated sum payable at certain regular intervals (1) during the lifetime of one or more persons, or (2) for a specified period only.

annuity unit The number of annuity units denotes the share of funds an annuitant will receive from a variable annuity account after the accumulation period ends and benefits begin. A formula is used to convert accumulation units to annuity units.

any occupation A definition of total disability that requires the insured to be unable to perform any job for which he is, "reasonably suited by reason of education, training, or experience," in order to receive disability income benefits.

apparent authority The authority the general public assumes an agent has due to his actions, regardless of whether the authority has been given to the agent by law or contract.

application Form supplied by the insurance company, usually filled in the by the agent and medical examiner (if applicable) on the basis of information received from the applicant. It is signed by the applicant and is part of the insurance policy if it is issued. It gives information to the home office underwriting department so it may consider whether an insurance policy will be issued and, if so, in what classification and at what premium rate.

appointment The authorization or certification of an agent to act for or represent an insurance company.

approval receipt Rarely used today, this is a type of conditional receipt that provides that coverage is effective as of the date the application is approved (before the policy is delivered).

Armstrong Investigation An investigation of a large number of insurance companies in the United States in 1905 that led to the enactment of stricter state supervision and insurance requirements.

assessment insurance A plan by which either the amount of insurance or the number and amount of the assessments are variable. It is offered by either pure or advance assessment associations.

assessment mutual insurer An insurance company characterized by member-insureds who are assessed an individual portion of each loss that occurs. No premium payment is payable in advance.

assignee A person (including a corporation, partnership or other organization) to whom a right or rights under a policy are transferred by means of an assignment

assignment The legal transfer of a policyowner's rights or interests in an insurance policy to another party. The insured requests the assignment, and, barring state law, the company can either accept or reject the request.

assignment provision (health contracts) A commercial health policy provision that allows the policyowner to assign benefit payments from the insurer directly to the health care provider.

assignor A person (including a corporation, partnership or other organization or entity) who transfers a right or rights under an insurance policy to another by means of an assignment.

attained age With reference to an insured, the current insurance age.

authority The actions and deeds an agent is authorized to conduct on behalf of an insurance company, as specified in the agent's contract.

authorized company An insurer that meets the licensing criteria of the state it wishes to do business in and has received a certificate of authority. Also known as an admitted company.

automatic premium loan provision This authorizes an insurer to pay any premium in default automatically at the end of the grace period and charge the amount so-paid against the life insurance policy as a policy loan.

average indexed monthly earnings (AIME) The basis used for calculating the primary insurance amount (PIA) for Social Security benefits.

average monthly wage (AMW) The average wage base for computing virtually all Social Security benefits prior to 1979.

aviation exclusion This excludes from coverage certain deaths or disabilities due to aviation for those, other than fare-paying passengers. May be attached by rider or included in standard policy language.

B

back dating The practice of making a policy effective at a date earlier than the present.

basic medical expense policy This is a health insurance policy that provides first dollar benefits for specified (and limited) health care, such as hospitalization, surgery, or physician services and that is characterized by limited benefit periods and relatively low coverage limits.

beneficiary A person to whom the proceeds of a life or accident policy are payable when the insured dies. The various types of beneficiaries are: primary (those first entitled to proceeds), secondary (those entitled to proceeds if no primary beneficiary is living when the insured dies), and tertiary (those entitled to proceeds if no primary or secondary beneficiaries are alive when the insured dies).

benefit May be either the money or the right(s) given to the policyowner if the conditions set out in the policy come to pass.

benefit period The maximum length of time that insurance benefits will be paid for any one accident, illness, or hospital stay.

Best's Insurance Report A guide, published by A.M. Best, Inc., that rates insurers' financial integrity, managerial, and operational strengths.

binder A written note that temporarily obligates an insurer to provide insurance in the amount of $1 million or more; it effectively puts insurance into force before a contract has been written or the premium paid. A binder is usually good for 90 days.

binding receipt This is given by a company upon an applicant's first premium payment. The policy, if approved, becomes effective from the date of the receipt.

blackout period The period following the death of a family breadwinner during which no Social Security benefits are available to the surviving spouse.

blanket policy This covers a number of individuals who are exposed to the same hazards, such as members of an athletic team or company officials who are passengers in the same company plane.

Blue Cross Independent, nonprofit membership organization providing protection against the costs of hospital care in a limited geographical area. Benefit payments are made directly to the hospital; benefits vary among Blue Cross organizations.

Blue Shield Independent, nonprofit membership organization providing protection against the costs of surgery and other items of medical care in a limited geographical area. Benefit payments are made directly to the company.

broker A licensed insurance representative who does not represent a specific company, but places business among various companies. Legally, the broker is usually regarded as a representative of the insured rather than the company.

business continuation plan Arrangements between the businessowners that provide that the shares owned by any one of them shall be sold to and purchased by the other co-owners or the business in the event of death or disablement.

business health insurance This is insurance issued primarily to indemnify a business for the loss of services of a key employee, partner, or active close corporation stockholder.

business overhead expense insurance A form of disability income coverage designed to pay necessary business overhead expenses, such as rent, should the insured businessowner become disabled.

buyer's guides Informational consumer guide books that explain insurance policies and insurance concepts; in many states, they must be given to applicants when certain types of coverages are being considered.

buy-sell agreement An agreement that a decreased businessowner's interest will be sold and purchased at a predetermined price or according to a predetermined formula.

C

cafeteria plan An employee benefit arrangement in which employees can select from a range of benefits.

cancellable contract A health insurance contract that may be terminated by the company or renewed at its option.

capital sum The amount provided for accidental dismemberment or loss of eyesight. Indemnities for loss of one member or sight of one eye are percentages of the capital sum.

career agency system A method of marketing, selling, and distributing insurance, represented by agencies or branch offices committed to the ongoing recruitment and development of career agents.

carrier Another term for an insurer or an entity responsible for the payment of benefits under an insurance policy; i.e., an insurer carries the risk for the policyowner(s).

case management The professional arrangement and coordination of health services through assessment, service plan development, and monitoring.

cash or deferred arrangements A qualified employer retirement plan under which employees can defer amounts of their salaries into a retirement plan. These amounts are not included in the employee's gross income and so are tax-deferred. Also called 401(k) plans.

cash refund annuity This provides that, upon the death of an annuitant before payments totaling the purchase price have been made, the excess of the amount paid by the purchaser over the total annuity payments received will be paid in one sum to designated beneficiaries.

cash surrender option A nonforfeiture option that allows whole life insurance policyowners to receive a payout of their policy's cash values.

cash surrender value Amount available to the owner when a life insurance policy is surrendered to the company. During the early policy years, the cash value is the reserve less a surrender charge; in later policy years, it usually equals or closely approximates the reserve value at time of surrender.

cash value The equity amount or savings accumulation in a whole life policy.

chronic condition A treatable but incurable illness, such as arthritis or hypertension.

class designation A beneficiary designation. Rather than specifying one or more beneficiaries by name, the policyowner designates a class or group of beneficiaries. For example, my children.

classification Occupational category of a risk.

cleanup fund A basic use for life insurance; this is a reserve to cover costs of last illness, burial, legal, and administrative expenses, miscellaneous outstanding bills, etc. Also called a final expense fund.

close corporation A corporation owned by a small group of stockholders, each of whom usually has a voice in operation the business.

closed-panel HMO A group of physicians who are salaried employees of an HMO and who work in facilities provided by the HMO.

Consolidated Omnibus Budget Reconciliation Act (COBRA) of 1985 This law extended group health coverage to terminated employees and their families for up to 18 or 36 months.

coinsurance (percentage participation) The principle under which the company insures only part of the potential loss, and the policyowners paying the other part. For instance, in a major medical policy, the company may agree to pay 75% of the insured expenses, and the insured must pay the other 25.

collateral assignment The assignment of a policy to a creditor as security for a debt. The creditor is entitled to be reimbursed out of policy proceeds for the amount owed. The beneficiary is entitled to any excess of policy proceeds over the amount due the creditor in the event of the insured's death.

combination company A company whose agents sell both weekly premium life and health insurance as well as ordinary life insurance.

commercial health insurers Insurance companies that function on the reimbursement approach, which allows policyowners first to seek medical treatment and then to submit the charges to the insurer for reimbursement.

commissioner The head of a state insurance department; public officer charged with supervising the insurance business in a state and administrating insurance laws. Called superintendent in some states, and director in others.

commissioner's standard ordinary (CSO) table The table of mortality based on intercompany experience over a period of time, which is legally recognized as the mortality basis for computing maximum reserves on policies issued within past years. The 1980 CSO Table replaced the 1958 CSO Table.

common disaster provision This is sometimes added to a policy and designed to provide an alternative beneficiary in the event that both the insured and the original beneficiary die as the result of a common accident.

competent parties A person capable of understanding the contract being agreed to; to be enforceable, a contract must be entered into by competent parties.

comprehensive major medical insurance This is designed to give the protection offered by both a basic medical expense and major medical policy. It is characterized by a low deductible amount, coinsurance clause and high maximum benefits.

concealment The deliberate withholding of material facts that would affect the validity of an insurance policy or a claim under the policy.

conditional contract A contract that is in force only if certain obligations are met or events come to pass. In regard to an insurance contract, the payment of benefits is dependent on or a condition of the occurrence of the risk insured against.

conditionally renewable contract A health insurance policy that provides that the insured may renew the contract from period to period or continue it to a stated date or an advanced age, subject to the right of the insurer to decline renewal under the conditions defined in the contract.

conditioned receipt This is given to the policyowners when they pay a premium at the time of application. Such receipts bind the insurance company if the risk is approved as applied for, subject to any other conditions stated on the receipt.

conservation The activities involved in taking over and managing the affairs of a financially troubled insurer; the efforts involved in keeping insurance policies in force and/or reinstating lapsed policies.

consideration The inducement to complete a contract, for example, the premium paid by the insured and the promise to pay made by the insurer.

consideration clause The part of an insurance contract that sets forth the amount of initial and renewal premiums and frequency of future payments.

contestable period The period during which the company may contest a claim on a policy because of misleading or incomplete information furnished in the application.

contingent beneficiary The person or persons named to receive proceeds in case the original beneficiary is no longer living. Also referred to as secondary or tertiary beneficiary.

contract An agreement (offer and acceptance) between two parties that have legal capacity to contract that involves valuable consideration and that does not violate any statute or other legal rule.

contract of agency A legal document that contains the terms of the contract between the agent and company, signed by both parties. Also called an agency agreement.

contributory plan A group insurance plan issued to an employer under which both the employer and employees contribute to the cost of the plan. Generally, 75% of the eligible employees must be insured. *See also* noncontributory plan.

conversion privilege This allows the policyowner, before an original insurance policy expires, to elect to have a new policy issued that will continue the insurance coverage. Conversion may be effected at attained age (premiums based on the age attained at time of conversion) or at original age (premiums based on age at time of original issue).

convertible term An insurance contract that may be converted to a permanent form of insurance without medical examination.

coordination of benefits (COB) provision This is designed to prevent duplication of group insurance benefits. It limits benefits from multiple group health insurance policies in a particular case to 100% of the expenses covered and designates the order in which the multiple carriers are to pay benefits.

corridor deductible In superimposed major medical plans, this is the deductible amount between the benefits paid by the basic plan and the beginning of the major medical benefits.

cost of living (COL) rider A rider available with some policies that provides for an automatic increase in benefits (typically tied to the Consumer Price Index) to offset the effects of inflation.

coverage requirements The standards of coverage that prevent retirement plans from discrimination in favor of highly compensated employees. A plan must pass an IRS coverage test to be considered qualified.

covering note A written note prepared by an agent or broker, usually good for 90 days, that informs the insured that coverage is in effect before a contract has been written or the premium paid. *See also* binder.

credit accident and health insurance This pays policy premiums during the disability period or pays off an outstanding loan if the insured debtor becomes totally disabled due to an accident or sickness. May be individual or group policy.

credit life insurance This is usually written as a decreasing term on a relatively small decreasing balance installment loan that may reflect direct borrowing or a balance due for merchandise purchased. If the borrower dies, benefits pay the balance due. May be individual or group policy.

credit report A summary of an insurance applicant's credit history, made by an independent organization that has investigated the applicant's credit standing.

cross-purchase plan An agreement that provides that upon a businessowner's death, surviving owners will purchase the deceased interest, often with funds from life insurance policies owned by each principal on the lives of all other principals.

currently insured A status of limited eligibility under Social Security that provides only death benefits.

custodial care The level of health or medical care given to meet daily personal needs, such as dressing, bathing or getting out of bed. Though it does not require medical training, it must be administered under a physician's order.

D

death rate The proportion of persons in each age group who die within a year; usually expressed as so many deaths per thousand persons. *See also* expected mortality.

debit insurer *See* home service insurer.

decreasing term insurance This is term life insurance on which the face value slowly decreases in scheduled steps from the date the policy comes into force to the date the policy expires, while the premium remains level. The intervals between decreases are usually monthly or annual.

deductible The amount of expense or loss to be paid by the insured before a health insurance policy starts paying benefits.

deferred annuity This provides for the postponement of the commencement of an annuity until after a specified period or until the annuitant attains a specified age. May be purchased either on single-premium or flexible premium basis.

deferred compensation plan The deferral of an employee's compensation to some future age or date. These plans are frequently used to provide fringe benefits, such as retirement income, to selected personnel.

defined benefit plan A pension plan under which benefits are determined by a specific benefit formula.

defined contribution plan A tax-qualified retirement plan in which annual contributions are determined by a formula set for those in the plan. Benefits paid to a participant vary with the amount of contributions made on his or her behalf and the length of service under the plan.

delayed disability provision A disability income policy provision that allows a certain amount of time after an accident for a disability to result during which the insured remains eligible for benefits.

dental insurance A relatively new form of health insurance coverage typically offered on a group basis. It covers the costs of normal dental maintenance as well as oral surgery and root canal therapy.

dependency period The period following the death of the breadwinner up until the youngest child reaches maturity.

deposit term An insurance product with a modest endowment feature. It is normally sold for 10-year terms with a higher first-year premium than for subsequent years. If policy lapses, insured forfeits his or her deposit and receives no refund.

disability A physical or mental impairment that makes a person incapable of performing one or more duties of his or her occupation.

disability buy-sell agreement An agreement between business co-owners that provides that shares owned by any one of them who becomes disabled shall be sold to and purchased by the other co-owners or by the business using funds from disability income insurance.

disability income insurance A type of health insurance coverage that provides for the payment of regular, periodic income should the insured become disabled illness or injury.

disability income rider This is typically a rider to a life insurance policy that provides benefits in the form of income in the event the insured becomes totally disabled.

discrimination In insurance, this is the act of treating certain groups of people unfairly in the sale or pricing of policies; or of treating any of a given class of risk differently from other like risks. Discrimination is expressly prohibited in most state insurance codes.

dividend The policyowner's share in the divisible surplus of a company issuing insurance on the participating plan.

dividend options The different ways in which the insured under a participating life insurance policy may elect to receive surplus earnings: in cash, as a reduction of premium, as additional paid-up insurance, left on deposit at interest, or as additional term insurance.

domestic insurer An insurance company that writes business in the state or province of its incorporation or charter.

dread disease policy *See* limited risk policy.

E

elimination period The duration of time between the beginning of an insured's disability and the commencement of the period for which benefits are payable.

employee benefit plans Plans through which employers offer employees benefits such as coverage for medical expenses, disability, retirement, and death.

employee stock ownership plan (ESOP) A form of defined contribution profit-sharing plan that ESOP invests primarily in the securities or stock of the employer.

endowment A contract that provides for payment of the face amount at the end of a fixed period, at a specified age of the insured or at the insured's death before the end of the stated period.

endowment period The period specified in an endowment policy during which, if the insured dies, the beneficiary receives a death benefit. If the insured is still living at the end of the endowment period, he or she receives the endowment as a living benefit.

enhanced whole life A whole life insurance policy issued by a mutual insurer, in which policy dividends are used to provide extra death benefits or to reduce future premiums.

enrollment period The period during which new employees can sign up for coverage under a group insurance plan.

entire contract provision An insurance policy provision that states that the application and policy contain all provisions and constitute the entire contract.

entity plan An agreement in which a business assumes the obligation of purchasing a deceased owner's interest in the business, thereby proportionately increasing the interests of surviving owners.

equity-indexed annuity A fixed deferred annuity that offers the traditional guaranteed minimum interest rate and an excess interest feature that is based on the performance of an external equities market index.

errors and omissions (E&O) insurance This is professional liability insurance that protects an insurance producer against claims arising from service he or she rendered or failed to render.

estate This is, most commonly, the quantity of wealth or property remaining at an individual's death.

estate tax The federal tax imposed on the value of property transferred by an individual at his or her death.

estoppel The legal impediment to denying the consequences of one's actions or deeds if they lead to detrimental actions by another.

evidence of insurability Any statement or proof of a person's physical condition or occupation that affects acceptance of the applicant for insurance.

examiner A physician authorized by the medical director of an insurance company to make medical examination person assigned by a state insurance company.

excess interest The difference between the rate of interest the company guarantees to pay on proceeds left under settlement options and the interest actually paid on such funds by the company.

exclusion ratio A fraction used to determine the amount of annual annuity income exempt from federal income tax. The exclusion ratio is the total contributions or investment in the annuity divided by the expected ratio.

exclusion rider A health insurance policy rider that waives the insurer's liability for all future claims on a pre-existing condition.

exclusions These are specified hazards listed in a policy for which benefits will not be paid.

exclusive provider organization (EPO) A variation of the PPO concept, an EPO contracts with an extremely limited number of physicians and typically only one hospital to provide services to members; members who elect to get health care from outside the EPO receive no benefits. *See also* preferred provider organization.

expected mortality The number of deaths that theoretically should occur among a group of insured persons during a given period, according to the mortality table in use. Normally, a lower mortality rate is anticipated and generally experienced.

experience rating The review of the previous year's claims experience for a group insurance contract in order to establish premiums for the next period.

express authority The authority given to an agent or agency directly by means of the agency agreement or contract.

extended term insurance A nonforfeiture option that provides for the cash surrender value of a policy to be used as a net single premium (at the insured's attained age) to purchase term insurance for the face amount of the policy, less indebtedness, for as long a period as possible (but no longer than the term of the original policy.)

extra percentage tables Mortality or morbidity tables that indicate the percentage amount increase of premium for certain impaired health conditions.

F

face amount This commonly refers to the principal sum involved in the insurance contract. The actual amount payable may be decreased by loans or increased by additional benefits payable under conditions specified or stated in the rider.

facility of payment provision A clause permitted under a uniform health insurance policy provision that allows the company to pay up to $1,000 in benefits or proceeds to any relative who appears entitled to it if there is no named beneficiary or if the insured or beneficiary is a minor or legally incompetent.

facultative reinsurance The reinsurance of individual risks at the reinsurer's option. *See also* reinsurance; treaty reinsurance.

fair credit reporting act A Federal law requiring an individual to be informed if he or she is being investigated by an inspection company.

family income policy A combination of ordinary life and decreasing term insurance covering a period of 5,10,15, or 20 years. The term insurance is sufficient to provide (often when supplemented by interest on the ordinary life insurance) a specified monthly income from the date of death until the end of the specified income period. The principal sum of the ordinary insurance is payable when monthly income from the term insurance ceases or upon subsequent death.

family maintenance (family protection) policy Similar to the family income policy, this combines ordinary and term insurance, but without the decreasing insurance feature. Beginning at the insured's death, it provides for payment of an income for a fixed period of 10, 15, or 20 years from the date of death (not from the date of issue, as in the family income policy), with payment of the principal sum of the ordinary insurance at the end of the fixed period.

family plan policy An all-family plan of protection, usually with permanent insurance on the primary wage earner's life and with spouse and children automatically covered for lesser amounts of protection, usually term, all included for one premium.

Federal Insurance Act (FICA) The contributions made by employees and employers to fund Social Security benefits.

fiduciary A person who occupies a position of special trust and confidence regarding the handling or supervision of the affairs or funds of another. Examples are trustees, executors, administrators, corporate directors, and insurance agents.

final expense fund *See* cleanup fund.

fixed-amount settlement option A life insurance settlement option whereby the beneficiary instructs that proceeds be paid in regular installments of a fixed dollar amount. The number of payment periods is determined by the policy's face amount, the amount of each payment and the interest earned.

fixed annuity A type of annuity that provides a guaranteed fixed benefit amount payable for the life of the annuitant.

fixed-period settlement option A life insurance settlement option in which the number of payments is fixed by the payee, with the amount of each payment determined by the amount of proceeds.

flat deductible The amount of covered expenses that must be paid by the insured before medical benefits are payable.

foreign insurer An insurance company that operates in a state other than the one in which it is incorporated or chartered.

franchise insurance A life or health insurance plan for covering groups of persons with individual policies uniform in provisions, although perhaps different in benefits. Solicitation usually takes place in an employer's business with the employer's consent. It is generally written for groups too small or that qualify for regular group coverage. May be called wholesale insurance when the policy is life insurance.

fraternal benefit insurer A nonprofit benevolent organization that provides insurance to its members.

fraud An intentional concealment or false representation of a material fact that intends to take something of value or to force the surrender of a right. Fraud can only be determined by a court of appropriate jurisdiction.

free look A provision required in most states whereby policyholders have either 10 or 20 days to examine their new policies at no obligation.

fully funded In a retirement plan, a status in which the funds necessary to meet the financial obligations of the plan are accumulated in a reserve while the plan is in operation.

fully insured A status of complete eligibility for the full range of Social Security benefits: death benefits, retirement benefits, disability benefits and Medicare benefits.

funding In a retirement plan, the setting aside of funds for the payment of benefits.

G

general agent An independent agent with the authority, under contract with the company, to appoint soliciting agents within a designated territory and fix their compensation.

gift tax A Federal tax imposed on the (lifetime) transfer of property for less than full consideration.

government insurer An organization that, as an extension of the federal or state government, provides a program of social insurance.

grace period The period of time after the due date of a premium during which the policy remains in force without penalty.

graded premium whole life This is a variation of a traditional whole life contract that provides for lower than normal premium rates during the first few policy years, with premiums increasing gradually each year. After the preliminary period, premiums level off and remain constant.

gross premium The total premium paid by the policyowner, it generally consists of the net premium plus the expense of operation minus interest.

group credit insurance A form of group insurance issued by insurance companies to creditors to cover the lives of debtors for the amounts of their loans.

group insurance This is insurance that provides coverage for a group of persons, usually employees of a company, under one master contract.

group model HMO *See* closed-panel HMO.

guaranteed insurability (guaranteed issue) A arrangement, usually provided by rider, whereby additional insurance may be purchased at various times without evidence of insurability.

guaranteed renewable contract A health insurance contract that the insured has the right to continue in force by payment of premiums for a substantial period of time during which the insurer has a unilateral right to make any change in any provision, other than a change in premium rate for classes of insureds.

guaranty association An association established by each state to support insurers and protect consumers in the case of insurer insolvency. They are funded by insurers through assessments.

H

hazard A specific situation or condition that increases the probability or severity of a loss.

health insurance This is insurance against loss through sickness or accidental bodily injury. Also called accident and health, accident and sickness, sickness and accident or disability insurance.

health maintenance organization (HMO) Health care management that stresses preventive health care, early diagnosis and treatment on an outpatient basis. Persons generally enroll voluntarily by paying a periodic fixed fee.

home health care Skilled or unskilled care provided in an individual's home, usually on a part-time basis.

home service insurer An insurer that offers relatively small policies with premiums payable on a weekly basis, collected by agents at the policyowner's home.

hospital benefits The benefits payable for charges incurred while the insured is confined to or treated in a hospital, as defined in a health insurance policy.

hospital expense insurance Health insurance benefits subject to a specified daily maximum for a specified period of time while the inured is confined to a hospital, plus a limited allowance up to a specified amount for miscellaneous hospital expenses, such as operating rooms, anesthesia or laboratory fees. Also called hospitalization insurance. *See also* medical expense insurance.

hospital indemnity A form of health insurance that provides a stipulated daily, weekly or monthly indemnity during hospital confinement; payable on an unallocated basis without regard to actual hospital expense.

human life value An individual's economic worth, measured by the sum of his or her future earnings that are devoted to his or her family.

I

immediate annuity This provides of the payment of an annuity benefit at one payment interval from date of purchase. Can only be purchased with a single payment.

implied authority Authority that, although it is not expressed in a contract (express authority) is necessary to perform the duties expressly authorized.

incidents of ownership Any power or interest over a life insurance policy that would subject the policy to inclusion in a decedent's gross estate.

incontestable clause This places a time limit (one to two years after issue) on the insurer's right to void a policy or refuse benefits because of material misstatements made in the application.

increasing term insurance This is term life insurance in which the death benefit increases periodically over the policy's term. Usually purchased as a cost of living rider to a whole life policy. *See also* cost of living rider.

indemnity approach A method of paying health policy benefits to insureds based on a predetermined, fixed rate set for the medical services provided, regardless of the actual expenses incurred.

independent agency system A system for marketing, selling and distributing insurance in which independent brokers are not affiliated with any one insurer but represent any number of insurers.

indexed whole life A whole life insurance policy whose death benefit increases according to the rate of inflation. Such policies are usually tied to the Consumer Price Index (CPI).

individual insurance These are policies that provide protection to the policyowner, as distinct from group and blanket insurance. Also called personal insurance.

individual retirement account (IRA) A personal qualified retirement account through which eligible individuals accumulate tax-deferred income up to a certain amount each year, depending on their tax bracket.

industrial insurance A life insurance policy that provides modest benefits and a relatively short benefit period. Premiums are collected on a weekly or monthly basis by an agent calling at insured's homes. *See also* home service insurer.

inspection receipt A receipt obtained from an insurance applicant when a policy (upon which the first premium has not been paid) is left with him or her for further inspection. It states that the insurance is not in effect and that the policy has been delivered for inspection only.

inspection report An investigator report that provides facts required for a proper underwriting decision on applications for new insurance and reinstatements.

installment refund annuity An annuity income option that provides for the funds remaining at the annuitant's death to be paid to the beneficiary in the form of continued annuity payments.

insurability All conditions pertaining to individuals that affect their health, susceptibility to injury, or life expectancy; an individual's risk profile.

insurability receipt A type of conditional receipt that makes coverage effective on the date the application was signed or the date of the medical exam (whichever is later), provided the applicant proves to be insurable.

insurable interest The interest from which monetary loss will result if the peril insured against occurs; possibility of financial loss that can be protected against by insurance.

insurance A contractual means of transferring the risk of loss to an entity (insurer) that pools similar exposures.

insurance code The laws that govern the business of insurance in a given state.

insurer An entity that provides insurance coverage, typically through a contract of insurance. *See also* carrier.

insuring clause This defines and describes the scope of the coverage provided and limits of indemnification.

integrated deductible In superimposed major medical plans, this is a deductible amount between the benefits paid by the basic plan and those benefits paid by the major medical. All or part of the integrated deductible may be absorbed by the basic plan.

interest adjusted net cost method A method of comparing the costs of similar policies by using an index that takes into account the time value of money.

interest-only option (interest option) A mode of settlement under which all or part of the policy proceeds are left with the company for a definite period at a guaranteed minimum interest rate. Interest may either be added to the proceeds or paid annually, semiannually, quarterly, or monthly.

interest-sensitive whole life A whole life policy whose premiums vary depending upon the insurer's underlying death, investment, and expense assumptions.

interim term insurance Term insurance for a period of 12 months or less by special agreement of the company; it permits a permanent policy to become effective at a selected future date.

intermediate nursing care A level of health or medical care that is occasional or rehabilitative, ordered by a physician, and performed by skilled medical personnel.

irrevocable beneficiary A beneficiary whose interest cannot be revoked without his or her written consent, usually because the policyowner has made the beneficiary designation without retaining the right to revoke or change it.

J

joint and last survivor policy A variation of the joint life policy that covers two lives but pays the benefit upon the death of the second insured.

joint and survivor annuity This covers two or more lives and continues in force as long as any one of them survives.

joint life policy This covers two or more lives and provides for the payment of the proceeds at the death of the first among those insured, at which time the policy automatically terminates.

juvenile insurance This is written on the lives of children who are within specified age limits and generally under parental control.

K

Keogh plans These are designed to fund retirement of self-employed individuals; the name is derived from the author of the Keogh Act (HR-10), under which contributions to such plans are given favorable tax treatment.

key-person insurance This provides protection of a business against financial loss caused by the death or disablement of a vital number of the company, usually individuals possessing special managerial or technical skill or expertise.

L

lapse Termination of a policy because of the nonpayment of premiums.

law of large numbers A statistical principle which states that the larger the number of observations, the more accurate and reliable a prediction will be.

legal purpose The concept that the purpose of a contract must be legal, moral and in the public good. *See also* contract.

legal reserve The standard levels for policy reserves established thorough the insurance laws of the various states.

level premium funding method The insurance plan (used by all regular life insurance companies) under which, instead of an annually increasing premium that reflects the increasing chance of death, an equivalent level premium is paid. Reserves that accumulate from more than adequate premiums paid in the early years supplement inadequate premiums in later years.

level term insurance this is term coverage on which the face value remains unchanged from the date the policy comes into force to the date the policy expires.

license The certification issued by a state insurance department that an qualifies individual to solicit insurance applications for the period covered; usually issued for one year, renewable on application without need for repeat on the original qualifying requirements.

licensed insurer *See* admitted insurer.

lien system A plan for issuing coverage for substandard risks. A standard premium is paid but there is a lien against the policy to reduce the amount of insurance if the insured dies from a cause that resulted in the substandard rating.

life annuity This is payable during the continued life of the annuitant. No provision is made for the guaranteed return of the unused portion of the premium.

life expectancy The average duration of the life remaining to a number of persons of a given age, according to a given mortality table. Not to be confused with probable lifetime, which refers to the difference between a person's present age and the age at which death is most probable, i.e., the age at which most deaths occur.

life income settlement option A settlement option that provides for life insurance or annuity proceeds to be used to buy an annuity payable to the beneficiary for life, often with a specified number of payments certain or a refund if payments don't equal or exceed premiums paid.

life insurance This is insurance against loss due to the death of a particular person (the insured) upon whose death the insurance company agrees to pay a stated sum or income to the beneficiary.

limited pay life insurance A form of whole life insurance characterized by premium payments only being made for a specified or limited number of years.

limited policies These restrict benefits to specified accidents or diseases, such as travel policies, dread disease policies, ticket policies and so forth.

limited risk policy This provides coverage for specific kinds of accidents or illnesses, such as injuries received as a result of travel accidents or medical expenses stemming from a specified disease. *See also* special risk policy.

Lloyd's of London An association of individuals and companies that underwrite insurance on their own accounts and provide specialized coverages.

loading The amount added to net premiums to cover the company's operating expenses and contingencies; includes the cost of securing new business, collection expenses, and general management expenses.

loan value The amount that can be borrowed from the issuing company by the policyowner using the value of the life insurance policy as collateral.

long-term care The broad range of medical and personal services for individuals (often the elderly) who need assistance with daily activities for an extended period of time.

long-term care policy A health insurance policy that provides daily indemnity benefits for extended care confinement.

loss sharing A basic principle of insurance whereby a large number of insureds contribute to cover the losses of a few.

lump sum The payment of the entire proceeds of an insurance policy in one sum. This is the method of settlement provided by most policies unless an alternate settlement is elected by the policyowner or beneficiary.

M

major medical expense policy A health insurance policy that provides broad coverage and high benefits for hospitalization, surgery, and physician services. Characterized by deductibles and coinsurance cost-sharing.

managed care A system of delivering health care and health care services characterized by arrangements with selected providers, programs of ongoing quality control and of utilization review, and financial incentives for members to use providers and procedures covered by the plan.

mandatory second opinion Requires insureds to get a second opinion before receiving nonlife-threatening surgery in order to be eligible for benefits.

master policy A policy issued to the employer under a group plan; contains all the insuring clauses defining employee benefits. Individual employees participating in the group plan receive individual certificates that outline highlights of the coverage. Also called master contract.

material Having influence or effect; a representation relating to a matter that is so substantial as to influence an outcome or actions.

maturity value The proceeds payable on an endowment contract at the end of the specified endowment period, or payable on an ordinary life contract at the last age of the mortality table if the insured is still living at that age. Maturity value of a policy is the same as the face amount of the policy and is equal to the reserve value of the contract on this maturity date. Actual amount payable by the company may be increased by dividend additions or accumulated dividend deposits, or decreased by outstanding loans.

McCarran-Ferguson Act Also know as Public Law 15, this 1945 act exempted insurance from federal antitrust laws in all matters regulated by the states.

Medicaid This provides medical care for the needy under joint federal-state participation (Kerr-Mills Act).

medical cost management The process of controlling how policyholders utilize their policies. *See also* mandatory second opinion, precertification, ambulatory surgery, and case management.

medical examination This is usually conducted by a licensed physician; the medical report is part of the application, becomes part of the policy contract, and is attached to the policy. A nonmedical is a short-form medical report filled out by the agent. Various company rules, such as amount of insurance applied for or already in force, or applicant's age, sex, past physical history and data revealed by inspection report, etc., determine whether the examination will be medical or nonmedical.

medical expense insurance This pays benefits for nonsurgical doctors' fees commonly rendered in a hospital; sometimes pays for home and office calls.

Medical Information Bureau (MIB) A service organization that collects medical data on life and health insurance applicants for member insurance companies.

medical report A document completed by a physician or other approved examiner and submitted to an insure to supply medical evidence of insurability (or lack of insurability) or in relation to a claim.

Medicare A federally sponsored health insurance and medical care program for persons age 65 or older; administered under provisions of the Social Security Act.

Medicare Part A This is compulsory hospitalization insurance that provides specified in hospital and related benefits. All workers covered by Social Security finance its operation through a portion of their FICA tax.

Medicare Part B A voluntary program designed to provide supplementary medical insurance to cover physician services, medical services and supplies not covered under Medicare Part A.

Medicare Part C A program that offers a variety of Medicare managed care choices, a private fee-for-service plan (PFFS), and a Medicare medical savings account plan (MSA). Also known as Medicare Advantage (MA).

Medicare Part D A prescription drug benefit program that will be offered to Medicare beneficiaries beginning in 2006. Medicare beneficiaries will pay a projected monthly premium and annual deductible. Beneficiaries will share the costs of prescription drugs with Medicare.

Medicare supplement policy This is health insurance that provides coverage to fill the gaps in Medicare coverage.

minimum deposit insurance A cash value life insurance policy having a first-year loan value that is available for borrowing immediately upon payment of the first-year premium.

minimum premium plan (MPP) Designed to support a self-insured plan, a minimum premium plan helps insure against large, unpredictable losses that exceed the self-insured level.

miscellaneous expenses Hospital charges, other than for room and board, e.g., x-rays, drugs, laboratory fees, etc., in connection with health insurance.

misrepresentation The act of making, issuing, circulating, or causing to be issued or circulated, an estimate, illustration, circular, or statement of any kind that does not represent the correct policy terms, dividends or share of the surplus or the name or title for any policy or class of policies that does not in fact reflect its true nature.

misstatement of age or sex provision This provides that, if the insured's age or sex is misstated in an application for insurance, the benefit payable usually is adjusted to what the premiums paid should have purchased.

misuse of premium The improper use of premiums collected by an insurance producer.

modified endowment contract (MEC) A life insurance policy under which the amount a policyowner pays in during the first years exceeds the some of net level premium that would have been payable to provide paid-up future benefits in seven years.

modified whole life A whole life insurance with premium payable during the first few years (usually five) only slightly larger than the rate of term insurance. Afterwards, the premium is higher for the remainder of life than the premium for ordinary life at the original age of issue, but lower than the rate at the attained age at the time of charge.

money-purchase plan A type of qualified plan under which contributions are fixed amounts or fixed percentages of the employees' salary. An employee's benefits are provided in whatever amount the accumulated or current contributions will produce for him or her.

moral hazard Effect of person reputation, character, associates, personal living habits, financial responsibility and environment (as distinguished from physical health) upon an individual's general insurability.

morale hazard The effect(s) that indifference loss has on the risk to be insured.

morbidity The relative incidence of disability due to sickness or accident within a given group.

morbidity rate This shows the incidence and extent of disability that may be expected from a given large group of persons; used in computing health insurance rates.

mortality The relative incidence of death within a group.

mortality table A listing of the mortality experience of individuals by age; permits an actuary to calculate, on average, how long a male or female of a given age group may be expected to live.

mortgage insurance A basic use of life insurance, so-called because many breadwinners leave insurance to pay off any mortgage balance outstanding at their death. The insurance generally is made payable to a family beneficiary instead of to the mortgage holder.

multiple employer trust (MET) This is made up of several small groups of individuals that need life and health insurance but do not qualify for true group insurance who band together under state trust laws to purchase insurance at a more favorable rate.

multiple employer welfare arrangement (MEWA) This is similar to a multiple employer trust (MET) with the exception that in a MEWA, a number of employers pool their risks and self-insure.

multiple protection policy A combination of term and whole life coverage that pays some multiple of the face amount of the basic whole life portion (such as $10 per month per $1,000) throughout the multiple protection period (such as to age 65).

mutual insurer An insurance company that is owned by its policyholders and managed by a board of directors.

N

National Association of Health Underwriters (NAHU) An organization of health insurance agents that is dedicated to supporting the health insurance industry and to advancing the quality of service provided by insurance professionals.

National Association of Insurance Commissioners (NAIC) An association of state insurance commissioners active in the analysis of insurance regulations and in the formation and recommendation of uniform and model regulations and legislation.

National Association of Insurance and Financial Advisors (NAIFA) An organization of life insurance agents that is dedicated to supporting the life insurance industry and to advancing the quality of service provided by insurance professionals.

National Service Life Insurance (NSLI) Created by Congress in 1940 to provide policies for individuals on active duty in military service. Persons entering military service after December 31, 1956 cannot purchase this insurance. However, persons discharged with a service-connected disability may purchase it within a certain time limit.

natural group A group formed for a reason other than to obtain insurance.

needs approach A method for determining how much insurance protection a person should have by analyzing a family's or business' needs and objectives should the insured die, become disabled, or retire.

net premium This is calculated on the basis of a given mortality table and a given interest rate, without any allowance for loading.

nonadmitted insurer An insurance company that has not been licensed to operate within a given state.

noncancelable and guaranteed renewable contract A health insurance contract that the insured has the right to continue in force by payment of premiums set forth in the contract for a substantial period of time, during which the insurer has no right to make unilaterally any change in any contract provision.

noncontributory plan An employee benefit plan under which the employer bears the full cost of the employees' benefits; must insure 100% of eligible employees.

nondisabling injury An injury that requires medical care, but does not result in loss of time from work.

nonduplication provision This stipulates that insureds shall be ineligible to collect for charges under a group health plan if the charges are reimbursed under their own or spouse's group plan.

nonforfeiture options The privileges allowed under terms of a life insurance contract after cash values have been created.

nonforfeiture values Those benefits in a life insurance policy that by law the policyowner does not forfeit even if he or she discontinues premium payments; usually cash value, loan value, paid-up insurance value and extended term insurance value.

nonmedical insurance This is issued on a regular basis without requiring a regular medical examination. In passing on the risk, the company relies on the applicant's answers to questions regarding his or her physical condition and on personal references or inspection reports.

nonparticipating This is insurance under which the insured is not entitled to share in the divisible surplus of the company.

nonqualified plan A retirement plan that does not meet federal government requirements and is not eligible for favorable tax treatment.

notice of claims provision A policy provision that describes the policyowner's obligation to provide notification of loss to the insurer within a reasonable period of time.

O

offer and acceptance The offer may be made by the applicant by signing the application, paying the first premium and, if necessary, submitting to a physical examination. Policy issuance, as applied for, constitutes acceptance by the company. Or, the offer may be made by the company when no premium payment is submitted with application. Premium payment on the offered policy then constitutes acceptance by the applicant.

Old Age, Survivors, Disability and Hospital Insurance (OASDI) Retirement, death, survivor's disability income, health, and hospital insurance benefits provided under the Social Security system. It is better known as Social Security.

open certificate This stipulates that rates and policy provisions may be changed. Fraternal benefit societies are required by law to issue this type of certificate. Also called open policy.

open-panel HMO A network of physicians who work out of their own offices and participate in the HMO on a part-time basis.

optionally renewable contract A health insurance policy in which the insurer reserves the right to terminate the coverage at any anniversary or, in some cases, at any premium due date, but does not have the right to terminate coverage between such dates.

ordinary insurance Life insurance of commercial companies not issued on the weekly basis; amount of protection usually is $1,000 or more.

Occupational Safety and Health Administration (OSHA) This establishes federal work safety guidelines.

other insureds rider A term rider that covers a family member other than the insured and that is attached to the base policy covering the insured.

outline of coverage The informational material about a specific plan or policy of insurance that describes the policy's features and benefits; in many states, an outline of coverage is required to be given to consumers when certain types of coverages are being considered.

overhead insurance A type of short-term disability insurance that reimburses the insured for specified, fixed, monthly expenses, normal, and customary in operating the insured's business.

overinsurance An excessive amount of insurance; an amount of insurance that would result in payment of more than the actual loss or more than incurred expenses.

own occupation A definition of total disability that requires that the insured must be unable to work at his or her own occupation in order to receive disability income benefits.

P

paid-up additions The additional life insurance purchased by policy dividends on a net single premium basis at the insured's attained insurance age at the time additions ar purchased.

paid-up policy A contract on which no further premiums are to be paid and for the benefits of which the company is held liable.

parol evidence rule A rule of contract law that brings all verbal statements into the written contract and disallows any changes or modifications to the contract by oral evidence.

partial disability An illness or injury that prevents an insured from performing at least one or more, but not all, of their occupational duties.

participating An insurance plan under which the policyowner receives shares (commonly called dividends) of the divisible surplus of the company.

participating physician A doctor or physician who accepts Medicare's allowable or recognized charges and will not charge more than this amount.

participation standards The rules that must be followed for determining employee eligibility for a qualified retirement plan.

partnership A business entity that allows tow or more people to strengthen their effectiveness by working together as co-owners.

payor rider This is available under certain juvenile life insurance policies, upon payment of an extra premium; provides for the waiver of future premiums if the person responsible for paying them dies or is disabled before the policy becomes fully paid or matures as a death claim, or as an endowment, or the child reaches a specific age.

***per capita* rule** This stipulates that death proceeds from an insurance policy are to be divided equally among the living primary beneficiaries.

peril The immediate, specific event that causes loss and gives rise to risk.

period certain annuity An annuity income option that guarantees a definite minimum period of payments.

periodical publication group A group representative of those eligible for blanket life insurance. In this case, the policy is issued to a newspaper, farm paper, magazine, or other periodical. The policy insures independent contractors and others engaged in the marketing and delivery of periodical publications.

permanent flat extra premium A fixed charge added per $1,000 of insurance for substandard risks.

personal producing general agency system (PPGA) A method of marketing, selling, and distributing insurance in which personal producing general agents (PPGAs) are compensated for business they personally sell and business sold by agents with whom they subcontract. Subcontracted agents are considered employees of the PPGA, not the insurer.

***per stirpes* rule** This stipulates that death proceeds from an insurance policy are to be divided equally among the named beneficiaries. If a named beneficiary is deceased, his or her share then goes to the living descendants of that individual.

policy The insurance contract and all attached endorsements.

policy loan A loan made by the insurance company to the policyowner with the policy's cash value assigned as security. One of the standard nonforfeiture options.

policy provisions The term or conditions of an insurance policy as contained in the policy clauses.

precertification The insurer's approval of an insured's entering a hospital. Many health policies require precertification as part of an effort to control costs.

pre-existing condition An illness or medical condition that existed before a policy's effective date; usually excluded from coverage through the policy's standard provisions or by waiver.

preferred provider organization (PPO) An association of health care providers, such as doctors and hospitals, that agree to provide health care services to members of a particular group at fees negotiated in advance.

preferred risk A risk whose physical condition, occupation, mode of living and other characteristics indicate a prospect for longevity or an unimpaired life.

preliminary term insurance This is term insurance attached to a newly issued permanent life insurance policy that extends term coverage of a preliminary period of 1 to 11 months, until the permanent insurance becomes effective. The purpose is to provide full life insurance premium and the anniversary to a later date.

premium The periodic payment required to keep an insurance policy in force.

premium factors The three primary factors considered when computing the basic premium for insurance: mortality, expense and interest.

Presbyterian Minister's Fund The oldest life insurance company in existence; founded in 1759 as "A Corporation for the Relief of Poor and Distressed Presbyterian Ministers and of Poor and Distressed Widows and Children of Presbyterian Ministers."

prescription drug coverage This is usually offered as an optional benefit to group medical expense plans and covers some or all of the cost of prescription drugs.

presumptive disability benefit A disability income policy benefit that provides that if an insured experiences a specified disability, such as blindness, he or she is presumed to be totally disabled and entitled to the full amount payable under the policy, whether or not he or she is able to work.

primary beneficiary In life insurance, this is the beneficiary designated by the insured as the first to receive policy benefits.

primary insurance amount (PIA) Amount equal to a covered worker's full Social Security retirement benefit at age 65 or disability benefit.

principal A person whose obligations are guaranteed under a bond (also called the obligor); the applicant for or subject of insurance; the one (usually the insurer) from whom an insurance agent derives authority.

principal sum The amount under an AD&D policy that its payable as a death benefit if death is due to an accident.

private insurer An insurer that is not associated with federal or state government.

probationary period The specified number of days after an insurance policy's issue date during which coverage is not afforded for sickness. Standard practice for group coverages.

proceeds The net amount of money payable by the company at the insured's death or at policy maturity.

producer A general term applied to an agent, broker, personal producing general agent, solicitor, or other person who sells insurance.

professional liability insurance *See* errors and omissions insurance.

profit-sharing plan Any plan whereby a portion of a company's profits is set aside for distribution to employees who qualify under the plan.

proof of loss A mandatory health insurance provision stating that the insured must provide a completed claim form to the insurer within 90 days of the date of loss.

proper solicitation A high professional standard that requires an agent to identify himself or herself properly as an agent soliciting insurance on behalf of an insurance company.

pure endowment A contract providing for payment only upon survival of a certain person to a certain date and not in event of that person's prior death. This type of contract is just the opposite of a term contract, which provides for payment only in event that a certain person dies within the term period specified.

pure risk The uncertainty as to whether loss will occur; offers no chance for gain. Insurance may be provided against many types of pure risk.

Q

qualified plan A retirement or employee compensation plan established and maintained by an employer that meets specific guidelines spelled out by the IRS and consequently receives favorable tax treatment.

R

Railway Passengers Assurance Company Founded in 1848, this company made the first real attempt to protect the general public against accidents by writing ticket insurance to railway passengers for injury or death while riding the railways.

rate-up in age A system of rating substandard risks that involves assuming the insured to be older than he or she really is and charging a correspondingly higher premium.

rating The premium classification given an applicant for life or health insurance.

reasonable and customary charge The charge for a heath care service consistent with the going rate of charge in a given geographical area for an identical or similar service.

rebating The act of returning part of the commission or giving anything else of value to the insured as an inducement to buy the policy. It is illegal and cause for license revocation in most states. In some states, both the agent and the person receiving the rebate may be punished.

reciprocal insurer An association of individuals known as subscribers, managed by an attorney-in-fact, who agree to exchange insurance risks.

recurrent disability provision A disability income policy provision that specifies the period of time during which the reoccurrence of a disability is considered a continuation of a prior disability.

reduced paid-up insurance A nonforfeiture option contained in most life insurance polices that allows the insured to elect to have the cash surrender vale of the policy used to purchase a paid-up policy for a reduced amount of insurance.

re-entry option An option in a renewable term life policy under which the policyowner is guaranteed, at the end of the term, to be able to renew his or her coverage without evidence of insurability at a premium rate specified in the policy.

refund annuity This provides for the continuance of the annuity during the annuitant's lifetime at least until total payment equal to the purchase price has been made by the company.

rehabilitation benefit This is offered as an optional benefit to a disability income policy is designed to cover the cost of retraining in order to re-enter the work force following a period of disability.

reimbursement approach The payment of health policy benefits to insured based on actual medical expenses incurred.

reinstatement The act of putting a lapsed policy back in force by producing satisfactory evidence of insurability and paying any past-due premiums required.

reinsurance The act of sharing or spreading a risk that is too large for one insurer by transferring part of the risk to a reinsurer. The insurance company obtaining the reinsurance is called the ceding company; the insurance company issuing the reinsurance is called the reinsurer.

relative value scale A method for determining the benefits payable under a basic surgical expense policy. Points are assigned to each surgical procedure and a dollar per point amount, or conversion factor, is used to determine the benefit.

renewable term A term policy prove that may be renewed on the same plan for one or more years without medical examination, but with rates based on the insured's advanced age.

renewable option An option that allows the policyowner to renew a term policy before its termination date without having to provide evidence of insurability.

replacement The act of replacing one life insurance policy with another; may be done legally under certain conditions. *See also* twisting.

representation A statement of material fact that is reasonably accepted as substantially true.

reserve Funds held by the company to help fulfill future claims.

reserve basis In life insurance, this is the mortality table and assumed interest rate used in computing rates.

residential care A type of health or medical care designed to provide a benefit for elderly individuals who live in a retirement community; addresses full-time needs, both social and medical.

residual disability benefit A disability income payment based on the proportion of income the insured has actually lost, taking into account the fact that he or she is able to earn some income.

respite care A type of health or medical care designed to provide a short rest period for a caregiver. Characterized by its temporary status.

results provision *See* accidental bodily injury provision.

retention The act of keeping a policy in force and on the books.

revocable beneficiary A beneficiary whose right in a policy are subject to the policyowner's reserved right to revoke or change the beneficiary designation and the right to surrender or make a loan on the policy without the beneficiary's consent.

rider Strictly speaking, a rider adds something to a policy. However, the term is used loosely to refer to any supplemental agreement attached to and made a part of the policy, whether the policy's conditions are expanded and additional coverages added, or a coverage or conditions is waived.

risk The uncertainty regarding loss; a term indicating the person or property insured. *See also* pure risk; speculative risk.

risk pooling *See* loss sharing.

risk selection The method a home office underwriter uses to choose applicants that the insurance company will accept. The underwriter must determine whether risks are standard, substandard, or preferred and adjust the premium rates accordingly.

rollover IRA An individual retirement account established with funds transferred from another IRA or qualified retirement plan that the owner had terminated.

S

salary continuation plan An arrangement whereby an income, usually related to an employee's salary, is continued upon employee's retirement, death, or disability.

salary reduction SEP (SARSEP) A qualified retirement plan limited to companies with 25 or fewer employees. It allows employees to defer part of their pretax income to the plan, lowering their taxable income. *See also* Simplified Employee Pension Plan.

savings incentive match plan for employees (SIMPLE) A qualified employer retirement plan that allows small employers to set up tax-favored retirement savings plans for their employees.

schedule A list of specified amounts payable, usually for surgical operations, dismemberment, fractures, etc.

secondary beneficiary An alternative beneficiary designated to receive payment, usually in the event the original beneficiary predeceases the insured.

Section 457 plans Deferred compensation plans for employees of state and local governments in which amounts deferred will not be included in gross income until they are actually received or made available.

Self-Employed Individuals Retirement Act Passed by Congress in 1962, this act enables self-employed persons to establish qualified retirement plans similar to those available to corporations.

self-insurance Provided by a non-insurance company that has the financial ability to retain the risk of loss without the use of an insurance policy.

self-insured plan A health insurance plan under which an employer (usually a large one), labor union, fraternal organization or other group retains the risk of covering its employees' medical expenses.

service insurers Companies that offer prepayment plans for medical or hospital services; well-known examples are Blue Cross/Blue Shield plans and health maintenance organizations.

servicemembers' group life insurance (SGLI) All servicemembers on active duty are automatically covered for a specified amount of this group term life insurance, unless they elect no coverage or lesser amounts. The insurance is written by commercial companies and premiums are shared by insured and federal government.

service provider An organization that provides health coverage by contracting with service providers, to provide medical services to subscribers, who pay in advance through premiums. Examples of such coverages are HMOs and Blue Cross/Blue Shield plans.

settlement options Optional modes of settlement provided by most life insurance policies in lieu of lump-sum payment. Usual options are lump-sum cash, interest-only, fixed-period, fixed-amount and life income.

simplified employee pension plan (SEP) A type of qualified retirement plan under which the employer contributes to an individual retirement account set up and maintained by the employee.

single dismemberment The loss of one hand, one foot, or the sight of one eye.

single-premium whole life insurance This is whole life insurance for which the entire premium is paid in one sum at the beginning of the contract period.

skilled nursing care The daily nursing care ordered by a doctor; often medically necessary. It can only be performed by or under the supervision of skilled medical professionals and is available 24 hours a day.

Social Security The programs first created by Congress in 1935 and now comprised of Old Age, Survivors and Disability Insurance (OASDI), Medicare, Medicaid and various grants-in-aid, which provide economic security to nearly all employed people.

sole proprietorship The simplest form of business organization whereby one individual owns and controls the entire company.

special agent An agent who represents an insurance company in a given territory.

special class These are applicants who cannot qualify for standard insurance, but may secure policies with riders waiving payment for losses involving certain existing health impairments.

special questionnaires The forms used when, for underwriting purposes, the insurer needs more detailed information from an applicant regarding aviation or avocation, foreign residence, finances, military service, or occupation.

special risk policy This provides coverage for unusual hazards normally not covered under accident and health insurance, such as a concert pianist insuring his or her hands for a million dollars. *See also* limited risk policy.

specified disease insurance *See* limited risk policy.

speculative risk A type of risk that involves the chance of both loss and gain; not insurable.

spendthrift provision This stipulates that, to the extent permitted by law, policy proceeds shall not be subject to the claims of creditors of the beneficiary or policyowner.

split-dollar life insurance An arrangement between two parties where life insurance is written on the life of one, who names the beneficiary of the net death benefits (death benefits less cash value), and the other is assigned the cash value, with both sharing premium payments.

spousal IRA An individual retirement account that persons eligible to set up IRAs for themselves may set up jointly with a nonworking spouse.

standard provisions The forerunners of the Uniform Policy Provisions in health insurance policies today.

standard risk A person who, according to a company's underwriting standards, is entitled to insurance protection without extra rating or special restrictions.

stock bonus plan A plan under which bonuses are paid to employees in shares of stock.

stock insurer An insurance company owned and controlled by a group of stockholders whose investment in the company provides the safety margin necessary in issuance of guaranteed, fixed premium, and nonparticipating policies.

stock redemption plan An agreement under which a close corporation purchases a deceased stockholder's interest.

stop-loss provision This is designed to stop the company's loss at a given point, as an aggregate payable under a policy, a maximum payable for any one disability or the like; also applies to individuals, placing a limit on the maximum out-of-pocket expenses an insured must pay for health care, after which the health policy covers all expenses.

straight life income annuity (straight life annuity, life annuity) An annuity income option that pays a guaranteed income for the annuitant's lifetime, after which time payments stop.

straight whole life insurance *See* whole life insurance.

subscriber The policyowner of a health care plan underwritten by a service insurer, such as Blue Cross/Blue Shield.

substandard risk A person who is considered an under-average or impaired insurance risk because of physical condition, family or personal history of disease, occupation, residence in unhealthy climate, or dangerous habits. *See also* special class.

successor beneficiary *See* secondary beneficiary.

suicide provision This provides that if the insured commits suicide within a specified period, usually two years after the issue date, the company's liability will be limited to a return of premiums paid.

supplemental accident coverage This is often included as part of a group basic or major medical plan and is designed to cover expenses associated with accidents to the extent they are not provided under other coverages.

supplementary major medical policy A medical expense health plan that covers expenses not included under a basic policy and expenses that exceed the limits of a basic policy.

surgical expense insurance This provides benefits to pay for the cost of surgical operations.

surgical schedule A list of cash allowances payable for various types of surgery, with the respective maximum amounts payable based upon severity of the operations; stipulated maximum usually covers all professional fees involved, such as surgeon and anesthesiologist.

surplus The amount by which assets exceed liabilities.

surplus lines broker An individual licensed to place coverage not available in his or her state (or not available in sufficient amount) through insurers not licensed or not admitted to do business in the state where the broker operates.

surrender value *See* cash surrender value.

T

taxable wage base The maximum amount of earnings upon which FICA taxes must be paid.

tax-sheltered annuity An annuity plan reserved for nonprofit organizations and their employees. Funds contributed to the annuity are excluded from current taxable income and are only taxed later, when benefits begin to be paid. Also called tax-deferred annuity and 403(b) plan.

temporary flat extra premium A fixed charge per $1,000 of insurance added to substandard risks for a specified period of years.

temporary insurance agreement *See* binding receipt.

term insurance This provides protection during a limited number of years and expires without value if the insured survives the stated period, which may be one or more years.

term of policy The period for which the policy runs. In life insurance, this is to the end of the term period for term insurance, to the maturity date for endowments and to the insured's death (or age 100) for permanent insurance. In most other kinds of insurance, it is usually the period for which a premium has been paid in advance; however, it may be for one year or more, even though the premium is paid on a semiannual or other basis.

tertiary beneficiary A beneficiary designated as third in line to receive the proceeds or benefits if the primary and secondary beneficiaries do not survive the insured.

third-party administrator (TPA) An organization outside the members of a self-insurance group which, for a fee, processes claims, completes benefits paperwork and often analyzes claims information.

third-party applicant A policy applicant who is not the prospective insured.

three-year rule Under estate tax law, this rule brings into the gross estate the value of any life insurance policy in which the decedent had incidents of ownership if the policy had been transferred within three years of his or her death.

time limit on certain defenses A provision stating that an insurance policy is incontestable after it has been in force a certain period of time. It also limits the period during which an insurer can deny a claim on the basis of a pre-existing condition.

total disability A disability that prevents insureds from performing any duty of their usual occupations or any occupation for remuneration; actual definition depends on policy wording.

traditional net cost method A method of comparing costs of similar policies that does not take into account the time value of money.

travel-accident policies These provided coverage limited to indemnities for accidents while traveling, usually by common carrier.

treaty reinsurance An arrangement under which two or more insurers agree to share large insurance risks; the reinsurer automatically reinsures risks of a certain type written by the other, subject to the agreement.

trust Arrangement in which property is held by a person or corporation (trustee) for the benefit of others (beneficiaries). The grantor (person transferring the property to the trustee) gives legal title to the trustee, subject to terms set forth in a trust agreement. Beneficiaries have equitable title to the trust property.

trustee A person who holds legal title to property for the benefit of another; may be either an individual or a company, such as a bank and trust company.

twisting The practice of inducing a policyowner with one company to lapse, forfeit, or surrender a life insurance policy for the purpose of taking out a policy in another company. Generally classified as a misdemeanor, subject to fine, revocation of license and sometimes imprisonment. *See also* misrepresentation.

U

unallocated benefit A reimbursement provision, usually for miscellaneous hospital and medical expenses, that does not specify how much will be paid for each type of treatment, examination, dressing, etc., but only sets a maximum that will be paid for all such treatments.

underwriter A company that receives premiums and accepting responsibility for fulfilling the policy contract or a company employee who decides whether or not the company should assume a particular risk; the agent who sells the policy.

underwriting The process through which an insurer determines whether, and on what basis, an insurance application will be accepted.

Unfair Trade Practices Act A model act written by the National Association of Insurance Commissioners (NAIC) and adopted by most states empowering state insurance commissioners to investigate and issue cease and desist orders and penalties to insurers for engaging in unfair or deceptive practices, such as misrepresentation or coercion.

Uniform Individual Accident and Sickness Policy Provisions Law An NAIC model law that established uniform terms, provisions and standards for health insurance policies covering loss resulting from sickness or from bodily injury or death by accident or both.

Uniform Simultaneous Death Act A model law that states that when an insured and beneficiary die at the same time, it is presumed that the insured survived the beneficiary.

unilateral A characteristic of an insurance contract in that only one party, the insurance company, makes an enforceable promise.

uninsurable risk A person who is not acceptable for insurance due to excessive risk factors.

universal life A flexible premium, two-part contract containing renewable term insurance and a cash value account that generally earns interest at a higher rate than a traditional policy. The interest rate varies. Premiums are deposited in the cash value account after the company deducts its fee and a monthly cost for the term coverage.

urgent care center A health care establishment that allows patients to see a physician without an appointment at any time; serves as an alternative to a hospital emergency room.

utilization review A technique used by health care providers to determine after the fact if health care was appropriate and effective.

V

valued contract A contract of insurance that pays a stated amount in the event of a loss.

variable annuity Similar to a traditional, fixed annuity in that retirement payments will be made periodically to the annuitants, usually over the remaining years of their lives. Under the variable annuity, there is no guarantee of the dollar amount of the payments; they fluctuate according to the value of an account invested primarily in common stocks.

variable life insurance This provides a guaranteed minimum death benefit. Actual benefits paid may be more, however, depending on the fluctuating market value of investments behind the contract at the insured's death. The cash surrender value also generally fluctuates with the market value of the investment portfolio.

variable universal life (VUL) insurance A life insurance policy combining characteristics of universal and variable life policies. A VUL policy contains unscheduled premium payments and death benefits and a cash value that vary according to the underlying funds whose investment portfolio is managed by the policyowner.

vesting The right of employees under a retirement plan to retain part or all of the annuities purchased by the employer's contributions on their behalf or, in some plans, to receive cash payments or equivalent value, on termination of their employment, after certain qualifying conditions have been met.

veterans' group life insurance (VGLI) This is low-cost nonrenewable, but convertible, five-year term insurance to which Servicemembers' Group Life Insurance (SGLI) is converted automatically at the time an insured servicemember is discharged, separated or released from active duty. At the end of the five-year period, the veteran may convert his or her VGLI to an individual policy with any company participating in the program.

vision insurance An optional coverage available with group health insurance plans, vision insurance typically pays for charges incurred during eye exams; eyeglasses and contact lenses are usually excluded.

void contract An agreement without legal effect; an invalid contract.

voidable contract A contract that can be made void at the option of one or more parties to the agreement.

voluntary group AD&D A group accidental death and dismemberment policy paid for entirely by employees, rather than an employer.

W

waiting period *See* elimination period.

waiver An agreement waiving the company's liability for a certain type or types of risk ordinarily covered in the policy; a voluntary giving up of a legal, given right.

waiver of premium A rider or provision included in most life insurance policies and some health insurance policies that exempts the insured from paying premiums after he or she has been disabled for a specified period of time, usually six months in life policies and 90 days or six months in health policies.

war clause This relieves or reduces the insurer's liability for specified loss caused by war.

warranties Statements made on an application for insurance that are warranted to be true; that is, they are exact in every detail as opposed to representations. Statements on applications for insurance are rarely warranties, unless fraud is involved. *See* representation.

whole life insurance This is permanent level insurance protection for the whole of life, from policy issue to the death of the insured. Characterized by level premiums, level benefits and cash values.

wholesale insurance *See* franchise insurance

workers' compensation The benefits paid to workers for injury, disability, or disease contracted in the course of their employment. Benefits and conditions are set by law, although in most states the insurance to provide the benefits may be purchased from regular insurance companies. A few states have monopolistic state compensation funds.

Y

yearly renewable term insurance (YRT) *See* annually renewable term.

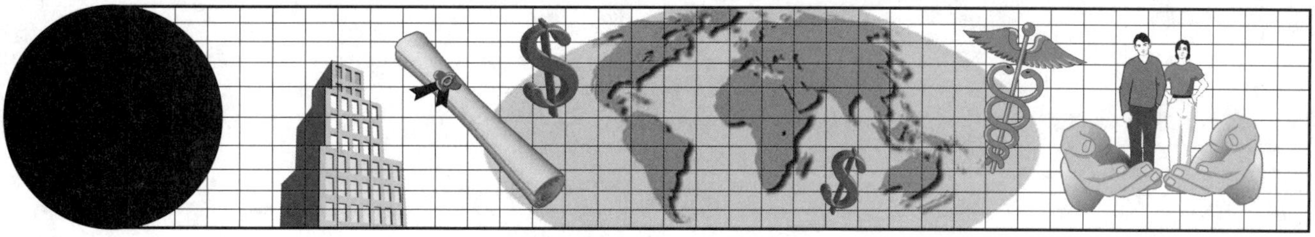

Appendix

This appendix contains both a sample whole life participating life insurance policy and sample application, as well as a sample health insurance policy and sample application. They are both representative of typical policies and applications issued by insurance companies in the United States and contain the standard language and provisions found in actual forms.

ERIE HEALTH INSURANCE COMPANY OF AMERICA

Erie Health agrees, in accordance with the provisions of this policy, to pay the benefits provided in this policy due to injury or sickness.

Twenty-Day Right to Examine Policy You may return this policy by delivering it to the Home Office or to an agent of the Company within 20 days after receiving it. Immediately on such delivery, the policy will be void as of the date of issue and any premium paid will be refunded.

Robert Johnson
President

John Birdy
Secretary

Insured:	Bill Dempsy
Policy Number:	0000-0000-00
Policy Date:	November 5, 2004

Individual Health Policy

Contents

Index

DEFINITIONS

"You," "Your" and "Yours" means the insured named on the Policy Schedule. "Time," "Us" and "Ours" means the Company.

COVERED PERSON: Covered person means the insured and all eligible dependents shown on the policy schedule, or added by endorsement.

CUSTODIAL CARE means care given to a covered person if the person:

1. is mentally or physically disabled and such disability is expected to last for an indefinite time;
2. needs a protected, monitored and/or controlled environment;
3. needs help to support the essentials of daily living; and
4. is not under active and specific medical, surgical and/or psychiatric treatment, which will reduce the disability to the extent necessary for the person to function outside a protected, monitored and/or controlled environment.

DENTAL SERVICE means any medical or surgical procedure that involves the hard or soft tissue of the mouth that requires treatment as a result of a disease or condition of the teeth and gums. Treatment for neoplasms is not considered a dental service.

DISABLED DEPENDENTS: This section amends the Eligible Dependents section. An unmarried child who cannot support himself due to mental incapacity or physical handicap may continue to be insured. This child must be fully dependent upon you for support. The Company may inquire of you two months prior to attainment by a dependent of the limiting age set forth in this policy, or at any reasonable time thereafter, whether such dependent is in fact a disabled and dependent person. In the absence of proof submitted within 60 days of such inquiry that such dependent is a disabled and dependent person, the Company may terminate coverage of such person at or after attainment of the limiting age. In the absence of such inquiry, coverage of any disabled and dependent person shall continue through the term of such policy or any extension or renewal thereof.

EFFECTIVE DATE OF COVERAGE; A covered person's effective date of coverage is: (1) the policy date, if the covered person is listed on the application and the policy schedule; or (2) the date of policy endorsement, if the covered person is added

ELIGIBLE DEPENDENTS: Eligible dependents are those dependents shown on the policy schedule or added by endorsement. This may include: (1) Your lawful spouse; and (2) Unmarried dependent children, including step-children and adopted children (or children who are in your custody pursuant to an interim court order of adoption), if they are legally dependent on you for their support and under 21 years of age.

Your newborn children, born while the policy is in force, will be covered for 60 days after birth. For coverage beyond 60 days after birth, written application must be made to the Company within that 60-day period. An additional premium will be required retroactive to date of birth. Other eligible dependents may be added by you upon evidence of insurability satisfactory to the Company. Additional premium will be required.

ELIGIBLE FOR MEDICARE means that the covered person is either:

1. covered by both Part A and Part B of Medicare; or
2. not covered for both Part A and Part B of Medicare because of:
   a. a failure to enroll when required;
   b. a failure to pay any premium that may be required for full coverage of the person under Medicare; or
   c. a failure to file any written request, claim or document required for payment of Medicare benefits.

HOSPICE PROGRAM means a coordinated interdisciplinary program for meeting the special physical, psychological, spiritual and social needs of dying covered persons and their immediate families. The covered person must be enrolled in the program by a physician.

HOSPITAL means a place other than a convalescent, nursing or rest home, that:

- provides facilities for medical, diagnostic and acute care on an inpatient basis. If these services are not on its own premises, they must be available through a prearranged contract;
- provides 24-hour nursing care supervised by registered nurses;
- has X-ray and lab facilities either on its premises or available through a prearranged contract;
- charges for these services.

A special ward, floor or other accommodation for convalescent, nursing or rehabilitation purposes is not considered a hospital.

IMMEDIATE FAMILY means you, your spouse, and the children, brothers, sisters and parents of either you or your spouse.

INJURY: Injury means accidental bodily injury sustained by a covered person while covered under this policy.

MEDICALLY NECESSARY CARE means confinement, treatment or service that is rendered to diagnose or treat a sickness or injury. Such care must be (1) prescribed by a physician; (2) considered to be necessary and appropriate for the diagnosis and treatment of the sickness or injury; and (3) commonly accepted as proper care or treatment of the condition by the U.S. medical community. Medically necessary care does not include care considered to be: (1) experimental or investigative in nature by any appropriate technological assessment body established by any state or federal government; (2) provided only as a convenience to the covered person or provider; and (3) in excess (in scope, duration or intensity) of that level of care which is needed to provide safe, adequate and appropriate diagnosis and treatment. The fact that a physician may prescribe, order, recommend or approve a service or supply does not, of itself, make the service or supply medically necessary.

MEDICARE: Medicare means the Health Insurance for the Aged Act, Title XVIII of the Social Security Act as amended.

MENTAL ILLNESS: Mental illness means a mental or nervous disorder, including neuroses, psychoneurosis, psychopathy, psychosis and other emotional disorders. Affective disorders (including bipolar disorders and major depression), alcoholism, drug addiction and chemical dependency are also included in this definition.

OTHER HEALTH INSURANCE PLAN: This means any plan that provides insurance, reimbursement or service benefits for hospital, surgical or other medical expenses. This includes: (1) individual or group health insurance policies; (2) nonprofit health service plans, including Blue Cross and Blue Shield; (3) health maintenance organization subscriber contracts; (4) self-insured group plans; (5) welfare plans; (6) medical coverage under homeowners or automobile insurance; and (7) service provided or payment received under laws of any national, state or local government. This does not include Medicaid.

If coverage is provided on a service basis, the amount of benefits under such coverage will be taken as the cost of the service in the absence of such coverage.

PART A means the Hospital Insurance Benefits for the Aged portion of Medicare.

PART B means the Supplementary Medical Insurance for the Aged portion of Medicare.

PHYSICAL MEDICINE means the diagnosis and treatment of physical conditions relating to bone, muscle or neuromuscular pathology.

PHYSICIAN: A person licensed by the state to treat the kind of injury or sickness for which a claim is made. The physician must be practicing within the limits of his or her license.

POLICY OWNER: The insured shown on the policy schedule unless someone else is designated the owner on the application.

PRE-EXISTING CONDITIONS: A pre-existing condition is a condition not fully disclosed on the application for insurance:

1. for which the covered person received medical treatment or advice from a physician within the six-month period immediately preceding that covered person's effective date of coverage; or
2. which produced signs or symptoms within the six-month period immediately preceding that covered person's effective date of coverage.

   The signs or symptoms must have been significant enough to establish manifestation or onset by one of the following tests:

   a. The signs or symptoms would have allowed one learned in medicine to make a diagnosis of the disorder; or
   b. The signs or symptoms should have caused an ordinarily prudent person to seek diagnosis or treatment.

Pre-existing conditions will be covered after the covered person has been insured for two years, if the condition is not specifically excluded from coverage.

REASONABLE AND CUSTOMARY CHARGE means the lesser of:

1. The actual charge;
2. What the provider would accept for the same service or supply in the absence of insurance; or

PAGE 3

3. The reasonable charge as determined by the Company, based on factors such as:
   a. the most common charge for the same or comparable service or supply in a community similar to where the service or supply is furnished;
   b. the amount of resources expended to deliver the treatment and the complexity of the treatment rendered; and
   c. charging protocols and billing practices generally accepted by the medical community or specialty groups; or
   d. inflation trends by geographic region.

SICKNESS: Sickness means an illness, disease or condition of a covered person that manifests itself after the covered person's effective date of coverage. For sickness that manifests itself during the first 15 days following the effective date, coverage is provided only for covered expense incurred after that 15-day period.

SKILLED NURSING FACILITY means a nursing home, licensed as a skilled nursing facility, operating in accordance with the laws of the state in which it is located and meeting the following requirements:

1. Is primarily engaged in providing room, board and skilled nursing care for persons recovering from sickness or injury;
2. Provides 24-hour-a-day skilled nursing service under the full-time supervision of a physician or graduate registered nurse;
3. Maintains daily clinical records;
4. Has transfer arrangements with a hospital;
5. Has a utilization review plan in effect;
6. Is not a place for rest, the aged, drug addicts, alcoholics or the mentally ill; and
7. May be a part of a hospital.

COVERAGE DESCRIPTION

DEDUCTIBLE AMOUNT: The deductible amount for each covered person during each calendar year is the larger of:

- the basic deductible amount shown in the policy schedule; or
- the amount of benefits paid for covered expenses by any other health insurance plan as defined in the policy.

The deductible amount must be:

- incurred each calendar year; and
- deducted from covered expenses.

A calendar year begins on January 1 and ends December 31.

MAXIMUM FAMILY DEDUCTIBLE AMOUNT: A maximum family deductible amount equal to three times the basic deductible amount will satisfy the deductible requirements for all covered persons in a family during a calendar year.

FAMILY CAP MAXIMUM: The maximum expense amount incurred per family for covered expense will not exceed the family cap maximum shown in the policy schedule for any calendar year.

CARRY-OVER DEDUCTIBLE: Any covered expense incurred and applied to a covered person's basic deductible amount during the last three months of a calendar year may also be used to reduce that person's basic deductible amount for the next calendar year.

The maximum family deductible and the carry-over deductible provisions will not apply if the benefits paid by other health insurance are used as the deductible.

RIGHT TO CHANGE DEDUCTIBLE AMOUNT: You may apply for an increase or decrease in the basic deductible amount within a 60-day period after a premium rate change, or during the first 30 days of a calendar year, provided that: (1) the new basic deductible amount is one that is available on this form, (2) a request for the change is made in writing to the Company, and (3) no claims have been incurred during that calendar year.

If you request a decrease in the deductible amount, the Company will require proof of continued insurability of all covered persons.

PAYMENT OF BENEFITS: Benefits for covered expense incurred will be paid in accordance with Sections A and B of the covered expense provision.

If benefits paid by other health insurance are used as the deductible amount, all covered expense will be paid at 100 percent, but payment will not exceed the amount that would have been paid in the absence of other health insurance.

Where applicable, the rate of payment starts again for each covered person each new calendar year after the deductible amount has been met. The Company will pay up to the lifetime maximum benefit shown in the policy schedule for each covered person.

If the payment by other health insurance is used as the deductible amount, the lifetime maximum benefit will be increased. The maximum benefit will be increased by $3 for each $1 paid by other coverage over the basic deductible.

PAYMENT OF BENEFITS WHEN ELIGIBLE FOR MEDICARE: When any covered person is eligible for Medicare, he or she will be deemed to have Part A and Part B Medicare coverage that is primary to the coverage under this policy. Services covered by Medicare will not be covered by this policy to the extent that benefits are payable by Medicare. If there is remaining covered expense after Medicare pays for assigned services, benefits will be paid at 100 percent up to the amount approved by Medicare; for unassigned services, benefits will be paid at 100 percent up to our reasonable and customary charge limit. Payment of benefits for services not covered by Medicare will be determined by the terms and limits of this policy.

COVERED EXPENSE: Covered expense means expense that is (a) incurred for services, treatment or supplies prescribed by a physician and described in Section A or B below; (b) incurred by a covered person as the result of sickness or injury as defined; (c) incurred for medically necessary care; and (d) incurred while the covered person's coverage is in force. Covered expense does not include any charge in excess of the reasonable and customary charge.

A. The following items of covered expense are subject to the deductible and rate of payment as described in this policy and shown in the policy schedule.

1. Room, board and general nursing care while confined in a semi-private room, ward, coronary care or other intensive care unit in a hospital. For confinement in a private room, the covered expense is limited to the hospital's most common daily charge for a semi-private room.
2. Other hospital services including services performed in a hospital outpatient department or in a free-standing surgical facility.
3. Physician services and surgical services, including second surgical opinions by board-certified specialists. This does not include services rendered by members of your immediate family.
4. Reconstructive surgery to restore function for conditions resulting from accidental injury provided the injury occurred while the covered person is insured under this plan. Reconstructive surgery that is incidental to or follows covered surgery performed as the result of trauma, infection or other diseases of the involved part.

   Reconstructive surgery for congenital defects provided the covered person has been insured continuously under this plan since the time of birth.
5. Hospice programs when (a) the physician projects a life expectancy of six months or less; and (b) the physician enrolls a covered person in the program. Notification is to be made in writing to the Company within seven days of admission to a licensed hospice facility. Covered expense includes up to 30 days of inpatient treatment at a hospice facility. Hospice home care is covered in addition to benefits provided under item 6. Benefits for services that include inpatient hospice services, hospice home care and counselling under the authorized hospice program are limited to $15,000 during the covered person's lifetime.
6. Up to 40 home health care visits in any 12-month period. One visit consists of up to four hours of home health aide service within a 24-hour period by anyone providing services or evaluating the need for home health care.

   For home health care to be a covered expense, the physician must certify that:
   a. hospitalization or confinement in a skilled nursing facility would otherwise be required;
   b. medically necessary care is not available from members of the covered person's immediate family or persons living with the covered person without causing undue hardship; and
   c. the home health care will be provided by a state-licensed or Medicare-certified home health agency.

   Home health care does not include:
   a. services not included in the home health care plan established for the covered person by the physician;

PAGE 5

b. services provided by the covered person's immediate family or anyone residing with the covered person;
c. homemaker services; or
d. custodial care.

7. Professional ambulance service to the nearest hospital that is able to handle the sickness or injury. One trip to a hospital for a covered person for each sickness or injury is covered.
8. X ray, radioactive treatment, laboratory tests and anesthesia services.
9. Outpatient physical medicine benefits to a maximum of $500 for each covered person per calendar year. Physical medicine benefits include but are not limited to: rehabilitative speech, physical, occupational and cognitive therapies; biofeedback; sports medicine; cardiac exercise programs; adjustments and manipulations. The limitation does not apply to the treatment of burns, fractures, complete dislocations; joint replacements or related conditions for which a covered person is hospitalized for surgery and physical medicine that immediately follows hospitalization.
10. Rental, up to the purchase price, or purchase, when approved in advance by the Company, of (a) a basic wheelchair, basic hospital bed or basic crutches; (b) the initial permanent basic artificial limb, eye or external breast prosthesis; and (c) oxygen and the equipment needed to administer oxygen.

    Casts, orthopedic braces, splints, dressings and sutures.

    Dental braces, dental appliances, corrective shoes, orthotics or repairs to or replacement of prosthetic devices are not covered expenses.
11. Drugs that require the written prescription of a licensed physician. However, if a prescription drug benefit rider is attached to this policy, covered drugs will be paid under that rider (to age 65 or prior Medicare eligibility) instead of under this policy.
12. Whole blood, blood plasma and blood products, if not replaced.
13. Dental service for an injury to a sound natural tooth when the expense is incurred within six months following the injury.

    "Sound" is defined as:

    a. organic and formed by nature;
    b. not extensively restored or endodontically treated; and
    c. not extensively decayed or involved in periodontal disease.
14. Treatment of mental illness. Expense incurred by a covered person while confined as an inpatient to a hospital or psychiatric hospital for mental illness as defined in the policy. Coverage is limited to a maximum benefit of $2,500 for a covered person during a calendar year. Outpatient treatment, drugs or medications are not covered.
15. Sterilization, if the covered person has been insured on this policy for at least two years.
16. Treatment of temporomandibular joint dysfunction except for: crowns that correct vertical dimension; splints, orthopedic repositioning appliances, biteplates and equilibration treatments (including splint equilibration and adjustments); bite functional or occlusal registration, with or without splints, and kinesiographic analysis; any orthodontic treatment, including extraction of teeth; study models, except for the complete model made necessary when surgical intervention is completed. Surgical charges for correction of orthognathic conditions are covered.

B. The following items 1, 2 and 3 of covered expense will not be subject to the basic deductible amount of the 80 percent rate of payment. Covered expense will be considered for payment under this section before it is considered under any other section of the policy. Covered expense for which a benefit is payable under this section will not be considered for payment under any other section of the policy.

1. Skilled nursing care: Medically necessary care in a skilled nursing facility for up to 30 days provided (a) the covered person enters the skilled nursing facility within 14 days after discharge from an authorized hospital confinement; (b) the skilled nursing facility confinement is for the same condition that required the hospital confinement; and (c) such care is authorized by the Company within seven days following admission to the skilled nursing facility. The daily benefit for confinement in a skilled nursing facility will not exceed one-half of the semi-private hospital room rate for the area.
2. Second and third opinions required by the Company's authorization service. Only an exam, X ray and lab work, and a written report by the physician rendering the opinion are

PAGE 6

included. You will be supplied with a list of three recommended physicians from whom the second or third opinion may be sought. The service may allow another physician to be consulted if the physician is (a) a board-certified specialist in the field of the proposed treatment; (b) is not financially associated with the first physician; and (c) does not perform the treatment.

3. Pre-admission testing. X rays and lab work performed on an outpatient basis before an authorized hospital admission provided (a) the tests are related to a scheduled admission; (b) the charges for the tests would have been covered expense if the individual was confined as an inpatient in a hospital; and (c) the tests were not repeated in or by the hospital, or elsewhere.

HUMAN ORGAN/TISSUE TRANSPLANT OR REPLACEMENT: Covered expense incurred by a covered person for the following human organ or tissue transplants or replacements if the procedure is authorized as indicated below, to a maximum lifetime benefit of $250,000 for each covered person.

Human organ transplant. The following procedures are covered if the procedure is authorized in writing by the Company prior to the beginning of the donor search and selection:

a. Bone marrow transplant
b. Heart transplant
c. Liver transplant

No benefits will be paid if the procedure has not been authorized by the Company prior to the beginning of the donor search and selection. To begin the authorization process, the physician or the physician's assistant must contact the Company's authorization service.

Tissue transplant or replacement. The following procedures are covered if authorized according to the procedures outlined in the authorization provision:

a. Cornea transplant
b. Prosthetic tissue replacement, including joint replacement
c. Vein or artery graft
d. Heart valve replacement
e. Implantable prosthetic lens in connection with cataracts

Donor Expenses. Expense incurred for surgery, storage and/or transportation service related to donor organ acquisition is also covered, up to a maximum benefit of $10,000 per covered procedure.

If the transplanted organ is from a live donor, expense incurred by the donor that is not paid by any other plan of insurance will be covered as though the donor's expense were the expense of the covered person.

No benefits will be paid for any transplant not authorized in writing by the Company prior to the beginning of donor search and selection or any transplant or replacement procedure not specifically listed above.

Kidney Disease or End Stage Renal Disease. Expense incurred for dialysis, transplantation and donor-related services to a maximum of $30,000 for each covered person during a calendar year. The transplant must be authorized in writing by the Company prior to the beginning of the donor search and selection. No benefits will be paid if the procedure has not been authorized by the Company prior to the beginning of such search.

Together with expense for dialysis and/or transplantation, expense incurred for surgery, storage and/or transportation service related to donor organ acquisition is limited to the $30,000 annual maximum. If the transplanted organ is from a live donor, expense incurred by the donor that is not paid by any other plan of insurance will be covered as though the donor's expense were the expense of the covered person, and included in the $30,000 annual maximum.

The limits in this provision for kidney disease or end stage renal disease provide for coordination with the governmental coverage for end stage renal disease.

COVERED COMPLICATIONS OF PREGNANCY: You, your spouse or a dependent child are covered for complications of pregnancy as defined below. Benefits are provided on the same basis as any covered sickness. Covered complications of pregnancy are limited to:

1. Conditions (when pregnancy is not ended) whose diagnoses are distinct from pregnancy, but are caused or adversely affected by pregnancy. Some examples: acute nephritis, nephrosis and cardiac decompensation.
2. Non-elective caesarean section
3. Ectopic pregnancy that is terminated
4. Spontaneous termination of pregnancy (mis-

carriage) that occurs before the 26th week of gestation; or missed abortion

Covered complications of pregnancy do not include: high-risk pregnancy or delivery, false labor, premature labor, occasional spotting, physician prescribed rest, morning sickness, pre-eclampsia or placenta previa.

CONGENITAL ILLNESS OR DEFECT OF A NEWBORN CHILD: Congenital illness or defect of a child of the insured born while this policy is in force will not be considered a pre-existing condition. Benefits will be provided on the same basis as any other sickness.

AUTHORIZATION PROVISION

This plan requires pre-authorization of all hospital admissions, inpatient surgeries, outpatient surgeries and transplants. The payment of benefits for covered expense described under the "Coverage Description" section of this policy may be reduced if the authorization procedure described below is not followed.

AN AUTHORIZATION DOES NOT GUARANTEE THAT BENEFITS WILL BE PAID. PAYMENT OF BENEFITS WILL BE DETERMINED BY THE TERMS AND LIMITS OF THE POLICY.

ELECTIVE ADMISSION OR SURGERY: For non-emergency hospital confinement, inpatient surgery, outpatient surgery or day surgery performed in a hospital, you must have the physician ordering the confinement or surgery obtain authorization before the patient is admitted to the hospital or has surgery performed. The authorization is obtained by the physician or physician's assistant from the Company's authorization service. The service can be reached by telephone during normal business hours, each Monday through Friday. A toll-free number and the name of the Company's authorization service is provided on the ID card given to you by the Company. You must instruct the physician to obtain the authorization by using the authorization form provided by the Company.

The service may require a second opinion prior to granting authorization. In such cases, you will be supplied with a list of three recommended physicians from whom the second opinion may be sought. However, the service may allow another physician to be consulted who (a) is a board-certified specialist in the field of the proposed treatment or surgery; (b) is not financially affiliated with the first physician; and (c) does not perform the surgery or provide the treatment. If the second opinion confirms the need for admission, then the admission will be considered AUTHORIZED. If the second opinion does not confirm the need for surgery or treatment, the service may allow a third opinion to be sought from a physician meeting the qualifications described for second opinions.

The physician may proceed with treatment on the basis of verbal authorization from the service. This will be followed by a written authorization sent to you, the hospital and the physician. The authorization remains valid for 60 days from the date of the written authorization. For treatment beginning after the 60-day period, a new authorization must be obtained.

EMERGENCY ADMISSIONS: Emergency admissions are admissions for life-threatening conditions or for a condition for which the absence of immediate treatment would cause permanent disability. An emergency admission must also be authorized in the same manner as an elective admission or surgery, as soon as it is reasonably possible to give notice of such confinement. Otherwise that portion of an emergency confinement occurring beyond 48 hours after admission (excluding Saturdays, Sundays and legal holidays) is considered UNAUTHORIZED.

UNAUTHORIZED ADMISSION, CONFINEMENT, OR SURGERY: If authorization is obtained in accordance with the above procedures, the hospital admission or surgery will be considered authorized; otherwise, it will be considered UNAUTHORIZED. An admission, confinement or surgery for which authorization was obtained shall be considered UNAUTHORIZED if (a) the authorization is no longer valid when confinement begins or surgery is performed; or (b) the type of treatment, admitting physician or hospital differs from the authorized treatment, physician or hospital.

Also, that portion of a hospital confinement, whether non-emergency or emergency, that exceeds the number of authorized days will be considered UNAUTHORIZED, unless an extension is granted. To receive an extension, the physician must call the Company's authorization service at least 24 hours prior to the originally scheduled discharge date and request an extension. The authorization service may or may not authorize an extension. Unauthorized extensions will be considered on the same basis as an unauthorized admission.

REDUCTION OF PAYMENT: The first $500 of covered expense incurred for unauthorized hospital admissions, confinements (or the unauthorized portion thereof) or any surgery shall not be paid by the Company; nor will that $500, or any portion thereof, be applied to the basic deductible amount requirement or rate of payment determination. As described under the Coverage Description section, to be a covered expense, the services, treatment and supplies must be medically necessary and the resulting charges reasonable and customary.

EXCLUSIONS AND LIMITATIONS

EXPENSES NOT COVERED BY THIS POLICY:
This policy does not provide benefits for the following:

1. pre-existing conditions during the first two years coverage is in force; except as provided by the policy;
2. expense incurred for a sickness during the first 15 days after a covered person's effective date of coverage;
3. intentionally self-inflicted injury, suicide or suicide attempt, whether sane or insane;
4. care, treatment or services while in a government hospital, unless the covered person is legally required to pay for such services in the absence of insurance;
5. injury or sickness to the extent that benefits are paid by Medicare or any other government law or program (except Medicaid); or any Motor Vehicle No-Fault Law;
6. injury or sickness covered by any Worker's Compensation Act or Occupational Disease Law;
7. war or any act of war; injury or sickness while in the military service of any country (any premium paid for a time not covered will be returned pro-rata);
8. treatment of Temporomandibular Joint Dysfunction except as provided in item 16 of the covered expense provision;
9. dental service including X rays, care or treatment except as provided under item 13 of the covered expense provision;
10. treatment for infertility; confinement, treatment or services related to artificial insemination; restoration of fertility, reversal of sterilization or promotion of conception; or expense incurred for genetic counselling, testing or treatment.
11. eyeglasses, contact lenses, hearing aids, eye exams, eye refraction or eye surgery for correction of refraction error;
12. normal pregnancy or childbirth (except as may be provided by rider), routine well-baby care including hospital nursery charges at birth; abortion or caesarean section except as provided in the Covered Complications of Pregnancy provision;
13. expense incurred for weight reduction or weight-control programs, including surgery; treatment, medication or hormones to stimulate growth;
14. reconstructive or plastic surgery that is primarily a cosmetic procedure, including medical or surgical complications therefrom; except as provided in item 4 of the covered expense provision;
15. the first $500 of otherwise covered expense incurred during any unauthorized hospital confinement or the unauthorized portion of a confinement or unauthorized surgery (see Reduction of Payment Provision);
16. treatment, removal or repair of tonsils or adenoids during the first six months of coverage, except on an emergency basis;
17. expense incurred due to injury or sickness due to committing a felony or while under the influence of illegal narcotics;
18. sales tax or gross receipt tax;
19. custodial care.

CLAIMS

NOTICE OF CLAIM: If a covered person incurs covered expense, you must give the Company written notice of claim. The notice must be given within 60 days after the claim begins, or as soon as is reasonably possible. The notice must be given to the Company or its agent, and must include your name and policy number.

CLAIM FORMS: When notice of claim is received, the Company will send you claim forms. If you do not receive the forms within 15 days after the giving of such notice, you shall be deemed to have complied with the proof of loss requirements if: (1) you give the Company a written statement of the nature and the extent of the loss for which claim is made; and (2) such statement is given within the time limit stated in the Proofs of Loss provision.

PROOFS OF LOSS: You must give the Company written proof of loss within 90 days after the covered expense is incurred. If written proof is not given in the time required, this will not make the claim invalid as long as the proof is given as soon as reasonably possible. In no event, except in the absence of legal capacity, may proof be given later than one year from the time otherwise required.

PAYMENT OF CLAIMS: Benefits will be paid to you unless you have assigned them to a doctor, hospital or other provider. Any benefits unpaid and unassigned at your death will be paid to the designated beneficiary or your estate.

TIME OF PAYMENT OF CLAIMS: Benefits for covered expense will be paid promptly upon receipt of written proof of loss. If not paid within 30 days of receipt of proof of loss, interest at the rate of 8 percent per annum will be paid, in addition, after the 30th day.

PHYSICAL EXAMINATION: While a claim is pending, the Company has the right to have a covered person examined as often as reasonably necessary. This will be at the Company's expense.

CONTRACT

CONSIDERATION: This policy is issued on the basis of the statements and agreements in the application and payment of the required premium. Premium payment in advance on or before the policy date will keep this policy in force from the policy date until the first renewal date. The premium is set out in the policy schedule. Each renewal premium is due on its due date subject to the grace period. All periods of insurance will begin and end at 12:01 A.M., standard time, at your residence.

ENTIRE CONTRACT; CHANGES: This policy, your attached application and any endorsements constitute the entire contract. No change in this policy is valid unless approved by an executive office of the Company. The approval must be endorsed by the officer and attached to the policy. No agent can change this policy or waive any of its provisions.

TIME LIMIT ON CERTAIN DEFENSES: After two years from the effective date of coverage, no misstatement made in the application (unless fraudulent) will be used to void the policy or deny any claim beginning after the two year period.

No claim for expense incurred by a covered person that begins more than two years from that person's effective date of coverage will be reduced or denied on the grounds that a disease or physical condition (not excluded from coverage by name or specific description) had existed prior to the covered person's effective date.

GRACE PERIOD: There is a grace period of 31 days for the payment of each premium due after the first premium. The policy will stay in force during this grace period. If the premium is not paid by the end of the grace period, this policy will lapse. No coverage will be provided during the grace period if the covered person has similar coverage available through another carrier and does not pay premium to the Company.

NON-RENEWAL: The grace period does not apply if the Company has given you written notice that it will not renew the policy. This notice must be sent to you at least 30 days before the premium is due. Notice will be mailed to your last known address in the Company's records. Coverage will continue for any period for which premium has been accepted.

The Company can only decline to renew the policy on the renewal date occurring on, or after and nearest, each anniversary. The anniversary will be based on the policy date or last reinstatement date. This does not apply if premiums are not paid. Non-renewal will not prejudice any expense incurred while the policy was in force.

LEGAL ACTION: You cannot bring legal action to recover on this policy before at least 60 days have passed from the time written proof has been given to the Company. No action can be brought after three years from the time written proof has been given to the Company. The time limit is five years in Kansas; six years in South Carolina.

TERMINATION OF INSURED'S COVERAGE: Your coverage will end on the date the policy lapses or is non-renewed.

TERMINATION OF DEPENDENT COVERAGE: Coverage will end for your dependent children on the date the policy lapses or is non-renewed, or on the premium due date following the earliest to occur of (a) the date of their marriage, (b) the date they reach age 21 (or age 25 if the dependent is enrolled in and actively pursuing a full-time course of study at an accredited institution of higher learning), or (c) the date they are no longer dependent on you. Coverage will end on your spouse: (a) on the date the policy lapses or is non-renewed; or (b) on the premium due date following the date of a divorce. Benefits will still be paid to the end of the time for which premiums were accepted.

CONVERSION: A spouse or a dependent child who is no longer eligible for coverage on this policy can obtain a similar policy. No proof of good health will be required, but written application must be made within 60 days after that person's coverage terminates.

MISSTATEMENT OF AGE OR SEX: If any age or sex has been misstated, an adjustment in the benefits payable will be made to recover any past premiums due.

REINSTATEMENT: If you do not pay a renewal premium within the time granted, your policy will lapse. It will be reinstated if the Company or its agent accepts the premium without requiring an application.

If the Company or its agent requires an application for reinstatement, and the application and one modal premium are received within six months of the lapse date, the policy will be reinstated when approved by the Company. The Company has 45 days to act on your application. Your policy will be reinstated unless the Company notifies you in writing of its disapproval.

You will be covered for an injury sustained on or after the reinstatement date. You will be covered for a sickness that begins more than ten days after the reinstatement date.

After the policy is reinstated, you and the Company will have the same rights as existed just before the due date. These rights are subject to any provisions endorsed or attached to the policy. Premium cannot be required for more than 60 days before the date.

CONFORMITY WITH STATE STATUTES: If this policy, on its effective date, is in conflict with any laws in your state of residence, it is changed to meet the minimum requirements of such laws.

MAJOR MEDICAL INSURANCE APPLICATION

Name ______________________________ Occupation ______________ Sex ____
Last First Middle M/F

Billing Address ______________________________ Height ____ Weight ____
Street City State Zip Code Ft. In. Lbs.

Date of Birth ________ Place of Birth ______________ Phone (_____) __________
Mo./Day/Yr. City/State Area Code Number

Social Security # ______________ Business Phone (_____) __________
Area Code Number

1) I am a member actively at work at least 30 hours a week ❑ Yes ❑ No

YOUR CHOICE OF DEDUCTIBLE: ❑ PLAN A–$250 ❑ PLAN B–$500 ❑ PLAN C–$1,000

HOW WOULD YOU LIKE YOUR PREMIUM BILLED: ❑ Monthly ❑ Quarterly

WHICH PLAN ARE YOU APPLYING FOR: ❑ Comprehensive ❑ Basic

If you wish to include your spouse and/or eligible dependent children, complete this section:

NAME (First, Middle, Last)	SEX	DATE OF BIRTH	HEIGHT	WEIGHT
Your Spouse				
Your Children				

THE FOLLOWING QUESTIONS ARE TO BE ANSWERED FOR EACH PERSON APPLYING FOR COVERAGE. ANY MISSTATEMENTS MAY AFFECT YOUR COVERAGE—GIVE FULL DETAILS TO ALL "YES" ANSWERS IN THE SPACE PROVIDED.

In the last 10 years, has any person proposed for insurance been diagnosed, treated by or consulted a licensed physician or practitioner for any of the following:

Yes No

a. Abnormal blood pressure, chest pain, stroke, heart attach or murmur or any other heart, blood or circulatory disorder . . . . ❑ ❑

b. Cancer, tumor, growth, enlarged lymph nodes, skin disorder or discolored areas or lesions of the skin or mouth . . . . ❑ ❑

c. Emphysema, lung or respiratory disorder . . . . ❑ ❑

d. Arthritis, or any disorder of the back or neck, muscles, bones or joints . . . . ❑ ❑

e. Kidney or urinary system disorder, disorder of the prostate or reproductive system, or breast disorder . . . . ❑ ❑

Yes No

f. Ulcers, colitis, rectal disorder or any disorder of the digestive system, liver or gallbladder . . . . ❑ ❑

g. Diabetes, thyroid disorder, speech impairment or disorder of the eyes, ears, nose or throat . . . . ❑ ❑

h. Seizures or neurological disorder, mental, nervous or emotional disorder, psychiatric or psychological counseling or treatment . . . . ❑ ❑

i. Alcoholism, drug or chemical dependency or substance abuse . . . . ❑ ❑

j. Acquired Immune Deficiency Syndrome or AIDS Related Complex (ARC) . . . . ❑ ❑

For Office Use Only
Eff. ______________ Ren. Date ______________ Paid ______________
CC ______________ Cert. No. ______________

NOTICE OF INSURANCE INFORMATION PRACTICES

TO PROPERLY UNDERWRITE AND ADMINISTER YOUR INSURANCE COVERAGE A CERTAIN AMOUNT OF INFORMATION MUST BE COLLECTED. THE APPLICATION FOR INSURANCE CONTAINS INFORMATION OBTAINED FROM YOU NECESSARY FOR THIS PURPOSE. IN ADDITION, AS PART OF OUR REGULAR UNDERWRITING PROCEDURE, OTHER INFORMATION MAY BE COLLECTED FROM OTHER SOURCES ABOUT YOU OR YOUR ELIGIBLE DEPENDENTS WHO MAY BE PROPOSED FOR INSURANCE.

GENERALLY, DISCLOSURE OF PERSONAL INFORMATION WILL NOT BE MADE TO THIRD PARTIES. HOWEVER, IN SOME CIRCUMSTANCES, THE INSURANCE COMPANY OR YOUR AGENT WILL MAKE DISCLOSURE OF PERSONAL INFORMATION WITHOUT YOUR AUTHORIZATION TO THIRD PARTIES. THIS MIGHT INCLUDE THE DISCLOSURE OF PERSONAL INFORMATION TO PERSONS OR ORGANIZATIONS WHO MAY WISH TO MARKET PRODUCTS OR SERVICES, INCLUDING AFFILIATES OF THE INSURANCE COMPANY, BUT ONLY IF YOU HAVE NOT INDICATED TO US IN WRITING THAT YOU OBJECT TO OUR DOING SO.

YOU HAVE THE RIGHT TO OBTAIN ACCESS TO PERSONAL INFORMATION ABOUT YOU OR YOUR ELIGIBLE DEPENDENTS, IF PROPOSED FOR INSURANCE, COLLECTED BY THE COMPANY OR YOUR AGENT, EXCEPT INFORMATION RELATING TO A CLAIM, CIVIL OR CRIMINAL PROCEEDING. MEDICAL INFORMATION WILL ONLY BE RELEASED THROUGH A DOCTOR, PRACTITIONER, OR OTHER MEDICAL PROFESSIONAL SELECTED BY YOU WHO IS LICENSED TO PROVIDE PROFESSIONAL CARE RELEVANT TO THE NATURE OF THE INFORMATION. YOU ALSO HAVE THE RIGHT TO SEEK CORRECTION OF INFORMATION YOU BELIEVE TO BE INACCURATE.

Yes No

2) Are you or any of your dependents currently pregnant? **If yes, list name and due date.** ❑ ❑

____

3) In the last 2 years, has any person proposed for insurance taken prescription medication for more than 30 days? **If yes, state condition, name of medication, dosage and frequency in space provided below.** ❑ ❑

4) In the last 5 years, have you or any of your dependents to be insured had any physical disorder, illness, injury, surgery, or check-up, or consultation other than admitted above? ❑ ❑

Complete the following for each "YES" answer to questions 1 through 4:

Ques. No.	Name of Person	Date of Treatment From	Date of Treatment To	Reason for Checkup, Diagnosis, Illness or Condition Frequency of Attacks	Treatment or Findings, Medication, Recommendations, Hospitalization and/or Surgery Degree of Recovery	Name and Address of Each Physician, Practitioner and Medical Facility

If additional space is needed use a separate sheet. Sign, date and return it with this form.

Yes No

5) Has any person proposed for insurance had health insurance declined, postponed, ridered, rated, canceled or had reinstatement or renewal refused? **If yes, state the name of the company, action, reason and date in the space below.** ❑ ❑

6) Does any person proposed for insurance now carry health insurance or have an application pending with another company? **If yes, state name of applicant, company, type and amount of coverage in the space provided below.** ❑ ❑

7) Will the coverage you are applying for replace any coverage listed above? **If yes, give details below.** ❑ ❑

____

____

____

____

I understand and agree that the statements and answers in this application are complete and true to the best of my knowledge and belief and shall form a part of the contract of insurance. I also understand and agree that the insurance applied for, if issued, shall be subject to such statements and answers and will take effect on the effective date stated on the schedule provided the applicable first premium has been paid.

I AUTHORIZE any physician, medical practitioner, hospital, clinic, other medical or medically related facility, insurance or reinsuring company, Medical Information Bureau, consumer reporting agency, employer, or the Veterans Administration, having information available as to advice, diagnosis, treatment, or care of any physical or mental condition concerning me, my spouse, or my minor children, including information about drugs, alcoholism, or mental illness, and any other non-medical information concerning me, my spouse, or my minor children to give to the Company, its affiliates, its legal representative, or its reinsurers any and all such information.

I UNDERSTAND the information obtained by use of the Authorization will be used by the Company or its affiliates to determine eligibility for insurance.

I KNOW that I may request to receive a copy of this Authorization.

I ACKNOWLEDGE having received and read the Notice Regarding Medical Information Bureau and the Notice of Insurance Information Practices (where applicable).

I AGREE that a copy of this Authorization shall be as valid as the original.

I AGREE that this Authorization shall remain valid for two years from the date shown below.

______________ X ______________________ X ______________________

DATE SIGNATURE OF PROPOSED INSURED SIGNATURE OF SPOUSE (IF APPLYING)

NATIONAL ASSOCIATION OF HEALTH UNDERWRITERS
PROTECTING THE CONSUMER'S FUTURE
NAHU

NAHU—America's Benefit Specialists

Code of Ethics

To hold the selling, servicing, and distribution of Disability Income and Health Insurance Plans as a professional and a public trust and do all in my power to maintain its prestige.

To keep the needs of those whom I serve paramount.

To respect my client's trust in me, and never do anything which would betray that trust or confidence.

To give all service possible when service is needed.

To present policies factually and accurately—providing all information necessary for the issuance of sound insurance coverage to the public I serve.

To use no advertising which may be false or misleading.

To consider the sale of Disability Income and Health Insurance Plans as a career, know and abide by the insurance laws of my state, and seek constantly through study to increase my knowledge and improve my ability to meet the needs of my client.

To be fair and just to my competitors, and engage in no practice which might reflect unfavorably on myself or my industry.

To treat prospects, clients, and companies fairly by submitting applications which reveal all available information pertinent to the underwriting of a policy.

To be loyal to my clients, associates, fellow agents and brokers, and the company or companies whose products I represent.

Dear Student,

What did you think of your Dearborn PASSTRAK study materials? We'd like to know!

We invite you to complete the PASSTRAK survey below. Your responses will help us to develop even better exam preparation materials. Please tear this page out of your book, fold it into thirds, seal it and mail it to us. We'll pay the postage. Your comments are greatly appreciated.

Dearborn™
Financial Services
A **Kaplan Professional** Company
30 S Wacker Drive
Suite 2500
Chicago IL 60606-7481

Book title and edition number: ______________________________

Please rate the PASSTRAK materials using the following scale:

1 = Poor 2 = Satisfactory 3 = Very Good

License Exam Manual

Easy to read	1	2	3
Easy to understand	1	2	3
Organized	1	2	3
Up-to-date	1	2	3
Complete	1	2	3
Accurate	1	2	3

Questions & Answers

Challenging	1	2	3
Number of questions	1	2	3
Accurate	1	2	3
Up-to-date	1	2	3
Matches the test	1	2	3

How well do you believe the PASSTRAK materials prepared you for the exam? 1 2 3

What did you like about the PASSTRAK materials?

What would you like us to do to improve the PASSTRAK materials?

Which topic or subject did you find most difficult to study?

What other Dearborn products do you use? Please check them here:

Classroom ____ AnswerPhone ____ Online Drill & Practice ____ Continuing Education Materials ____

Practice Finals ____ Diagnostic Exams ____ Course software ____ Audiotapes ____

How likely would you be to use an online product? Very likely ____ Somewhat likely ____ Not likely ____

Did you take the licensing exam? No ____ Yes ____ Date ____________ Score ____

Name (optional): ______________________________

State of Residence ______ Firm ________________

May we contact you?
If so, please provide us with your phone number or email address: ______________________

You can reach us with your comments and questions at Dearborn's AnswerPhone, a toll-free service.
Securities AnswerPhone: (800) 621-9621, ext. 3598
Insurance AnswerPhone: (800) 621-9621, ext. 2444

You can also contact us at our website, www.dearborn.com.

NOTE: This page, when folded over and taped, becomes a postage-free envelope that has been approved by the United States Postal Service. It has been provided for your convenience.

▼ Important—please fold over and tape before mailing ▼

NO POSTAGE NECESSARY IF MAILED IN THE UNITED STATES

BUSINESS REPLY MAIL

FIRST-CLASS MAIL PERMIT NO. 88175 CHICAGO, IL

POSTAGE WILL BE PAID BY ADDRESSEE

ATTN FINANCIAL SERVICES MARKETING
DEARBORN FINANCIAL SERVICES
30 S WACKER DRIVE
SUITE 2500
CHICAGO IL 60606-7481

▲ Important—please fold over and tape before mailing ▲

NOTE: This page, when folded over and taped, becomes a postage-free envelope that has been approved by the United States Postal Service. It has been provided for your convenience.

Please cut along dotted line

LIGHT

A National Gallery Touring Exhibition in partnership with
Bristol Museums and Art Gallery and the Laing Art Gallery, Newcastle upon Tyne

NO REPRESENTATIONAL ARTIST can ignore the role of light in making visible the things he or she depicts, but in some paintings the role played by light is fundamental. In landscape painting particularly, light may effectively become the chief subject to which all else is subordinated. This exhibition looks at some of the ways artists have used light in their paintings to create meaning and suggest mood, and how they have found ways in paint to represent its diverse effects. Light has also played a pivotal role in several important movements in art and many of those developments are represented in this exhibition.

In figure painting, dramatic use of artificial illumination was at the centre of the new pictorial approach initiated by the Italian artist Caravaggio around the beginning of the seventeenth century. In this style shadowy backgrounds and bright foreground highlights propelled powerfully naturalistic figures startlingly close to the viewer. The new approach was tremendously influential in Italy and parts of Northern Europe.

While the effects of artificial lighting could be exploited for particular artistic ends, unsurprisingly it is within the evolution of landscape painting that artists have been faced more consistently with the problems of painting light effects. A beautifying and all-enveloping golden glow is one of the defining features of the idealised landscape tradition, developed especially by Claude Lorraine in the seventeenth century in Italy. In the Netherlands at the same period, artists began to paint naturalistic landscapes, drawing on their actual experience of light and weather under the more turbulent northern skies. Over a long period the practice of studying details from nature, encouraged in art academies from the sixteenth century onwards, was transformed into the process of open-air sketching, designed to capture the atmospheric effects of particular times of day, weather conditions and seasons. In the nineteenth century Turner drew on both the idealised and naturalistic landscape traditions for his wonderful representations of luminous colour radiating from the sun. At the time, Turner's pictures provoked both admiration and criticism for the way light flooded the image, overwhelming the ostensible subject.

Impressionism, one of the most innovative and influential movements of modern times, was primarily concerned with light. The Impressionists' pictures are now so often seen simply as pretty, uncomplicated images that it is difficult to appreciate the rawness of their efforts to depict transient light effects, and the shocking boldness of the colour with which they represented the intensity of light.

Symbolic Light

Light has been used as a manifestation of the presence and power of God in Western religious painting for many centuries. This is the role light fulfils in G.F. Watts's canvas, which is almost filled with the blaze of the sun. In *The Agony in the Garden of Gethsemane*, painted by a follower of El Greco, luminous rays represent God communicating directly with Jesus. Light has a similar function in Berchem's *Annunciation to the Shepherds*, in which shining beams from the heavens transport angelic messengers.

Divine light is traditionally depicted as more intense than any earthly illumination. The glow emanating from the Christ Child in Rembrandt's *Adoration of the Shepherds* outshines the shepherds' lanterns and dazzles the onlookers. This illumination is also a representation of the concept of Jesus as the 'Light of the World', metaphorically lighting the path to redemption.

Light can also represent the opposite of the divine. The fiery light engulfing John Martin's *Destruction of Sodom and Gomorrah* evokes the flames of hell and eternal damnation. In paintings by Goya and Salvator Rosa, flames are associated with satanic practices. These pictures are set in darkness, excluding the light of salvation and reason. Moonlight, inextricably linked to darkness, is also associated with evil, madness and dreams. It illuminates both Rosa's scene of witchcraft and Paul Delvaux's surreal and disturbing dreamscape.

G.F. WATTS (1817–1904)
After The Deluge; The Forty-First Day, about 1885–91
The Watts Gallery, Compton, Guildford

ACCORDING TO THE ARTIST'S WIFE, WATTS DESCRIBED this picture as showing: 'The hand of the Creator moving by light and by heat to re-create. I have not tried to paint a portrait of the sun – such a thing is unpaintable – but I wanted to impress you with the idea of its enormous power.'

The painting depicts the ending of the mighty flood sent to punish mankind, as described in the Old Testament book of Genesis. The sun is shining above a featureless world, empty and black apart from the reflections on the water.

At its sides the sun's radiance illuminates vapour trails as the waters begin to disperse into mist. Light has tremendous symbolic significance since, according to the Bible, it was the first element of the universe created by God.

The representation of the sun as the sublime power and the powerfully abstract treatment were both influenced by the work of Turner. Watts greatly admired Turner's paintings, which he saw on visits to the National Gallery in London.

STUDIO OF EL GRECO (EL GRECO 1541–1614)
The Agony in the Garden of Gethsemane, late sixteenth century
National Gallery, London

EL GRECO AND HIS FOLLOWERS WERE CONCERNED WITH light's symbolic function and the ways it could be used to dramatise and underline meaning.

This image represents the events shortly before Christ's arrest and subsequent death, as told in the Bible. Jesus, abandoned by the sleeping disciples, prays alone to his Father that he be spared his coming suffering with the words: 'O my Father, if it be possible, let this cup pass from me' (Matthew 26:39). The shaft of light could be seen as symbolising the Holy Spirit, linking God the Father and God the Son: the three aspects of the Trinity.

On the right, Judas,who will betray Jesus, approaches with a group of Roman legionaries. Their figures are outlined by light spilling out from the blazing rent in the sky. In contrast, the moon above them and the torches they hold shine with a paler light.

In a strange oval-shaped cave on the left are the sleeping figures of the disciples, their forms also emphasised with dramatic contrasts of light and shade. Above an angel holds the 'cup of sorrow' that Christ asked to be taken from him, but it is also a communion cup and so a reference to Jesus' lifeblood.

REMBRANDT VAN RIJN (1606–1669)
The Adoration of the Shepherds, 1646
National Gallery, London

THE PRINCIPAL LIGHT OF REMBRANDT'S PICTURE emanates in a golden glow from the form of the Christ Child. The dark shadow of the foreground figure emphasises the brightness of the illumination. Dazzled, the kneeling shepherd with the stick starts back, his hands raised. This divine light completely outshines the lantern carried by the figure on the right. In the background, a warm glow behind the heads of the standing group reveals another light carried by an unseen figure.

This picture shows Rembrandt's mastery of the painting of soft light and deep shade known as *chiaroscuro*. A soft haziness surrounds the lights and dim pools of illumination fall in patches on the ground. These lights of varying strengths help establish a feeling of space around the figures. The soft shadows fading imperceptibly into darkness create a sense of intimacy, which complements the family atmosphere of the scene. Women, children and a dog have joined the shepherds mentioned in the biblical account given by Luke (2:16).

NICOLAES BERCHEM (1620–1683)
The Annunciation to the Shepherds, 1656
City of Bristol Museum and Art Gallery

THIS PICTURE, ONE OF BERCHEM'S RELATIVELY few religious subjects, depicts the announcement of Christ's birth to the shepherds, as described in the Bible. Shafts of light supporting angels and cherubim radiate from the heavens, a motif characteristic of Italian Baroque painting. Like many other Netherlandish artists of the period, Berchem was influenced by the work of Italian painters, particularly their use of light effects.

The divine radiance bathes the proclaiming angel in white illumination so powerful it casts a deep shadow at the feet of the standing shepherd in the centre of the picture who gazes up awestruck, blinded by its brilliance. But if the light is a clear symbol of divine revelation it is also a direct illustration of the Gospel text: 'And, lo, the angel of the Lord came upon them, and the glory of the Lord shone round about them' (Luke 2:9). The light picks out the reclining figures of a mother and her child, who do not appear in the Bible story. They provide a link between the divine event of Christ's birth and ordinary family life.

In the foreground is a group of cattle (also an addition to the story), whose forms are bathed in a golden haze. This group is very characteristic of Berchem, whose usual subjects were pastoral landscapes lit by a warm Italianate light.

SALVATOR ROSA (1615–1673)
Witches at their Incantations, about 1646
National Gallery, London

THE DARKNESS OF NIGHT WAS OFTEN ASSOCIATED with witchcraft, death and fearful things. This gathering of witches is lit by a moon that is not visible, but shines down from a position above the viewer. In the background the approaching dawn lightens the sky, but it is not yet strong enough to throw its illumination over the ground and banish the witches.

There are several other light sources within the picture. A tray of candles is held by a mysterious shrouded figure on the left and a woman holds up a flaming pot to the nostrils of the hanged man in the centre. A figure clad in dark armour also uses a burning torch to illuminate a magical manuscript. Light gleams on naked flesh, on the bony surface of a skull and shiny metal, and glitters on the eyes, shell and skin of grotesque creatures. The illumination of the moon and the firelight is not realistic. Instead it is used to draw the viewer's eye to and fro across the parade of horrid events, as the witches cast their spells.

FRANCISCO DE GOYA (1746–1828)
A Scene from El Hechizado por Fuerza ('The Forcibly Bewitched'), 1798
National Gallery, London

THE SUBJECT OF DREAMS AND FEARS TAKING FANTASTIC shape as they emerge out of the darkness of night was a theme that ran throughout Goya's work.

This painting depicts a scene in a comic play of the time by Antonio de Zamore in which the character of Don Claudio has been tricked into believing he will live only as long as the oil lamp he is refilling remains alight. The power of light has long been associated with salvation from the forces of evil. The lamp itself flares up, creating a grotesque mask of Don Claudio's features, while behind him the shadows resolve into the devilish shapes of huge prancing donkeys. (In the play these were merely a picture hung up to frighten Don Claudio.)

Satan was often thought to assume the form of a goat, and the element of horror is increased by the half-goat, half-female figure holding the lamp.

The first parts of the words '*lampara descomunal*' (monstrous lamp), spoken by Don Claudio in the play, appear on the edge of a book at the front of the picture.

JOHN MARTIN (1789–1854)
The Destruction of Sodom and Gomorrah, 1852
Laing Art Gallery, Newcastle upon Tyne

THIS BIBLE SUBJECT, PAINTED TOWARDS THE END OF Martin's life, was a return to the huge, theatrical scenes of mass destruction that had made his reputation many years before. The painting is dominated by the blazing light of God's wrath, as fire engulfs the twin cities of Sodom and Gomorrah in punishment for their inhabitants' wickedness. A great red-tipped orange arc fills the sky, burning an intense yellow at the centre of the conflagration. The design owed much to the looming, swirling appearance of massive storms in paintings by Turner, combined with the image of the blinding light generated by intense heat.

Lightning strikes out of the sky, turning Lot's unfortunate wife to salt because she has disregarded the divine command not to look back at the destruction. Only Lot and his children escape the annihilation. The lightning is represented by the traditional zig-zag shape, though its true form had been drawn by scientific researchers and published many years before.

During his lifetime Martin often exhibited his pictures as theatrical spectacles, lighting them dramatically with oil lamps.

PAUL DELVAUX (1897–1994)
A Siren in Full Moonlight, 1940
Southampton City Art Gallery

IN THIS SURREAL PAINTING THE NIGHT IS LINKED WITH sexual licence and the world of dreams. The bonds of restraint and reason imposed by daylight are loosened. Lit by the cool, somewhat sinister light of a full moon, a mermaid reclines on a shallow-stepped plinth. The mermaid has long been linked in mythology with sex, and was sometimes used as a symbol for prostitutes in popular imagery. Abutting the mermaid's head a doorway, lit by a dim hanging bulb, leads to a marooned municipal tower. These features, combined with the strange curtained doorways of the porticoes on the left, add to the sexual undertones of the picture. Street lamps, shining with the bluish hue of electric arc light, add little to the illumination but evoke night-time city streets where assignations can be made. The title of the picture increases the general sense of unease, since sirens were the mythical creatures reputed to lure sailors to their deaths.

Natural Light

Landscape painters have always been concerned with the challenge of capturing different effects of light. The paintings shown here include pictures executed at various periods, representing light effects from dawn to dusk.

Seventeenth-century Netherlandish artists, including townscape painters such as Berckheyde, developed an extraordinary sensitivity to atmospheric light in their paintings. The sky and its light dominate their pictures, creating wide, airy vistas, within which the fall of light on individual objects is carefully described.

By the beginning of the nineteenth century artists were becoming more fascinated than ever before by natural light and weather. Open-air studies, made by Corot among many others, enabled artists to produce sensitive paintings of the landscape under specific light conditions.

For some artists, light was not just a means of describing landscape and atmosphere, but the real subject of their paintings. A wonderful golden glow of sunlight floods the pictures of Claude and other seventeenth-century painters of idealised landscapes in Italy. Two centuries later, Turner was also obsessed with light, creating in his paintings magnificent, near abstract swathes of colour that transmit not only light, but also the emotional charge that light in landscape can carry.

For the Impressionists, the expression of light in pure colour and its transient qualities in all conditions were at the heart of their work, and they sometimes painted the complete picture in the open air. The concept of light as colour was also central to the work of Post-Impressionist painters such as Seurat.

CLAUDE LORRAINE (1604/5?–1682)
A Seaport, 1644
National Gallery, London

TURNER ADMIRINGLY DESCRIBED THE EFFECTS OF LIGHT achieved by the French artist Claude Lorraine as: 'The golden orient or the amber-coloured ether ... rich, harmonious, true and clear, replete with all the aerial qualities of distance, aerial lights, aerial colour ...'

Claude spent his career in Rome, and this picture incorporates architectural features from the city: the antique Arch of Titus stands in the water and the palace façade is adapted from a Renaissance gateway. The subject, an imaginary seaport at sunset, is one of several similar scenes painted by the artist.

The golden light of the setting sun on the horizon is magnified by the water and its long reflection sends light rippling towards the shore. Its radiance heightens the feeling of space and shimmers on the surfaces of the buildings.

The light is observed naturalistically, but it also has an evocative role. The golden veil over the picture contributes a quality of serenity and timelessness to the elegantly elongated forms.

In the foreground, the setting sun outlines the figures with light and casts long shadows that softly dissolve into darkness at the edges of the picture.

THE NETHERLANDISH LANDSCAPE AND CITYSCAPE painters of the seventeenth century were celebrated for their ability to represent natural light. The precise observation of the daylight in this picture helps to convince the viewer of the reality of the scene it represents. A bright afternoon sun lights up the west front of the Haarlem church of Saint Bavo and the square beneath. The length of the afternoon shadows and the clothes the people wear suggest that it is a warm spring day. The low viewpoint ensures a wide expanse of sky, its pale tones contributing to the sense of luminosity.

Light, as much as the crisp perspective, establishes the three-dimensional effect of the buildings and the spacious orderliness of the scene. The church front and transept, lit by full sun, are relatively bleached in colour. As the space recedes, the colours take on the subdued bluish tones imposed by the haze of distance, while the depth of colour in the shadows reduces as they gradually become darker.

At the same time, the sparkle of light on the figures and the warm-toned buildings contributes a charming sense of liveliness to the scene.

GERRIT BERCKHEYDE, (1638–1698)
The Market Place and the Grote Kerk at Haarlem, 1674
National Gallery, London

JOSEPH MALLORD WILLIAM TURNER (1775–1851)
The Evening Star, about 1830?
National Gallery, London

TURNER STUDIED LIGHT IN EVERY ATMOSPHERIC condition. He also read the scientific literature of the period, in particular Joseph Priestley's *History and Present State of Discoveries Relevant to Vision, Light and Colour*, 1767.

In this picture, the faint reddish arc of the sun shoots its last weak beams up into a sky still lit by dim streaks of yellow. Above, the first star of evening has appeared, its reflection on the water shining more brightly than the star itself. As the light fades sea, sky and sand unite in a luminous veil of colour and tone that captures the subtle effect of twilight over water. A figure on the beach and the spars of a marine structure serve to anchor the almost abstract composition in the real world.

At the time, many critics responded to Turner's pictures in similar fashion to William Hazlitt, who in 1816 described them as: '... representations not properly of the objects of nature as of the medium through which they were seen. They are the triumph of the knowledge of the artist ... over the barreness [sic] of the subject.'

JEAN-BAPTISTE-CAMILLE COROT (1796–1875)
Peasants under the Trees at Dawn, about 1840–5
National Gallery, London

FILLED WITH LIGHT, THIS PICTURE PRESERVES MUCH of the spontaneity of a sketch in its informal composition and free brushwork – and it was for these features that Corot's work was admired by Impressionist artists. Throughout his life Corot made great numbers of open-air studies (part of a landscape painter's usual practice at the time), studying especially the effects of light.

In this painting the sun, low down in the sky, shines from directly behind the scene to create a particular light effect known as *contre-jour*. The line of houses is thrown into silhouette and a halo of light shines through the hair of the woman sitting on the bank. Sunlight sparkles through the foliage of the trees and illuminates the upper planes of the pile of logs. The optical effect of this bright light is increased by the contrast with the subdued tones of its surroundings.

The picture balances pale earth colours with cool grey-green hues. Relatively bright touches of green in the foliage emphasise the delicate illumination of the sky. This juxtaposition captures the sensation of freshness in the early morning, with a hint of heat to come.

PIERRE-AUGUSTE RENOIR (1841–1919)
Boating on the Seine
about 1879–80
National Gallery, London

FULL SUNLIGHT FLOODS THIS QUINTESSENTIALLY Impressionist painting showing boating on the Seine, probably at Chatou to the west of Paris. As Renoir intended, it is easy to respond to this picture as an instantaneous snapshot of colour and light.

The handling of the paint is free and spontaneous, and it is applied so sketchily that the canvas shows through in many places. White paint has been dashed in to create clouds, and it underlies the pale blue of the sky, increasing the luminosity of the colour.

The picture is laid out in horizontal bands across the canvas and relies on the unifying sparkle of light over the whole scene. The painting's feeling of depth is created by a gradual lessening of the strength of the colours. On the water, horizontal dabs of pink and orange create the shimmer of reflections, while the shadows of the background foliage reflect the blue of the sky. At the front of the picture, the strong orange of the boat creates a sensation of warmth and brightness, which is intensified by the complementary blue of the water. This contrast also contributes to the scintillating reflections on the river.

CLAUDE-OSCAR MONET
(1840–1926)
Lavacourt under Snow
about 1878–81
National Gallery, London

THIS PICTURE, WHICH WAS PAINTED AT THE VILLAGE of Lavacourt by the river Seine, explores the luminosity of snow and the effects produced by light reflected on its white surface. It is one of several snow subjects Monet painted during his career.

Impressionists recognised and exploited the fact that coloured light produces shadows of a complementary colour, and here the pale morning sun gives the shadowed foreground snow its bluey tinge, which deepens in the shaded areas of the roofs. The sky, flushed with yellow, is reflected in the predominantly greenish hues of the river. Horizontal brushstrokes of green, blue, yellow and pink, dragged in fairly stiff paint, indicate the tumbling surface of the water.

The angle of the sun means that the distant hills are caught most strongly in its light. Hues of pink with blue and yellow, heavily loaded with lead white to make them very pale and luminous, create the effect of bright light at a distance. Broken brushstrokes break up the paint surface, producing a sparkle of light reflecting from the picture itself.

THIS PICTURE, WHICH MAY HAVE BEEN PAINTED ONTO A cigar-box lid, was one of many little sketches Seurat made in the open air in the early part of his career.

In the radically simple composition, Seurat aimed to achieve a luminous intensity by juxtaposing complementary and contrasting colours. In the grass, subtle greenish-blues are set against bright blues, with areas of warm reddish colour showing through the irregular brushstrokes. In places, the orange-brown of the wood support is visible. Against the sky, the dark leaves of the trees create a startling contrast with the light behind. Touches of cream, yellow, orange and blue re-create the colours of the setting sun.

The blue tones of the picture reproduce a particular visual effect of twilight, when the human eye is adjusting from daylight vision to darkness. During this period, the ability of the eye to perceive tones in the blue range increases significantly.

Seurat's approach to colour and light was influenced by scientific theories such as those proposed in Hermann von Helmholtz's *On the Relation of Optics to Painting* of 1871.

GEORGES SEURAT (1859–1891)
Sunset, about 1881
City of Bristol Museum and Art Gallery

Artificial Light

The striking contrasts of lighting generated by candles and firelight were often used in figure compositions to add drama and impact. This is particularly true of pictures by followers of the Italian painter Caravaggio in the seventeenth century. Strongly directional lighting from individual light sources allowed artists to create sculpturally solid figures, while darkened background shadows focused attention on the main scene.

With artificial illumination, artists could easily manipulate their compositions to highlight symbolic elements or underline meaningful comparisons. One recurring theme in art over many centuries was the contrast between youth and age, which is illustrated here in differing ways by Matthias Stom and Joseph Wright of Derby. By emphasising different aspects of the light within a scene an artist could also develop a painting's narrative, as in Wright of Derby's *An Experiment on a Bird in the Air Pump*. This picture shows how artificial light could produce rich colour, brilliant reflections and sparkling surfaces. Sharply lit details add to the realism of the painting.

Using artificial light artists could experiment with dual light sources, developing atmospheric space, or perhaps contrasting the qualities of various types of illumination. Nineteenth-century progress in artificial gas and electric lighting created intriguing new visual effects – both in interior and open-air scenes – which were studied by Impressionist artists such as Degas and Pissarro.

The sensational spray of light from a firework explosion at night is the subject of John Duncan Fergusson's picture *Dieppe, 14 July 1905: Night*, which ends the exhibition. This picture also explores the potential of staccato bursts of light for suggesting movement.

MATTHIAS STOM (ABOUT 1600–AFTER 1649)
Salome receiving the Head of John the Baptist, before 1640
Collection of Sir Denis Mahon, National Gallery, London

THE SUBJECT OF THIS PICTURE IS BIBLICAL AND SHOWS Salome, daughter of King Herod, holding up a platter to receive the head of John the Baptist who was killed at her demand.

The head hangs from the apex of a triangle of light, closed on the left by the bright white of the executioner's shirt, and on the right by the light reflected from Salome's skin and the shiny surface of her robe.

The illumination from the burning brand held by the young boy reflects off the golden plate held by Salome, imparting a greenish hue to the skin of the severed head. Its lifeless flesh contrasts with the lined face of the old woman and the plump, gleaming features of Salome. Strong directional lighting gives the figures three-dimensional solidity and produces rich warm colours.

This picture was probably painted in Rome and shows the influence of the Italian painter Caravaggio, whose command of the dramatic properties of artificial illumination drew a number of followers, including Stom, from the Netherlands.

HENDRICK TER BRUGGHEN (1588?–1629)
The Concert, about 1626
National Gallery, London

THIS PAINTING WAS INSPIRED BY SIMILAR WORKS BY Caravaggio, which the Netherlandish artist ter Bruggen knew from a ten-year stay in Italy.

A central foreground candle, its flame flickering above translucent wax, lights the picture. The low-level illumination throws highlights onto the chins of the young man and woman, casting dark shadows on their noses and cheeks without disturbing the naturalism of their features. The dark shadows intensify our experience of the light itself and also create depth. At the same time, bright white illumination on the woman's sleeve projects her towards us, enhancing our sense of the figures' reality and the feeling of their nearness.

A small wall-hung lamp in the background throws out warm lights and shadows, establishing space in what is otherwise an undefined area. It also subtly lights the face of the young boy.

At the front of the picture a bowl of grapes and a glass of wine glint in the light. Their presence underlines the theme of the painting, the transient sweetness of life represented by the music, the flickering candle and the youthfulness of the musicians.

JOSEPH WRIGHT OF DERBY (1734–1797)
An Experiment on a Bird in the Air Pump, 1768
National Gallery, London

THIS WORK SHOWS A SCIENTIFIC DEMONSTRATION OF a vacuum, vividly represented by the last flutter of a bird as the air is extracted from the glass globe in which it is imprisoned. The illumination comes from a candle placed on the table behind a huge vase of liquid, which amplifies its light. Reflections from glass and metal items, and from the children's silky dresses, glitter on the polished surface of the table. Satins, fur and pearls also gleam in the candlelight.

Light is used to help tell the story, directing the viewer's eye upwards from the troubling sight of the skull in the illuminated goblet, past the fearful little girls to the captive bird and the demonstrator's hand poised above the globe's stopper. The cool light of the moon, contrasting with the warm candlelight within the room, directs our attention to the boy using a pole to bring down the bird's cage for its safe return.

Different types of illumination help underline the varying characters and ages of the figures. A pool of light illuminates the father comforting his tender-hearted daughter as he rests his weather-beaten hand on her shoulder. On the left, a youthful couple have eyes only for each other.

HILAIRE-GERMAIN-EDGAR DEGAS (1834–1917)
Miss La La at the Cirque Fernando, 1879
National Gallery, London

MISS LA LA IS SHOWN PERFORMING THE ACT THAT MADE her famous, suspended from the ceiling of the Cirque Fernando by a rope clenched between her teeth. Degas watched her performance several times in January 1879.

Degas was particularly interested in the pictorial problems of artificial lighting combined with the distorting viewpoints generally experienced in theatrical entertainments. Here the lighting is gas, which casts a warm yellow light on the circus interior, deepening to a strong orange in the shaded areas of the ceiling. The effect of gaslight was to reduce tonal contrasts, browning dark tones and lightening colours generally.

Miss La La's pose casts her face into shadow while light from below catches the outstretched hand behind her, blurring the definition of the fingers. Light shimmers on her costume, which is a delicate pink shot with light blue and green tones. Unlike the other Impressionists, Degas occasionally used grey paint, which he has applied here to describe the sheen of the fabric.

To preserve the purity of his colours and their ability to reflect light, Degas diluted the oil paints with turpentine, resulting in the picture's matt finish.

CAMILLE PISSARRO (1830–1903)
The Boulevard Montmartre at Night, 1897
National Gallery, London

THIS PICTURE OF THE LIGHTS OF THE BOULEVARD Montmartre on a rainy night was one of a series by Pissarro showing the street at different times. In a letter the same year, the artist wrote: 'I am delighted to be able to paint those Paris streets that people have come to call ugly, but which are so silvery, so luminous and vital ... This is completely modern!'

On the right, the wet pavement reflects the warm orange and yellow blaze of the shops' gaslights, described in vertical streaks and dabs of paint. The cooler hue of the streetlights produces a silvery shimmer on the wet roadway. A strong blue aura surrounds the white globes of the lamps themselves, which appear to be electric. Paris was one of the first cities in Europe to experiment with electric arc lighting and by 1897 many streets were lit this way. Warm yellow glints indicate the oil lamps of the vehicles that line the street. At the horizon a glow of light, rendered in broken streaks of pale blue with touches of a warm reddish tone, bursts into the deeper blue of the sky.

JOHN DUNCAN FERGUSSON (1874–1961)
Dieppe, 14 July 1905: Night, 1905
Scottish National Gallery of Modern Art, Edinburgh

FEW CONDITIONS OF LIGHT ARE AS MOMENTARY AS THE spectacular explosions of fireworks. In this picture, magnificent cascades of yellow, lilac and pink hang in the sky, their pale hues re-creating the brightness of the light. Smears of colour represent the fading sprays of illumination as they fall.

Reflected radiance from the fireworks spreads in a golden sheen across the dark water of the harbour. Warm yellow lamps shine along the sea wall and little dots of light glow from the harbour buildings on the right. Above the lamps and the buildings hangs a faint lilac aura created by the artificial lights, while the light of the fireworks brightens the dark blue of the night sky nearby.

The picture is an exploration of the interplay between light, tone and colour – and also the relationship between light and movement. In the foreground, the light of the fireworks palely gleams on the insubstantial forms of the strolling people. Behind them, the optical effect produced by the rapid bursts of light in the sky creates ghostly impressions of their position moments before.

Picture Credits

BERCHEM

BERCKHEYDE

CLAUDE

COROT

DEGAS

DELVAUX

EL GRECO

FERGUSSON

GOYA

MARTIN

MONET

PISSARRO

REMBRANDT

RENOIR

ROSA

SEURAT

STOM

TER BRUGGHEN

TURNER

WATTS

WRIGHT OF DERBY

Written by Sarah Richardson,
Keeper of Fine Art at the
Laing Art Gallery

City of Bristol Museum
and Art Gallery,
26 January – 7 April 2002
Laing Art Gallery, Newcastle upon Tyne
20 April – 7 July 2002
National Gallery, London,
18 July – 6 October 2002

Supported by the
Heritage Lottery Fund

Supported at the National Gallery by
The Bernard Sunley Charitable Foundation

ISBN 1-85709-972-9

525292

9 781857 099720 >